Single-Case Research Design and Analysis:

New Directions for Psychology and Education

SINGLE-CASE RESEARCH DESIGN AND ANALYSIS

New Directions for Psychology and Education

Edited by

THOMAS R. KRATOCHWILL
JOEL R. LEVIN
University of Wisconsin—Madison

LAWRENCE ERLBAUM ASSOCIATES, PUBLISHERS
1992   Hillsdale, New Jersey   Hove and London

Lawrence Erlbaum Associates, Inc., Publishers
365 Broadway
Hillsdale, New Jersey 07642

Library of Congress Cataloging-in-Publication Data

Single-case research design and analysis : new directions for
  psychology and education / edited by Thomas R. Kratochwill, Joel R.
  Levin.
    p.   cm.
    ISBN 0-8058-0515-X
      1. Single subject research.   I. Kratochwill, Thomas R.
  II. Levin, Joel R.
  BF76.6.S56S56   1992
  150'.72—dc20   92-9493
                                                                    CIP

Printed in the United States of America
10 9 8 7 6 5 4 3 2 1

Contents

Preface

With the proliferation of single-case research in basic and applied areas of the social sciences, writers have continued to develop applicable data-analysis strategies. In the Preface to *Single-Subject Research: Strategies for Evaluating Change* (Kratochwill, 1978), it was noted that at the time there was growing interest in and controversy over the analysis of single-subject data. This picture has not changed much over the past 14 years. There is still interest; there is still controversy; and there are those who use statistical tests (advocates), those who do not (neutrals), and those who recommend against use of any inferential statistical test (opponents). Although it is not possible to specify exact number in each of these categories, the balance has probably not shifted very much since 1978.

So, the reader might ask why have we edited a book devoted to single-case data analysis? First, there is need to take stock of where we are in the development of data analysis procedures for single-case research. Increased research on various aspects of single-case data analysis is of compelling interest for the scholar of research methodology.

Second, as will become apparent to individuals who read this text, there are misapplications of various statistical procedures, including both some old errors of application and some new problems that heretofore have remained unexamined. These errors of application need to be made explicit and considered within the context of new theoretical and empirical information.

Third, there are new developments in the analysis of data from single-case or small *n* experiments. These developments extend beyond some of the conventional single-case designs that have their origins in the experimental analysis of behavior, and therefore are worthy of close examination even by traditional skeptics of inferential statistical applications. As two examples, strategies for analyzing social interaction patterns and group-based interventions follow directly from the earlier formulations of single-case designs and analyses.

In this text we hope that the reader will select a data-analysis strategy that best reflects his or her methodological approach, statistical sophistication, and philosophical beliefs. To this end, we present a wide variety of topics and perspectives. These include: visual (graphical) analysis, nonparametric tests, time-series experiments, applications of statistical procedures for multiple behaviors, applications of meta analysis in single-case research, and a discussion of issues related to the application and misapplication of selected techniques.

ACKNOWLEDGMENTS

We are very pleased to have such an outstanding group of contributors to this book. We thank the authors for sharing their knowledge. We especially express our thanks to our wives, Carol Ann Kratochwill and Mary Levin, for their appreciation of the time commitment needed to complete this project. Finally, we thank Larry Erlbaum and the staff at LEA for their support of this project.

REFERENCES

Kratochwill, T. R. (Ed). (1978). *Single subject research: Strategies for evaluating change.* New York: Academic Press.

Dedicated to the loving memory of our mothers,
Marian and Sonia

1 Single-Case Research Design and Analysis: An Overview

Thomas R. Kratochwill
University of Wisconsin–Madison

There is little doubt that single-case designs play a major role in applied and clinical research in psychology, education, and related fields. The rapid proliferation of writings on single-case design is remarkable over the past 15 years, and especially since the author of this chapter edited a volume devoted to single-subject research and strategies for evaluating change (Kratochwill, 1978). At that time there was only a handful of professional books devoted to this methodology and related issues. At this writing, the picture has changed dramatically, with a considerable number of professional works on both design and data analysis in the literature. Table 1.1 provides a listing of major textbooks in the area of single-case research design and analysis. It can be observed that although work in this area has a solid foundation prior to 1980, many major works have appeared since that time.

An interesting phenomenon in reviewing these works is that authors have discussed single-case methodology as a specialized research application in a variety of fields. For example, beyond the more traditional discussion of the methodology within applied behavior analysis (e.g., Bailey, 1977; Johnson & Pennypacker, 1980), there are presentations in clinical psychology (e.g., Barlow & Hersen, 1985), social work (e.g., Fischer, 1978), special education (e.g., Tawney & Gast, 1984), and communicative disorders (e.g., McReynolds & Kearns, 1983). That is, whereas single-case research design once appeared to have origins within quasi-experimental investigations in the tradition of Campbell and Stanley (1963) and applied behavior analysis with origins in the experimental analysis of behavior (Sidman, 1960), this picture has rapidly changed and the contributions are apparent across a variety of professional fields.

This widening influence of single-case methodology as a primary contribution

TABLE 1.1
Major Textbooks in the Area of Single-Case Research Design and/or Analysis

Date	Author	Textbook Title
1960	Sidman, M.	*Tactics of scientific research.* New York: Basic Books.
1969	Davidson, P. O., & Costello, C. G. (Eds.)	*N = 1: Experimental studies of single cases.* New York: Van Nostrand/Reinhold.
1973	Jayaratne, S., & Levy, R. L.	*Empirical clinical practice.* Irvington, NY: Columbia University Press.
1975	Glass, G. V., Wilson, V. L., & Gottman, J. M.	*Design and analysis of time-series experiments.* Boulder, CO: Colorado Associated University Press.
1975	Bailey, J. S.	*A handbook of research methods in applied behavior analysis.* Gainesville, FL: University of Florida.
1978	Fischer, J.	*Efficient casework practice: An eclectic approach.* New York: McGraw-Hill.
1978	Kratochwill, T. R. (Ed.)	*Single subject research: Strategies for evaluating change.* New York: Academic Press.
1979	Cook, T. D., & Campbell, D. T. (Eds.)	*Quasi-experimentation: Design and analysis issues for field settings.* Chicago: Rand McNally.
1979	Robinson, P. W., & Foster, D. F.	*Experimental psychology: A small-n approach.* New York: Harper & Row.
1980	McCleary, R., & Hay, R. A., Jr.	*Applied time-series analysis for the social sciences.* Beverly Hills, CA: Sage.
1980	Johnson, J. M., & Pennypacker, H. S.	*Strategies and tactics of human behavioral research.* Hillsdale, NJ: Lawrence Erlbaum Associates.
1980	McDowall, D., McCleary, R., Meidfinger, E. E., & Hay, R. A., Jr.	*Interrupted time-series analysis.* Beverly Hills, CA: Sage.
1981	Gottman, J. M.	*Time-series analysis: A comprehensive introduction for social scientists.* Cambridge, England: Cambridge University Press.
1981	Wodarski, J. S.	*The role of research in clinical practice: A practical approach for human services.* Baltimore: University Park Press.
1982	Kazdin, A. E.	*Single-case research designs: Methods for clinical and applied settings.* New York: Oxford University Press.
1982	Kazdin, A. E., & Tuma, A. H. (Eds.)	*Single-case research designs.* San Francisco, Jossey-Bass.
1983	McReynolds, L. V., & Kearns, K. P.,	*Single-subject experimental designs in communicative disorders.* Baltimore: University Park Press.
1984	Barlow, D. H., Hayes, S. C., & Nelson, R. O.	*The scientist practitioner: Research and accoutability in clinical and educational settings.* New York: Pergamon.

1984	Tawney, J. W., & Gast, D. L.	*Single subject research in special education.* Columbus, OH: Merrill.
1984	Yin, R. K.	*Case study research: Design and methods.* Beverly Hills, CA: Sage.
1985	Barlow, D. H., & Hersen, M.	*Single case experimental designs: Strategies for stydying behavior change* (2nd ed.). New York: Pergamon.
1985	Behling, J. H., & Merves, E. S.	*The practice of clinical research: The single-case methods.* Lanham, MD: University Press of America.
1986	Bromley, D. B.	*The case-study method in psychology and related disciplines.* New York: Wiley.
1986	Cryer, J D.	*Time series analysis.* Boston, MA: Duxbury Press.
1986	Poling, A., & Fuqua, R. W. (Eds.)	*Research methods in applied behavior analysis: Issues and advances.* New York: Plenum Press.
1986	Valsinger, J. (Ed.)	*The individual subject and scientific psychology.* New York: Plenum Press.

Source: Adapted from Kratochwill and Williams (1988). Personal perspectives on pitfalls and hassles in the conduct of single subject research. *Journal of the Association of Persons with Severe Handicaps, 13,* 147-154. Reproduced by permission.

to scientific information in these fields is interesting. But more importantly, the application of this methodology has allowed a number of refinements of application to specific and unique problems that may not have occurred without such diverse application across a variety of scholarly fields. Indeed, several specific advances may be pinpointed. First of all, specific advances have occurred in reconceptualizing the contributions of traditional "case-study" methodology. Traditional case-study methodology has typically been relegated to a rather low level of scientific knowledge. In fact, most case-studies involve demonstrations that do not allow an investigator to rule out conventional threats to internal validity and, therefore such studies do not quality as "true experiments" (Campbell & Stanley, 1963).

Several writers have presented the contributions that case-studies make and have presented the features that allow one to draw valid inferences from case-study and single-case design (Kazdin, 1981, 1982; Kazdin, Kratochwill, & VandenBos, 1986; Kratochwill, 1985; Kratochwill, Mott, & Dodson, 1984). In this regard, two important points are necessary to reconsider the role of case-studies in contributing valid information to scientific information. First, this methodology can be distinguished along a series of *types* that provide contributions to research knowledge. Table 1.2 presents three major types of case-study investigations that can be distinguished in applied and clinical research.

TABLE 1.2
Types of Case-Study Investigations

Type	Characteristics
Nontherapeutic case study (1) descriptive/uncontrolled (2) biography/autobiography	Researcher is interested in nonclinical investigation. Such areas as developmental or educational psychology would be representative. Includes traditional baby biographies.
Assessment/diagnosis case study (1) descriptive case	Researcher uses various psychometric instruments for diagnosis or description of cognitive or social behavior.
Therapeutic/intervention case study (1) uncontrolled (2) pre-experimental (3) clinical replication case	Researcher is primarily interested in a clinical disorder and may either describe natural course of disorder or develop intervention to treat client's problem.

Source: Kratochwill, Mott, and Dodson (1984). Case study and single-case research in clinical and applied psychology. In A. S. Bellack and M. Hersen (Eds.), *Research methods in clinical psychology* (pp. 35-99). New York: Pergamon.

The most common case-study methods are those used within clinical and other areas of applied psychology and which focus on outcome evaluation of specific intervention techniques. These case-studies have the "appearance" of an experiment in that some independent variable is manipulated. Nevertheless, many of these traditional case-studies are characterized by the absence of experimental control, inasmuch as the researcher cannot rule out most rival interpretations that might account for the observed therapeutic change. Since considerable ambiguity surrounds the interpretation of case-study methodology, these studies have been correctly relegated to a rather poor standing in the scientific community. Nevertheless, when various internal validity criteria are applied to case-study or even more well-controlled single-case designs, it is clear that ruling out various threats to validity is not an all or none matter (Kazdin, 1982). Attention to a variety of methodological, conceptual, and assessment factors is required to rule out various plausible factors that could account for observed effects. That is, whether a specific threat to internal validity of an experiment has been eliminated is often a matter of degree and, depending on how the study is arranged, various threats to validity might actually be controlled or rendered implausible.

To understand how the researcher can draw valid inferences, it is useful to note that the traditional uncontrolled case-study is characterized by a variety of unsystematic assessment and anecdotal reports, as well as the lack of design structure. However, numerous tactics can be used to advance understanding of contributions of case-studies and draw more valid inferences from the investigation. Table 1.3 provides a list of some dimensions that can be taken into account in either designing the study or evaluating an intervention case-study in the

TABLE 1.3
Improving Valid Inferences from Case-Study Research

Research Characteristics	Low-Inference Strategies	High-Inference Strategies
Type of data	Subjective data are used. For example, subjective anecdote description of outcomes is the fofus of the report.	Objective data are used. For example, observational data with high accuracy and reliability are used to measure outcomes.
Assessment occasions	Single-point measurement. The subject(s) is measured pre- or posttreatment, but not continuously.	Repeated measurement. The subject is measured continuously across phases of the study.
Planned vs. ex post facto	The researcher draws inferences from an intervention that was not part of the planned study; no manipulation of an independent variable occurred.	The researcher draws inferences from an intervention that was part of a direct manipulation of an independent variable during the actual study.
Projections of performance	The history of the case suggests problems of short duration or brief periods which may change without treatment.	The history of case suggests problems of long duration that have proved intractable to treatment previously.
Effect size	The effect size is small when considering trend and level of change in the data.	The effect size is large when considering trend and level of change in the data.
Effect impact	The effect impact is delayed across the treatment phase.	The effect impact is immediate within the treatment phase.
Numbers of subjects	The treatment effect is demonstrated on one subject.	The treatment effect is demonstrated across several subjects consistently.
Heterogeneity of subjects	The treatment effect is demonstrated across similar subjects (e.g., age, gender, race, etc.).	The treatment effect is demonstrated across subjects who differ on a variety of characteristics (e.g., age, gender, race).
Standardization of treatment	The treatment is procedurally not outlined or formalized in written form.	The treatment is procedurally outlined and produced in written form (e.g., manual) so that treatment agents implement it consistently.
Integrity of treatment	The treatment is not monitored during the implementation phase.	The treatment is repeatedly monitored during implementation to determine its accuracy and reliability.
Impact of treatment	The impact of treatment is demonstrated on a single outcome measure.	The impact of treatment is demonstrated on multiple outcome measures with similar strong effects.
Generalization and follow-up assessment	Formal measures of generalization and follow-up are not included.	Formal measures of generalization and follow-up are included in the study.

Source: Adapted from Kratochwill, Mott, and Dodson (1984). Case study and single-case research in clinical and applied psychology. In A. S. Bellack and M. Hersen (Eds.), *Research methods in clinical psychology (pp. 55-99).* New York: Pergamon.

research literature. Such tactics can be applied to more conventional single-case experimental research designs to improve on these methods as well.

A second domain where advances have been made in single-case design are in the conceptualization of actual design types. Traditionally, single-case designs have been identified by a particular title that reflects their application in basic or applied research. Moreover, there were few conceptual strategies for organizing the various designs in terms of their structural and functional properties. For example, in their classic text, Hersen and Barlow (1976) reviewed designs in terms of base A/B/A, multiple-baseline, multiple-schedule, and concurrent schedule strategies. This labeling of designs followed convention in terms of their specific and unique applications in basic and applied research in behavior modification. Similarly, in 1978 Kratochwill presented designs in terms of single-N and multiple-N conceptualizations. Single-N designs involve measurement of a single subject or group and allow a within-subject or group comparison of intervention effects in the time-series framework. In contrast, multiple-N designs involve both a within-group (or subject) and a between-group (or subject) comparison. The primary issues in this conceptualization were the degree of generalization that could be drawn from a specific design type and the option for random assignment of subjects to conditions in multiple-N applications.

Although both of these conceptualizations have been helpful in various ways, a true advance is presented by Hayes (1981) and extended by Barlow, Hayes, and Nelson (1984) to include the within- , between- , and combined-series design framework. Table 1.4 presents a summary of the major design types and their associated characteristics. The major advance emanating from this conceptualization pertains to the way inferences are drawn from the design itself.

Third, specific advances have been made in designing methods to assess generalization and maintenance, and dismantle compound treatments in single-case design. Barrios and Hartmann (1988) noted that true generalization assessment basically involves an extension of continuous measures or probes in within-series, between-series, and combined-series design types. For example, nontarget or untrained (or nonintervention) outcome measures are monitored over the duration of the study, as would occur in the usual analysis of acquisition procedures in the various design options. Table 1.5 presents a summary of single-case strategies for assessing generalization. Maintenance assessment is scheduled by comparing two or more maintenance procedures. The contribution of compound treatments is determined through a summary of findings from a series of single-case investigations as well as using conventional experimental design types to supplement the findings from single-case investigation. Table 1.6 presents a summary of single-case strategies for assessing joint effects.

Finally, advances in the analysis of single-case designs and small-N experiments have appeared. The literature has included new issues in both visual and statistical analysis (e.g., Matyas & Greenwood, 1990; Ottenbacher, 1990) as well as various perspectives on the debate over autocorrelation in single subject

TABLE 1.4
Major Types of Single-Case Designs and Associated Characteristics

Design Type	Representative Example	Characteristics
Within-series elements	Simple phase change (e.g., A/B, A/B/A, A/B/A/B) Comples phase change (e.g.,) interaction element: B/B+C/B, C/B+C/C, B+C/C/B+C, B+C/B/B+C	In these design elements, estimates of variability, level, and trend within a data series are assessed under similar conditions, the independent variable is introduced, and concomitant changes are assessed in tho stability, level, and trend across phases of a single data series.
Between-series elements	Alternating treatments design	In these design elements, estimates of variability, level, and trend in a data series are assessed in measures within a specific condition and across time. Outcome is assessed by comparing two or more of the series.
Combined-series elements	Multiple baseline (e.g., across subjects, across behaviors, across situations)	In these design elements, comparions are made both between and within a data series. Repetitions of a single simple phase change are scheduled, each with a new series and in which both the length and timing of the phase change differ across repetitions.

Source: Adapted from Hayes (1981). Single-case experimental designs and empirical clinical practice. *Journal of Consulting and Clinical Psychology, 49,* 193-211.

designs (Wampold, 1988). Other advances have occurred in development of specific visual and statistical tests. These advances are the focus of this book, and in the next section I provide an overview of these contributions.

OVERVIEW OF THE CHAPTERS

The traditional method of data analysis in single-subject experiments has been visual inspection of the data patterns from a graphic display. In chap. 2, Parsonson and Baer discuss visual analysis of data in single-subject experimentation. The chapter begins with a brief review of the advantages of graphical analysis and then progresses to an overview of some variables controlling graph reading, including serial dependency, mean shift, level and trend, variability and overlap, the types of graphing, and trend lines. The chapter concludes with an overview of research on visual analysis and research investigating differences between visual and statistical analyses. Directions for future research are presented.

One of the more controversial applications of statistical tests in single-case designs pertains to the application of time-series analyses. In fact, a variety of technical articles on the application of time-series analysis have appeared and the application of this method in applied behavioral research has been presented by

TABLE 1.5
A Summary of the Principal Single-Subject Strategies for Assessing Generalization

Type of Strategy	Description	Appraisal
Single generalization probe	A single measure of a non-targeted behavior, person, or setting is taken upon demonstration of therapeutic control over the targeted response(s) via a reversal or multuple baseline across behaviors, persons, or settings design.	The strategy does not allow us to infer with any confidence the generality of therapeutic effects. From a single measure of nontargeted rsponse, we cannot legitimately infer the level of that response prior to treatment, or can we attribute its current level to the treatment.
Multiple generalization probe	(a) Repeated measurement of a nontargeted response or responses is carried out in conjunction with a demonstration of therapeutic control over the targeted response via either a reversal or simultaneous treatment design.	The strategy does not allow for an unequivocal demonstration of either response or person generality. The strategy gives rise to two equally plausible accounts for systematic fluctuations in targeted and nontargeted responded: the treatment and a recurrent historical event. But the strategy does not enable us to choose one of these explanations over the other; thus it does not allow us to attribute fluctuations in targeted and nontargeted responding to the treatment.
	(b) Repeated measurement of a nontargeted response or responses is carried out upon demonstration of therapeutic control over the targeted response via either a multiple baseline across settings or behaviors design.	The strategy does not allow us to infer with any confidence the generality of therapeutic effects over either behaviors or settings. From the repeated measures of the nontargeted response(s), we cannot legitimately infer the level of responding prior to treatment, nor can we attribute the current level to the treatment.
Continuous generalization probes	(a) Concurrent measures of targeted and nontargeted responses vis-a-vis reversal designs.	The strategy allows for a demonstration of both therapeutic control and generality of therapeutic effects across behaviors, persons, and settings. Systematic fluctuation in targeted and nontargeted responding can be legitimately attributed to the treatment given there is no orderliness to the designers repeated presentation-and-removal of treatment. A demonstration of setting generality is possible insofar as the treatment is conceptualized as being present merely by being operative in the targeted situation.
	(b) Concurrent measurement of targeted and nontargeted responses vis-a-vis a multiple baseline across behaviors, persons, or settings design.	With this strategy, a multiple-baseline across behaviors design allows for a demonstration of person and setting generality, a multiple-baseline across-persons design response and setting generality, and a multiple-baseline across-settings design response and person generality. Systematic fluctuations in targeted and nontargeted responding can be legitimately attributed to the treatment provided there is no orderliness to the treatment's sequential administration across three or more independent behaviors, persons, or situations.

Source: Barrios and Hartmann (1877). Recent developments in single subject methodology: Methods for analyzing generalization, maintenance, and multi-component treatments. In Hersen, Eisler, and Miller (Eds.), *Progress in behavior modification* (Vol. 22, pp. 11-47). New York: Academic Press. Reproduced by permission.

TABLE 1.6
A Summary of the Principal Single-Subject Strategies for Assessing Joing Effects

	Description	Appraisal
Reversal	Each treatment component and all possible combinations of the components are repeatedly presented and withdrawn in a sequential fashion	Dismantling a two-component treatment via a single reversal design is possible, but not probable. The large number of treatment and no-treatment phases required is seen as curtailing its usage. Dismantling via a series of reversal designs is feasible. The strategy is, however, predicated on the assumption of homogeneity across subjects; and the generality of the findings is always suspect, as they may be restricted to the exact order in which the individual components and their combinations are assessed (across the series).
Simultaneous treatment	Each treatment component and all possible combinations of the component are presented in an alternating (and counter-balanced) fashion over time.	Dismantling a two-component treatment via a single simultaneous treatment design is possible, but not probable. The lengthy sequence required to counterbalance the alternation of treatments is seen as precluding its wide-scale use. Dismantling a compound treatment through a series of simultaneous treatment designs is feasible. The strategy is, however, predicted on the assumption of homogeneity across subjects. And the generality of the findings is always suspect, as the findings may be restricted to the exact order in which the individual components and their combinations are assessed (across the series).
Multiple baseline across behaviors, persons, or settings.	Each treatment component and all possible combinations of the components are introduced sequentially cross independent behaviors, persons, or settings.	Dismantling a compound treatment via a single multiple-baseline design is possible, but not probable. The design's provision of concurrent measurement of a minimum of six independent behaviors, persons, or settings should preclude its usage. Dismantling a compound treatment via a series of multiple-baseline designs is feasible. Us of the strategy does, however, require homogeneity of behaviors, persons, or settings (across the series). And the generality of the findings is held as suspect as the findings may be restricted to the exact order in which they are assessed (across the series).

Source: Barrios and Hartmann (1988). Recent developments in single subject methodology: Methods for analyzing generalization, maintenance, and multi-component treatments. In Hersen, Eisler, and Miller (Eds.), *Progress in behavior modification* (Vol. 22, pp. 11-47). New York: Academic Press. Reproduced by permission.

Hartmann et al. (1980). Table 1.7 (from Hartmann et al.) presents an overview of some of the applied and technical references in this area. Building on their previous work, in chap. 3 McCleary and Welsh present the philosophical and statistical foundations of time-series experiments. The authors begin their chapter with a review of time-series experiments and then progress through a variety of specific statistical applications that are unique to the time-series analysis format. The authors then turn attention to an analysis of some statistical problems

TABLE 1.7
Selected Applied and Technical References on ITSA

Applied

Deutsch and Alt (1977)	Controversial application if ITSA to assess the effects of gun-control legistration on gun-related crimes in Boston. See Hay and McCleary's (1979) critical evaluation and Deutsch's (1979) vigorous reply.
Gottman and McFall (1972)	Application of ITSA to evaluate the effects of self-monitoring on the school related behavior of high school dropouts.
McSweeney (1978)	Description of the effects of a response-cost procedure on the telephoning behavior of people in Cincinnati. The statistical analysis performed on the data are described in McCain and McCleary (1979).
Schnelle, Kirchner, McNees, and Lawler (1975)	Application of ITSA to assess the effectiveness of saturation patrols on burglary rates.

Technical

Jones, Vaught, and Weinrott (1977)	A nontechnical presentation of ITSA.
Kazdin (1976)	A discussion of the problems of serial dependency and several technical alternatives, including ITSA.
McCain and McCleary (1979)	The clearest technical introduction to ITSA.
Gottman and Glass (1978)	A restatement and updating of Glass et al. (1975).
Nelson (1973)	A summary of the Box-Jenkins theory in practice. Should be readable for those with a strong background in multiple regression. Applications illustrate the use of the ESP computer package.
Hibbs (1974)	Contains a good discussion of the problems of serial dependency in statistical tests of time series data. Requires a famiiarity with matrix algebra.
McCleary and Hay (1980)	A comprehensive applied treatment of the Box-Jenkins method designed for behavioral and social scientists.
Glass et al. (1975)S	Summary of the Box-Tiao method and the discussion of its application to behavioral and evaluation research.
Anderson (1976)	A well-written and mathematically sophisticated digest of Box-Jenkins.
Box and Tiao (1965)	A difficult but fundamental article on the analysis of interventions in time series.
Box and Jenkins (1976)	A treatise in mathematical statistics. The source for most of the other references.

Note. Technical articles are listed in order of difficulty.

Source: Hartmann et al. (1980). Interrupted time-series analysis and its application to behavioral data. *Journal of Applied Behavior Analysis, 13,* 543-559. Copyright by the Society of the Experimental Analysis of Behavior. Reproduced by permission.

3 rd 7 l annex,
       left - Red

in time-series, including stationarity and autocorrelation. The authors then present a number of sample analyses that involve estimating trend, estimating an impact of some intervention on this series, and estimating correlation. The chapter is especially interesting in view of recent microcomputer software providing applied researchers with access to time-series analyses for single-case experiments (Crosbie & Sharpley, 1989).

In chap. 5, Edgington describes statistical tests based on randomization schemes. The chapter begins with a discussion of the importance of randomization and then includes a presentation of the basis for nonparametric randomization tests and their assumptions in research. Thereafter, Edgington discusses various statistical tests that can be used in the major classes of single-subject designs, including within-series, between-series, and combined-series applications. Illustrations of the various applications are presented for the reader.

In chap. 6, Busk and Marascuilo provide a conceptual analysis of misconceptions and misunderstandings regarding the use of statistical procedures in single-case designs. They critically evaluate visual analysis as a method of single-case data analysis, present two issues concerning how autocorrelated errors influence single-case research and present issues surrounding the selection of a unit of analysis on which to base the statistical analysis of data. Specifically, they discuss appropriate summary measures that can be used in single-case designs. Thereafter, the chapter shifts to a focus on the use of randomization tests in within-series designs and combined-series multiple-baseline strategies.

In chap. 4, Wampold turns his attention away from conventional single-case design applications to the use of sequential analysis to study social interactions in single subjects. Like many traditional applications of single-case designs, these methods involve the intense analysis of behavior in single organisms. However, the applications can involve study of interactions among a single organism, system, or variations that allow the study of interactions among several interacting organisms. In his chapter, Wampold provides a mathematical model for methods to analyze sequences of behavior, examples of research that have used these strategies, and a conceptual discussion of issues and limitations of these methods in basic and applied research.

In the past several years, there has been a great deal of interest in using meta-analysis as a strategy to summarize research literatures (e.g., Glass, McGaw, & Smith, 1981; Hedges & Olkin, 1985; Rosenthal, 1984). Many conventional meta-analytical strategies have either not included single-case research investigations or have used statistical techniques to summarize results from these investigations in an inappropriate manner. Recently, White, Rusch, Kazdin, and Hartmann (1989) presented a technology for conducting a single-subject meta-analysis. In chap. 7, Busk and Serlin present an overview of methodological and statistical problems of meta-analysis applications to single-case designs.

In the final chapter, Levin comments and elaborates on issues raised throughout the book. The chapter includes a critical analysis of single-case statistical analysis, as well as an examination of conditions under which statistical analysis might prove useful in single-case designs.

REFERENCES

Anderson, O. D. (1976). *Time series analysis and forecasting: The Box–Jenkins approach*. London: Butterworth.

Bailey, J. S. (1977). *A handbook of research methods in applied behavior analysis*. Gainesville, FL: University of Florida.

Barlow, D. H., Hayes, S. C., & Nelson, R. O. (1984). *The scientist practitioner: Research and accountability in clinical and educational settings*. New York: Pergamon.

Barlow, D. H., & Hersen, M. (1985). *Single case experimental designs: Strategies for studying behavior change* (2nd ed.). New York: Pergamon.

Barrios, B. A. (1984). Single-subject strategies for examining joint effects: A critical evaluation. *Behavioral Assessment, 6,* 103–120.

Barrios, B. A., & Hartmann, D. P. (1988). Recent developments in single subject methodology: Methods for analyzing generalization, maintenance, and multi-component treatments. In M. Hersen, R. M. Eisler, & P. M. Miller (Eds.), *Progress in behavior modification* (Vol. 22, pp. 11–47). New York: Academic Press.

Behling, J. H., & Merves, E. S. (1985). *The practice of clinical research: The single-case methods*. Lanham, MD: University Press of America.

Box, G. E. P., & Jenkins, G. M. (1976). *Time-series analysis: Forecasting and control* (2nd ed.). San Francisco: Holden–Day.

Box, G. E. P., & Tiao, G. C. (1965). A change in level of a non-stationary time series. *Biometrika, 52,* 181–192.

Bromley, D. H. (1986). *The case-study method in psychology and related disciplines*. New York: Wiley.

Campbell, D. T., & Stanley, J. C. (1963). *Experimental and quasi-experimental designs for research*. Chicago: Rand McNally.

Cook, T. D., & Campbell, D. T. (Eds.) (1978). *Quasi-expiermentation: Design and analysis issues for field settings*. Chicago: Rand McNally.

Cryer, J. D. (1986). *Time series analysis*. Boston: Duxbury Press.

Davidson, P. O., & Costello, C. G. (Eds.) (1969). *N=1: Experimental studies of single cases*. New York: Van Nostrand/Reinhold Co.

Deutsch, S. J. (1979). Lies, damn lies, and statistics: A rejoinder to the comment by Hay and McCleary. *Evaluation Quarterly, 3,* 315–328.

Deutsch, S. J., & Alt, F. B. (1977). The effect of Massachusetts' gun control law on gun-related crimes in the city of Boston. *Evaluation Quarterly, 1,* 543–568.

Fischer, J. (1978). *Effective casework practice: An eclectic approach*. New York: McGraw-Hill.

Glass, G. V., McGaw, B., & Smith, M. L. (1981). *Meta-analysis in social research*. Beverly Hills, CA: Sage.

Glass, G. V., Willson, V. L., & Gottman, J. M. (1975). *Design and analysis of time-series experiments*. Boulder: Colorado Associated University Press.

Gottman, J. M. (1981). *Time-series analysis: A comprehensive introduction for social scientists*. Cambridge, England: Cambridge University Press.

Gottman, J. M., & Glass, G. V. (1978). Analysis of interrupted time-series experiments. In T. R. Kratochwill (Ed.), *Single subject research: Strategies for evaluating change* (pp. 197–235). New York: Academic Press.

Gottman, J. M., & McFall, R. M. (1972). Self-monitoring effects in a program for potential high school dropouts: A time-series analysis. *Journal of Consulting and Clinical Psychology, 39,* 273–281.

Hartmann, D. P., Gottman, J. M., Jones, R. R., Gardner, W., Kazdin, A. E., & Vaught, R. S. (1980). Interrupted time-series analysis and its application to behavioral data. *Journal of Applied Behavior Analysis, 13,* 543–559.

Hay, R. A., & McCleary, R. (1979). Box–Tiao time series models for impact assessment: A comment on the recent work of Deutsch and Alt. *Evaluation Quarterly, 3,* 277–314.

Hayes, S. C. (1981). Single-case experimental designs and empirical clinical practice. *Journal of Consulting and Clinical Psychology, 49,* 193–211.

Hedges, L. V., & Olkin, I. (1985). *Statistical methods for meta-analysis.* New York: Academic Press.

Hersen, M., & Barlow, D. H. (1976). *Single-case experimental designs: Strategies for studying behavior change.* New York: Pergamon.

Hibbs, D. A., Jr. (1974). Problems of statistical estimation and causal inference in time-series regression models. In H. L. Costner (Ed.), *Sociological methodology 1973–1974.* San Francisco: Jossey-Bass.

Jayaratne, S., & Levy, R. L. (1973). *Empirical clinical practice.* Irvington, NY: Columbia University Press.

Johnson, J. M., & Pennypacker, H. S. (1980). *Strategies and tactics of human behavioral research.* Hillsdale, NJ: Lawrence Erlbaum Associates.

Kazdin, A. E. (1976). Statistical analyses for single-case experimental designs. In M. Hersen & D. H. Barlow (Eds.), *Single case experimental designs: Strategies for studying behavior change.* Oxford, England: Pergamon.

Kazdin, A. E. (1981). Drawing valid inferences from case studies. *Journal of Consulting and Clinical Psychology, 49,* 183–192.

Kazdin, A. E. (1982). *Single-case research designs: Methods for clinical and applied settings.* New York: Oxford Press.

Kazdin, A. E., Kratochwill, T. R., & VandenBos, G. (1986). Beyond clinical trials: Generalizing from research to practice. *Professional Psychology: Research and Practice, 3,* 391–398.

Kazdin, A. E., & Tuma, A. H. (Eds.) (1982). *Single-case research designs.* San Francisco: Jossey-Bass.

Kratochwill, T. R. (Ed.). (1978). *Single subject research: Strategies for evaluating change.* New York: Academic Press.

Kratochwill, T. R. (1985). Case study research in school psychology. *School Psychology Review, 14,* 204–215.

Kratochwill, T. R., Mott, S. E., & Dodson, C. L. (1984). Case study and single-case research in clinical and applied psychology. In A. S. Bellack & M. Hersen (Eds.), *Research methods in clinical psychology* (pp. 55–99). New York: Pergamon.

Kratochwill, T. R., & Williams, B. L. (1988). Personal perspectives on pitfalls and hassles in the conduct of single subject research. *Journal of the Association of Persons with Severe Handicaps, 13,* 147–154.

Matyas, T. A., & Greenwood, K. M. (1990). Visual analysis of single-case time series: Effects of variability, serial dependence, and magnitude of intervention effects. *Journal of Applied Behavior Analysis, 23,* 341–351.

McCain, L. J., & McCleary, R. (1979). The statistical analysis of the simple interrupted time-series quasi-experiment. In T. D. Cook & D. T. Campbell, *Quasi-experimentation: Design and analysis issues* (pp. 233–293). Chicago: Rand McNally.

McCleary, R., & Hay, R. A., Jr. (1980). *Applied time series analysis for the social sciences.* Beverly Hills, CA: Sage.

McDowall, D., McCleary, R., Meidfinger, E. E., & Hay, R. A., Jr. (1980). *Interrupted time-series analysis.* Beverly Hills, CA: Sage.

McReynolds, L. V., & Kearns, K. P. (1983). *Single-subject experimental designs in communicative disorders.* Baltimore: University Park Press.

McSweeney, A. J. (1977). Time series analysis and research in behavior modification: Some answers. *AABT Newsletter, 4,* 22–23.

McSweeney, A. J. (1978). Effects of response cost on the behavior of a million persons: Charging for directory assistance in Cincinnati. *Journal of Applied Behavior Analysis, 11,* 47–51.

Nelson, C. R. (1973). *Applied time series analysis.* San Francisco: Holden–Day.

Ottenbacher, K. J. (1990). When is a picture worth a thousand p values? A comparison of visual and quantitative methods to analyze single subject data. *Journal of Special Education, 23,* 436–449.

Poling, A., & Fuqua, R. W. (Eds.). (1986). *Reserch methods in applied behavior analysis: Issues and advances.* New York: Plenum Press.

Robinson, P. W., & Foster, D. F. (1979). *Experimental psychology: A small-n approach.* New York: Harper & Row.

Rosenthal, R. (1984). *Meta-analytic procedures for social research.* Beverly Hills, CA: Sage.

Schnelle, J. F., Kirchner, R. E., McNeese, M. P., & Lawler, J. M. (1975). Social evaluation research: The evaluation of two police patrolling strategies. *Journal of Applied Behavior Analysis, 8,* 353–365.

Tawney, J. W., & Gast, D. L. (1984). *Single subject research in special education.* Columbus, OH: Merrill.

Valsinger, J. (Ed.) (1986). *The individual subject and scientific psychology.* New York: Plenum Press.

Wampold, B. E. (1988). Introduction. *Behavioral Assessment, 10,* 227–228.

White, D. M., Rusch, F. R., Kazdin, A. E., & Hartmann, D. P. (1989). Applications of meta-analysis in individual-subject research. *Behavioral Assessment, 11,* 281–296.

Wodarski, J. S. (1981). *The role of research in clinical practice: A practical approach for human services.* Baltimore: University Park Press.

Yin, R. K. (1984). *Case study research: Design and methods.* Beverly Hills, CA: Sage.

2 The Visual Analysis of Data, and Current Research into the Stimuli Controlling It

Barry S. Parsonson
University of Waikato

Donald M. Baer
University of Kansas

THE CASE FOR VISUAL ANALYSIS

Visual analysis is one of the oldest forms of data analysis. It is, in essence, simply the array of one set of information relative to one or more other sets of information, so that a viewer can draw a reasonable conclusion or make a reasonable hypothesis about any relationships or lack of them among these sets. Very often, the array takes the form called a graph, especially when at least one set of the information is quantitative; in other cases, especially when all the sets are qualitative, it takes the form of essentially a picture or diagram (cf. especially Tufte, 1990).

The point of the array is that the viewer can conclude or hypothesize about these relationships simply by visual inspection of the array: The viewer can *see*—not read, deduce, or derive, but see, and see quickly—the relationship or its absence. Thus a map shows where one place is relative to another; the relationships to be seen almost immediately are the distance and direction of any place from any other place. Certain maps show an additional relationship: where one place is relative to some means of getting there from another place. On one map, that additional element may be walking paths; on another, roads; and on another, airline terminals. The relationships that emerge from such maps are how to get from here to there by one or another means of transportation, and how long it will take—and occasionally the wry fact that you can't get there from here by that means.

The fact that visual display and analysis is one of the oldest forms of discovery and communication does not signal its obsolescence, not even in an age of ultrahigh technology. Indeed, some of our latest technology is dedicated to maximizing dramatically the efficiency of constructing and disseminating visual analyses; these are the modern computer graphics programs. Yet in behavioral research, which is the context for this book (and this chapter), by far the prevailing mode of analysis is statistical, not visual. The multivariate analysis of variance, culminating in a table not of data numbers but of numbers testifying primarily to the probability that the data patterns could have arisen by chance, is far more frequent than a picture of the underlying data numbers themselves. Yet we can have such a picture, often by the construction of lines or other geometrical forms to show the relationship of some behaviors to the variables that may control or otherwise relate to them.

Thus, the purpose of this chapter is to state again the case for the visual analysis of behavioral relationships through graphs, and most especially for the outcome of experiments in which an ongoing, repetitive behavior is altered in its time course by the deliberate, repetitive alteration of one or more of its environmental conditions. In that context, there are at least six advantages to be gained through graphic analysis:

1. It is visual, and thereby quick to yield conclusions and hypotheses.
2. Graphs can be quick and easy to make with no more technology than grid paper, pencil, and straight edge. However, if the latest computer graphics technology is to be used, then speed and ease are recaptured only after an initial high cost of money, time, and training.
3. Graphing comprises a remarkably wide range of formats, even outside of the latest computer graphics technology.
4. Graphed messages are immediately and enduringly accessible to students at unusually diverse levels of training.
5. In representing the actual data measured, graphs can and usually do transform those data as minimally as possible. In those paradigms of knowing wherein the measurable data under study are the reality to be understood (cf. Heshusius, 1982, for a presumably different paradigm), that is an obvious virtue.
6. The theoretical premises underlying graphs are minimal and well known— that what we are interested in can be made visual, and that almost all of us are skilled in responding to visual isomorphisms of the world in ways that make the world useful. By contrast, the theoretical premises underlying the defensible use of statistical analysis are numerous, complex, diverse, and frequently arcane to the majority of their users. Thus, statistical analysis users find themselves relying on techniques subject to apparently endless debate about their suitability for given problems—a debate often accessible to only a small minority of the users. Graphs do not present us with an estimate of the probability that the patterns and distributions of the data we have gathered could have arisen by chance if the variables coupled

with them are in fact not functional for them. Instead, graphs invite us to make that judgment ourselves (as well as many others exemplified herein). Thereby graphs create two audiences among researchers: (a) Some researchers will see that kind of judgment as merely a personal one. They seek a science based on objective rather than subjective judgments, so they must go further than graphic analysis in their search for an apparently objective estimate of the probability. Statistical analysis will seem to offer it to them—until they have studied its workings and underlying assumptions thoroughly enough to see how many essentially personal judgments they must make in order to estimate the suitability of each of the many models of statistical analysis for their problem and its data. (b) Some other researchers will prefer to make their own judgments about the patterns and distribution of the data; they will compare those judgments with interest but not submissively to the judgments of their peers. They will be glad to have all the data as accessible as possible, especially as simultaneously accessible as possible, and will avoid any technique that makes a decision for them in ways that are exceptionally difficult to inspect in its reduction, transformation, collation, and integration of each data point into some final decision.

To illustrate many of these points, suppose that we want to know if a certain well-measured but momentarily unnamed behavior, B, is affected differently by two well-controlled but unnamed environmental conditions, Condition 1 and Condition 2. We can experimentally alternate Condition 1 and Condition 2, each for varying lengths of time, holding everything else as stable as we can, and meanwhile measuring behavior B steadily and repeatedly under each repetition of each condition. If we do that, we can then compare the level of the behavior typical under the repeated applications of Condition 1 to the level of the behavior typical under the repeated applications of Condition 2. Table 2.1 shows every measurement of B in each of a mere two alternations of Conditions 1 and 2.

Certainly there are some clear messages to be derived from these numbers, testifying to a possibly complex differential relationship of the level of this behavior to Conditions 1 and 2. The interesting question here is only how long it takes the reader to extract and appreciate all of that message.

Now, here is a graph of the data in Table 2.1.

This graph shows us *at a glance* that Condition 2 produces more of this behavior than does Condition 1, and that initially it does so not all at once but gradually, as if a new skill were being shaped, whereas the second time that Condition 2 is applied, it produces its effect immediately, as would be expected from stimulus-control effects rather than reshaping. The possibility that the first application represents shaping and the second stimulus control is perhaps not clear enough to be affirmed flatly by every viewer, but it is clear enough to suggest further investigation of that possibility. The graph also shows us at a

TABLE 2.1
Hypothetical Data Gathered Under Two Conditions

Condition 1	Condition 2	Condition 1	Condition 2
1	5	4	11
1	6	2	10
2	6	0	11
0	8	2	9
1	7	1	9
2	9	1	8
1	8	2	7
0	11	0	7
1	10	0	9
1	10	1	8
	11	2	7
	9	1	6
	8		7
	8		5
	9		5
	8		
	10		

glance how much more of the behavior is produced by Condition 2 than Condition 1. It also suggests that the ability of Condition 2 to make this change in the behavior is perhaps decreasing by the end of its second application. That possibility, too, is perhaps not clear enough to be affirmed flatly by every viewer, but it, too, its clear enough to investigate further.

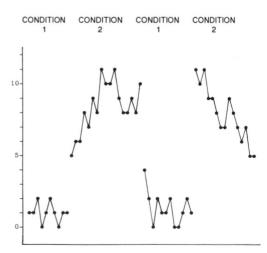

FIG. 2.1. A graphic representation of the hypothetical data of an ABAB single-subject experimental design offered in Table 2.1.

Of course, all of those conclusions and hypotheses can be extracted from the preceding table as well—the data are identical. The reader should ask how quickly and how fully both the clear and possible relationships of B to Conditions 1 and 2 were extracted from the table, relative to how quickly and how fully they were extracted from the graph. Each method of presentation offers us all the information that we collected; the table offers it to us as an array of numbers relative to their controlling variable, and the graph offers it to us as a picture of those numbers in that same array. The picture is a transformation of the numbers, certainly, but it is a remarkably minimal transformation of them. It still leaves the judgment of whether this behavior does indeed relate differentially to Conditions 1 and 2, and if so, exactly how, entirely up to us, the viewing researchers—the people who want those answers, and have been trained as best we know how to find them out.

Another interesting question is whether the viewer can decide whether the Condition 1 distributions of B are no more different from the Condition 2 distributions of B than could reasonably have arisen by chance if Conditions 1 and 2 are not functional for B. A fair variety of statistical analyses would assure these viewers that the differences in these two distributions could hardly have arisen by chance; a few other statistical methods would suggest to them that they could. Experienced visual analysts (we daresay) will typically decide fairly quickly that these differences are certainly not chance differences, and inexperienced visual analysts will come to the same conclusion even more quickly, interestingly enough. In our experience, they tend to respond to the entire picture as a clang! phenomenon, and not go on to examine the time course of each data path, point by point, and then reconsider them as a pattern of four aggregates, two with quite different internal trend patterns (the two Condition 2s), one without (the first Condition 1), and one either without or with a very short-lived one (the second Condition 1). But both kinds of visual analyst will decide that the conditions are functionally different for B far earlier than a statistical analysis could have agreed or disagreed with them. The experienced visual analysts will long since have gone on to consider those other possibilities in how B relates to Conditions 1 and 2; some of those analysts will affirm that the trends are real, and others will suspect (hypothesize) that they are but ask for more data before affirming that they are. Indeed, experienced visual analysts, studying their graphs as each point was added to the prior ones, would probably not have ended either of the Condition 2s when they were concluded in this hypothetical study: Those only hypothesizing that the trends were real would have gathered more data so as to be sure; those who were sure would have gathered more data to see how the trends would have ended (for there is always good reason to suppose that they will not continue as linear trends, especially on a graph with an arithmetical ordinate).

Graphic analysis is usually fast, clear, and easy; but it is important to consider why it is, so as to appreciate when it will not be. Graphic analysts often have the puzzling experience of finding normal adults who not only say that they cannot read graphs, but behave in a variety of other ways that confirm their premise. Yet most of us can see effortlessly when the lines of a graph, despite their local irregularities, as a whole are at different levels, and slant upward or downward or are horizontal, or change systematically from one of those states to another. Where did we learn that? One would think that these are easy generalizations from the facts that sighted people have already learned to appreciate–at a glance!–in the rest of their world. After all, their histories with lines are vastly more extensive than their histories with numerals: They constantly scan the world within which they move for the height, rise, fall, and stability of its contours, on which they must stand, sit, walk, ride, push, pull, drive, and place or retrieve something, and over which they will climb or jump. The "horizon" of "horizontal" is a key part of their eternal stimulus controls for where they are, where they are going, and for their balance. By contrast, their behavior with numerals is a mere occasional hobby.

On the other hand, sighted people read graphs quickly and easily only to the extent that they generalize from their extensive training in a real, three-dimensional visual world to the relatively new two-dimensional visual world of graphs; and behaviorists have learned that failures of generalization are never oddities. Of course there will be people who do not immediately and easily read in graphs everything that the graphs offer. By contrast, we learned to respond to numerals in the same domains in which they are used to represent data and their statistical analyses—on pages, chalkboards, and monitor screens. Numerals present no problem in setting generalization.

Thus, it is clear that despite the advantages of graphic analysis as a quick, easy, open, and widely accessible process, it is also true that both graph construction and graph reading are skills to be acquired. In recognition of that, a chapter like this in past years would sketch some skills from both of those skill classes. However, in 1983 and 1990, Edward R. Tufte published two classic texts on graphics: *The Visual Display of Quantitative Information* (1983) and *Envisioning Information* (1990). In our opinion, those texts thoroughly and engagingly display virtually everything there is to offer so far in constructing clear and evaluative graphics for both quantitative and qualitative data, and their relationships to controlling and other variables. Consequently, we earnestly recommend the reader to them both, and turn here to a consideration of recent research into the reading of graphs.

SOME VARIABLES CONTROLLING GRAPH READING

The past decade has shown increased attention to visual analysis, both as a skill to be taught in textbooks, especially behavior-analysis textbooks (e.g., Cooper, Heron, & Heward, 1986; Kazdin, 1982; Tawney & Gast, 1984), and as a skill to be analyzed, or at least assessed. Most of that research is stimulus-analytic; it is aimed at uncovering the stimuli that currently control visual analysts' judgments of what the data show, even if not illuminating the source or the modifiability of those judgments.

Thus, research to date has focused on the extent to which visual analysts can see the major kinds of effects that can be expected from experimental interventions into an ongoing baseline of behavior that can be graphed as a time course: simple changes from baseline in the mean level of the behavior under study, usually referred to as *mean shift*; changes in which each successive data point is an interactive function of the intervention and the level of the immediately prior data point(s), yielding at least changes in trend and sometimes simultaneous changes in both level and trend, and often referred to as *serial dependency*; degrees of such changes, simple or interactive, relative to both baseline and intervention variability, thereby affecting the degree to which the ranges of the baseline and intervention data points overlap; and changes only in degree of variability. Research has also considered a few factors orthogonal to the behavior change accomplished by the intervention, such as different graphing techniques: for example, adding trend lines (calculable of course in a variety of ways) to the data path(s), or choosing logarithmic rather than arithmetic scales for the ordinate. Most of these topics will be discussed.

Serial Dependency

A pioneering study by Jones, Weinrott, and Vaught (1978) found that mean agreement between visual and time-series analyses was both low (60%) and, what little there was of it, inversely related to the degree of serial dependency in the data—that serial dependency decreased agreement between the two methods of analysis. This study also pioneered in two frequently unexamined, sometimes implicit assumptions: (1) That it is relevant to compare the seemingly unforced, and often quite variable, judgments arrived at through visual analysis to the supposedly uniform judgments imposed by statistical analysis, as if the latter were somehow a standard—indeed, as if it were the truth; and (2) That uniformity across visual analysts in coming to their conclusions is a virtue.

Neither of these assumptions has much currency in modern visual analysis: (1) There is no single process called *statistical analysis* to provide that putative standard or truth; there are many of them, which in their diversity often allow quite different conclusions. When that happens, their users must finally make a judgment about which of them is "best" for the current problem, a judgment that frequently proves unreliable across the scientists considering the problem (as the most cursory examination of that literature will show); thus a supposedly objective, uniform process becomes instead a matter of individual scientific judgment. But that is exactly the point that visual analysts make about the behavior of doing science: (2) One of the central points of visual analysis is to leave with maximal clarity to each researcher and each member of the research audience any judgment about whether the current experimental intervention has had an effect on the behavior under study. Perhaps that is done in honor of the frequency with which science has been advanced by the disagreements of a few data analysts with the prevailing conventional wisdom about what the current data mean. One or both of these typically unexamined assumptions operates in virtually every study that will be reviewed here.

For example, to evaluate different types of serial dependency, Rojahn and Schulze (1985) used computer-generated AB-design graphs showing no, weak, or strong serial dependencies, some of the moving-average type and some of the autoregressive type; in addition, the graphs were constructed to represent five different significance levels of treatment effect (p = .50, .10, .05, .01, .001). These researchers then asked judges to rate 70 such graphs on a 5-point scale made up of just those probability values. The results did not support those of Jones et al. (1978), in that serial dependency did not much affect agreement between visual and statistical analyses. Rather, it was found that the more pronounced the moving-average and autoregressive effects, the greater the agreement between the two modes of analysis. The moving-average and autoregressive processes affected this agreement somewhat differently; strong autoregressive processes in particular led judges to overestimate treatment effects relative to statistical analysis.

Studies by Ottenbacher (1986) and Gibson and Ottenbacher (1988) investigated the effects of six graphical characteristics, including serial dependency, on interjudge agreement. Ottenbacher (1986) asked 46 occupational therapists to indicate if change had occurred between phases on five specially devised AB graphs. Gibson and Ottenbacher (1988) obtained ratings (0–5) of significance of change in 24 AB-design graphs from 20 rehabilitation therapists. Interjudge agreement was not affected by serial dependency in either study. Gibson and Ottenbacher (1988) also found no effect on the confidence in their decisions reported by the judges. However, these two studies appear to have confounded autocorrelation and mean shift, especially the Gibson and Ottenbacher data, in which the two variables intercorrelated at 0.73. Thus, judges may have confused high serial dependency with intervention effects. This would be consistent with the results of the previous studies. Still, one can always ask for further investigation into the relationship between mean shift and serial dependency. The amount and effects of serial dependency existent in applied behavior-analytic data are still much debated (Baer, 1988; Busk & Marascuilo, 1988; Huitema, 1986, 1988; Sharpley & Alavosius, 1988); thus it remains difficult to evaluate as a frequent "threat" to visual analysis.

Mean Shift

Pattern and degree of mean shift were among four data-path variables DeProspero and Cohen (1979) varied in the specially produced ABAB graphs they submitted for judgment to 108 editorial board members and guest reviewers of two behavior-analytic journals. Their graphs represented three patterns of mean shift: "ideal," in which the phase means changed as "expected" with "experimental" conditions; "inconsistent," in which the mean shifted only in the final B phase; and "irreversible," in which the mean shifted only in the first B phase and remained stable thereafter. In addition, three degrees of mean shift were displayed, and while this varied from graph to graph, it was held constant within graphs. In this study, the pattern of mean shift proved to be critical, on the average, in that mean ratings of "experimental control" were high only for at least some of the "ideal" graphs showing large degrees of mean shift. A statistical analysis revealed that pattern and degree of mean shift were highly significant main effects, yet together accounted for only a small proportion of the total variance. (It might be interesting, and certainly would be democratic, if similar analytic effort were invested to determine the extent to which highly significant p levels and proportion of variance accounted for are controlling variables in the conclusions of given populations of statistical-analysis consumers, especially in that typical publication greatly emphasizes the former over the latter.)

Knapp (1983) used AB graphs with a mean value of 5 in baseline and a range of nine mean values between 2 and 8 in the B phase, to see how that would affect the judgments of three different groups: that much-studied subpopulation, the editorial-board members of two behavior-analytic journals, as well as graduate behavior-analysis students and undergraduate psychology majors. A statistical analysis revealed significant main effects for mean shift, graph type, and their interaction. Extreme (e.g., 5-to-8 and 5-to-2) or zero (5-to-5) mean shifts were judged similarly regardless of graphing technique. At more moderate levels of mean shift (e.g., 5-to-3.5 or 5-to-6.5), graphing technique became critical. Judgments generally were comparable for those types of graphs commonly evaluated by applied behavior analysts, namely, arithmetic-ordinate and abscissa charts with a space or line between phase changes.

Ottenbacher's (1986) five graphs (discussed earlier) had also varied in degree of mean shift. Most judges saw "significant change" in the three graphs with the highest mean shift (which incidentally had the highest autocorrelation coefficients). Interjudge agreement about change was higher when the mean shifts across phases were large. Gibson and Ottenbacher (1988) (discussed earlier) had also included degree of mean shift as one their six variables, and again large mean shifts yielded higher interjudge agreement and greater confidence in judgments.

A major problem in studying the detection of mean shift is confounding it with other graphic characteristics, which may well be why it accounts for so little variance in judgment while emerging as a statistically significant main effect in the DeProspero and Cohen (1979) study. Mean shift will always accompany between-phase changes in trend and/or level, and may accompany changes in variability. And sometimes it is confounded with serial dependency (Gibson &

Ottenbacher, 1988; Ottenbacher, 1986). Mean shift will be present when there is no change in level or trend and no intervention effect between phases in the case of an upward/downward baseline trend continuing into an intervention attempt. In this case, a visual analyst relying only on mean shift as an indicator of an intervention effect will report change quite frivolously. Experience suggests that this misjudgment is more likely to be made if variability in the data paths masks perception of the absence of change in level and/or trend, or if phase means lines, emphasizing the shift, have been added to the graph. One way of minimizing such errors of judgment is to use trend lines (Baer & Parsonson, 1981).

Level and Trend

Half of the graphs generated by DeProspero and Cohen (1979) had a 30° upward trend, the remainder had zero slope. Their statistical analysis did not identify slope as a significant variable, although the data in their Table 1 reveal that judges' ratings almost always indicated less "experimental control" in graphs with that slope than in equivalent graphs without it. This points to some visual analysts responding to absence of trend as indicative of control. Indeed, it was the criterion most frequently mentioned by the judges.

In a study of teachers' abilities to discern trends, Munger, Snell, and Loyd (1989) investigated the effects of ascending, descending, flat, and flat but variable data paths, and four different weekly frequencies of probe-data collection (1, 2, 3, or 5 days per week). The teachers rated the degree of student progress in reading accuracy that they could see in the graphs, and also made mock decisions on program continuation. The graphs were derived from student records representing each of the data-path trends, modified to show different probe frequencies by removing enough of the intervening data points. In general, progress judgments showed accurate trend discrimination. Program-decision data showed that the average teacher would continue programs with ascending data paths and would recommend changing those with descending, flat, or flat but variable data paths. Changing the number of weekly probes did not affect judgments of progress on ascending data, but judgments were inconsistent for graphs with the other three types of data paths. Program decisions were affected by frequency of data collection (by the number of data points available for the decision) for all four classes of data path. With a very short baseline (five data points) and seven probe points spread over the 55 intervention days on the once-a-week probe graph, trend estimation is of course quite vulnerable to one or two disparate points (Cleveland, 1985). Different judgments might have been produced by plotting the dependent variable as a function simply of successive probes, rather than including in the visual display the number of days from start of baseline.

Judgments of changes in both level and/or trend were studied by Wampold and Furlong in two studies (Furlong & Wampold, 1982; Wampold & Furlong, 1981). They started with three prototypical AB graphs showing, respectively, changes in level, trend, and both level and trend. They transformed these graphs in three ways (referred to as standard, scaling, and variation transformations) to modify the visual appearance of these data paths. The judges were a group of graduate students studying single-subject research methodology, a group of students studying multivariate statistics (Wampold & Furlong, 1981), and the inevitable sample of editorial-board members of a behavior-analytic journal (JABA) (Furlong & Wampold, 1982). These judges were asked first to sort 36 graphs into whatever number of groups were justified as showing "similar effects" different from the effects of the other groups; and then to identify the common feature(s) of the graphs in each group. The single-subject students often responded primarily to the absolute size of the change from A to B; they were influenced most by those scaling transformations that enhanced both the variation and the size of the intervention effect. The multivariate students were mainly influenced by changes in level and/or trend, which often were not discriminated as such. The JABA reviewers typically did discriminate changes in level, trend, and level plus trend, and also attended frequently to absolute size of effect. The researchers suggested that the single-subject students and JABA reviewers were so strongly influenced by size of effect, rather than by more subtle relative variations in the data, because the identification of large changes has been emphasized as crucial to the character of applied behavior analysis (e.g., by Baer, 1977). (However, they drew this conclusion without evidence that their judges had ever even read those arguments, let alone agreed with them.) Ottenbacher (1986) also found that the detection of trend changes as such was made moderately difficult by the judges' ideas about clinically significant changes; the relevant correlation was 0.59. This finding was replicated by Gibson and Ottenbacher (1988), who obtained a similar correlation of 0.64, and also found raters' confidence in their judgments was lowest on graphs with trend changes across phases; they concluded that it was the characteristic most often associated with inconsistent interpretations.

The effects of level changes were studied by Gibson and Ottenbacher as well; they correlated negatively with interrater disagreement (-0.59), rater uncertainty (-0.45), and the raters' confidence in judgment (-0.52). The authors concluded that level change is the characteristic associated with the highest degrees of rater agreement, rater certainty, and rater confidence. Similarly, Bailey (1984) had special-education graduates of a course in applied behavior analysis judge whether or not significant between-phase changes in level or slope had occurred on arithmetic and semilogarithmic versions of five graphs previously used by Jones et al. (1978). Interjudge agreement on changes in level and trend on unmodified graphs (i.e., without trend lines) was consistently lower for trend changes.

The findings of Wampold and Furlong (1981), Gibson and Ottenbacher (1988), and Bailey (1984) agree: Change in level is more often agreed on than change in trend. The notion that slope can be difficult to judge is also supported by the work of Cleveland and his colleagues (Cleveland, 1985; Cleveland & McGill, 1987a; Cleveland, McGill, & McGill, 1988). In what may be a re-capitulation of the Weber–Fechner Law, their subjects' judgments of slope de-pended heavily on the magnitude of the relative angle that the data paths create when graphed, and that how steep an angle differential is needed to be seen as such varies widely across judges. Thus, research into ways to increase accurate discrimination of relative angle differential, independent of their absolute magni-tudes, is relevant. The use of trend lines for that purpose is reported later.

So far, the investigation of trend-change detection skills has focused on abrupt, sustained changes between phases. The detection of delayed or tempo-rary changes, especially within-phase changes, which also are relevant to visual analysis of behavioral data (Parsonson & Baer, 1978, 1986), remains un-analyzed. Similarly, the study of level-change detection has investigated either change in overall phase level (Furlong & Wampold, 1982; Wampold & Furlong, 1981) or abrupt change between the last data point in one phase and the first data point in the succeeding phase (Gibson & Ottenbacher, 1988). Delayed and tem-porary within-phase level changes (Parsonson & Baer, 1978) are also important real-world processes, but would not be caught (even if present) by the change-of-level judgments required in the studies reviewed so far. This is of course not a criticism of those studies, only a reminder that research examining judgments of within-phase changes, and their interaction with between-phase changes, is needed for a more complete understanding of visual analysis.

Variability and Overlap

The effect of variability in the data path has seen frequent study. DeProspero and Cohen (1979) included within-phase variation as a major variable. Absent trend, lower variability made the detection of experimental control more likely, but only in the "ideal" graphs (described earlier) and even there, only if the mean shift was of a suitable kind (p. 576). Of course large, stable mean shifts and low variability in ABAB patterns yield accurate detections of the effects that the researchers have programmed into the graphs to be seen. Indeed, control of variability is one of the goals of laboratory analysis, where it is often possible (Sidman, 1960); clear attainment of that control is usually indicative of thorough, correct analysis of the usually numerous controlling variables. In application, it often is possible to attain control of only one or two of those variables, and if they are not powerful, the effects of doing so will often escape detection. Thus, studies like these, which sometimes simulate the data of situations in which only one or a few variables have been brought under control, have great relevance for application. They also suggest that those visual analysts whose standard tactic is first to achieve thorough control of the variability of their baseline, and only then to introduce an experimental intervention, may well evaluate graphic data rather differently from those researchers who have rarely if ever had that possibility.

Perhaps that is why Ottenbacher (1986) found that changes in variability across phases did not cause very much disagreement between judges about significant changes between A and B phases of the graphs they viewed. Gibson and Ottenbacher (1988) replicated the finding, and again found only a weak correlation (0.41) between change in variability and the average judge's evaluation of the graphs. Unfortunately, that analysis did not reveal whether those judgments were influenced by the direction of the graphed change in variability: Is a variable "baseline" becoming a stable "intervention" different from a stable baseline becoming a variable intervention? In basic analysis, the two cases may be symmetrical; in applied research, they probably would not often be seen as that. The rehabilitation therapists serving as judges in this study may not have seen such cases as symmetrically as the "expert behavior analysts" of the DeProspero and Cohen (1979) study may have done.

The graphs of the Wampold and Furlong (1981) and Furlong and Wampold (1982) studies also included a variability transformation in which between-phase changes in level and/or trend were nonsignificant. They found that behavior analysts (both single-subject methodology students and JABA editors) separated these variability transformations less often than did the graduate students studying multivariate analysis, and that none of the groups made consistently sound judgments in the presence of enough variability (i.e., none grouped variability transformations separately as showing no effect). Thus, it appears that while variability did not greatly affect their judgments of change in level and/or trend, it still may have masked some intervention effects.

Furlong and Wampold (1982) suggest that graphs that are otherwise mathematically equivalent may be seen as different because judges fail to compare size of effect with variability in any systematic way (as the analysis of variance automatically does, and as its students probably learn to do implicitly, to the extent that they understand the technique that they are studying). After all, variability increases the number of slope and angle judgments necessary to judgment, both of which are associated with lower levels of accuracy in interpretation of quantitative information (Cleveland, 1985). The data presented by Munger et al. (1989) make the same point. When their teachers rated graphs with relatively few probes that showed variability but no trend, on the average they saw no student progress, and called for program changes. When probe frequency was increased, however, more teachers saw some progress and considered continuing the mock program. If general, these findings suggest that seeing an absence of trend in variable data is more difficult with many data points (i.e., with many angle and slope judgments to make and integrate into a whole pattern) than with few. Once again, research into angle discrimination seems recommended, much as Cleveland et al. (1988) have done in their investigations of orientation resolution and slope judgment. Any analogous effects of adding trend lines and smoothing data variability (e.g., plotting moving averages) also need study.

Overlap between the data points of adjacent phases has not been studied much. Gibson and Ottenbacher (1988) included it as a variable, and found that it had little influence on rater disagreement, but was weakly correlated (0.36) with the raters' uncertainty (the greater the overlap between baseline and intervention data, the lower the certainty of change). Overlap also was moderately correlated (-0.74), negatively, with the detection of between-phase changes.

Of course, there are no guidelines on how much overlap is too much to allow a conclusion that the intervention has produced a change. Perhaps applied judges will see early overlap as less contradictory of an eventually useful intervention effect than enduring or later overlap—that describes much of their work eventually taken as good enough. Ultimately, the applied evaluation of any difference, including overlapping ones, depends on a cost-benefit analysis; in the case of overlap, the question changes only a little, into asking whether the benefit of changing only some data points from the baseline range is still worth the cost of doing so. The answer obviously could be either Yes or No, depending on context.

Types of Graphing

In one of the few studies of its kind, Knapp (1983) investigated how graphing techniques could affect the detection of change, using three formats: the cumulative, semilogarithmic, and frequency-polygon types. (The last term refers to the modal arithmetic-scale line graphs of everyday journal use). In addition, the study incorporated three ways of representing the AB change (on the arithmetic frequency-polygon graphs): by a space between the A and B data paths, by a vertical line between them, or without separation—a continuous data path from the start of A to the end of B. Furthermore, various degrees of mean shift between phases were represented.

The judges comprised three groups: 12 behavior analysts per group, described as undergraduates, graduate students, and postgraduate reviewers (i.e., the inevitable editorial-board members/guest reviewers). They judged a total of 147 graphs, most of them generated by the author, mostly in the AB format, and some of them taken from those used by Jones et al. (1978). The three groups of judges did not differ significantly. A statistical analysis revealed some statistically significant ($p = .05$) differences due to graphing technique, the degree of mean shift, and their interaction. Semilogarithmic charts produced the least consensus, but only on "no change" judgments; line graphs with no visual separation of the A and B data points produced the most. It was of course mainly in the middle range of mean-shift amounts that judgment differences due to graphing techniques emerged. The author concluded that the graphing technique used influenced judgments of change at critical mean shifts.

These outcomes are not surprising, given that apparent slope and apparent size of mean shift are likely to vary between arithmetic, cumulative, and semilogarithmic charts, with the differences becoming more critical at moderate, rather than extreme, mean shifts. Once again, the judges' abilities to discriminate angle differentials independently of angle magnitude may be critical. Knapp sees the influence of connecting the baseline and intervention data paths as an "irrelevant structural feature" (p. 162), and argues that it should not affect judgment; but perhaps it should not be discounted (cf. Cleveland, 1984; Parsonson & Baer, 1978). Graphing technique may prove powerful; the Knapp (1983) study, and the Bailey (1984) study to be reported in the next section, are too few to allow a reliable judgment.

Trend Lines

In an effort to improve the discrimination of the angles that represent slope changes, especially in the face of extreme data-path variability, a number of authors have used trend lines as judgmental aids (e.g., Baer & Parsonson, 1981; Kazdin, 1982; Parsonson & Baer, 1978; White, 1973, 1974; White & Haring, 1980). Some recent studies have examined the effects of superimposing trend lines generated by the "split-middle" (White, 1974) and least-squares regression procedures. Bailey (1984) obtained judgments from 13 special-education graduate students on the significance of the change in level and/or slope in each phase of five graphs (from Jones et al., 1978); these were presented both in arithmetic and semilogarithmic form, and with and without split-middle trend lines. The trend lines increased interjudge agreement about level and trend changes in both arithmetic and semilogarithmic charts. However, while judgments not simply of change but of significant trend changes increased with arithmetic charts (from 51% to 77%), they declined with semilogarithmic (from 45% to 31%).

Clearly, the two kinds of graph can look quite different. Lutz (1949) suggests that many untrained judges simply misread semilogarithmic charts. Knapp (1983) later made a similar argument, citing the typical unfamiliarity of judges with the special characteristics of the logarithmic ordinate. Bailey (1984), quite commendably, did not compare his judges' accuracy in judging level or trend changes against any of the numerous statistical criteria available to him (or anyone); but he also did not investigate whether serial dependency affected those judgments differentially according to the kind of ordinate on which they were graphed, or the use of trend lines. Those problems thus remain unstudied.

True, the Rojahn and Schulze (1985) study (already described above in the serial-dependency section) did show that adding trend lines can increase the similarity between visual and statistical analysis; but no attempt was made to determine how trend lines might have affected rater consistency. However, this was one of the aims of a study by Skiba, Deno, Marston, and Casey (1989). They asked several special-education resource teachers to judge the reading-performance graphs of four of their students, specifically to say whether one of two interventions shown in the graphs was better than the other, to rate their confidence in that judgment, and to state the criteria they had used (level, trend, and/or variability). Their judgments were recorded twice, once prior to training in the use of the quarter-intersect trend-line procedure (White & Haring, 1980), and again afterward. Interrater agreement increased from 0.56 at pretraining to 0.78 after learning to use trend lines. After training, the teachers showed increased confidence in their judgments, and almost total reliance on trend, ignoring level and variability as criteria. Hojem and Ottenbacher (1988) compared the judgments of a group of health-profession students after one lesson in visual analysis ($N = 20$) with those of a group given similarly brief training in computing and projecting split-middle trend lines from baseline through intervention ($N = 19$). Five of the graphs used earlier by Ottenbacher (1986) were rated for significance of change in performance across the two phases. Statistical analysis revealed significant differences in the ratings assigned to four of the five graphs by the visual analysis and trend-analysis groups: The trend-analysis group showed greater confidence in their ratings; the visual-analysis group showed slightly lower overall agreement. Commendably, Hojem and Ottenbacher did not compare their subjects' judgments to the particular statistical criteria that Ottenbacher had provided in the earlier (1986) study. If made, those comparisons would have suggested that most of the visual-analysis group judged two of five graphs "incorrectly" (not in accord with the essentially arbitrary statistical judgment). Almost all of the trend-line group misjudged one of the assumed-to-be significant graphs. On the other hand, they were not misled by the large mean shift of another graph, which the researchers' statistical analysis had suggested could most parsimoniously be considered a continuation of a baseline trend after an ineffective intervention. Most of the visual-analysis group had seen this graph as a significant intervention effect. Thus, brief training in trend-line plotting had produced somewhat more agreement with at least one line of statistical analysis than was seen in the judgments of the visual-analysis group, in both the Ottenbacher (1986) and Hojem and Ottenbacher (1988) studies.

The results of these studies suggest that trend lines through the various phases of a study (Bailey, 1984; Rojahn & Schulze, 1985; Skiba et al., 1989) or projected from baseline through intervention (Hojem & Ottenbacher, 1988) may alter interjudge agreement by providing common stimuli for determining the direction and amount of change in overall trend and/or level occurring between phases. There also is evidence from the studies by Bailey (1984), Hojem and Ottenbacher (1988), and Skiba et al. (1989) that the presence of trend lines alters judges' confidence in their decisions. In addition, it seems that adding trend lines may increase the similarity between visual and at least some statistical analyses, but not at the price of the conservatism of visual judgments. The unanswered question is whether that is a good outcome.

These findings, coupled with the difficulties of accurate slope estimation by untrained viewers, might be seen as a recommendation that trend lines always be used. However, remember that Skiba et al. (1989) found that judges taught to use trend lines came to rely on them: They then attended much less to all other data-path characteristics, such as level and variability. Furthermore, while between-phase trend lines certainly do summarize trend and level changes instantly and clearly to the eye, they can also obscure from that same eye the within-phase changes in the variability, level, overlap, pattern, and latency of change, all of which can contribute important hypotheses about the nature of the behavior change under study (Parsonson & Baer, 1978, 1986). We need further research to show how trend-line analysis can be taught and used without paying any of that price. That research should be done under the assumption that this is only a training problem, not a fixed characteristic of visual analysis.

These studies used either median split (split-middle, quarter intersect) or least-squares regression procedures. Shinn, Good, and Stein (1989) studied the comparative predictive validity of these procedures. They asked special-education teachers to graph the reading progress of 20 mildly handicapped students. Each student's graph was offered in three versions, the first covering data points 1 to 10, the second, 1 to 20, and the third, 1 to 30. Times at 2, 4, and 6 weeks following the final data point on each partial graph were defined as the occasions when predictions based on trend-line projections from the partial graphs would be tested against actual student performance. Graduate students, well trained in the "split-middle" technique but unaware of the aims of the study, were given the partial graphs and asked to produce a split-middle trend line for each one, projecting it to the three designated prediction days. Reliability checks showed 0.91–0.99 agreement among them in generating these lines.

Then least-squares trend lines were obtained for the same data sets and projected over the same time spans. After that, actual student reading performance at each trend-line prediction point was taken as the median of the three actual data points nearest that day. Neither procedure systematically over- or under-predicted performance, but the least-squares procedure yielded better precision most consistently across all numbers of points and all three lengths of prediction.

Yet both procedures have disadvantages. In using the split-middle technique, Shinn et al. (1989) occasionally obtained very inaccurate predictions. This has also been the experience of the present authors, and the conditions that produce these deviant trend lines require examination. One contributing factor may be the requirement that the trend line must have the same number of data points on or above it as fall on or below it. Two disadvantages claimed for the least-squares procedure are its difficulty of computation, and the effects of extreme outlying data points on the trend line (Baer & Parsonson, 1981; Shinn et al., 1989). The former can be overcome by using the calculation algorithm provided by Baer and Parsonson (1981). However, the disproportionate effect of extreme outliers is inherent in the least-squares technique. Thus there is value in examining the applicability of alternative methods of generating trend lines, such as Cleveland's

LOWESS (1985) and the variety of ways of weighting regression calculations (Huber, 1973, cited in Cleveland & McGill, 1987a). The interesting question is what criteria we should use to evaluate these alternatives.

Problems in the Current Research

In all of the studies discussed here, raters evaluated only graphs. Thus, they were not evaluating data under the normal conditions of research and application.

First, there was an absence of the abundant and complex contextual information normally associated with evaluating data: the study's aims, the special characteristics of its subjects and its intervention personnel, all that is known about these intervention procedures and their interaction with these kinds of subjects and intervention personnel, all that is known about these kinds of measurement techniques and how they interact with these kinds of subjects and intervention personnel, and certainly not least, the graphing method, which in these studies may often have been different from the techniques the judges would have chosen. Indeed, the judges' additional opinions, when solicited, often enough included complaints about this (DeProspero & Cohen, 1979; Knapp, 1983).

Indeed, except for the graphs used by Jones et al. (1978), there was an absence or paucity of the usual information even on the graphs' axes—information about the dependent and independent variables, such as those considerations listed in the preceding paragraph. This point is important, in that it reminds us that there are two conceivable domains of reading graphs: the real-world domain, in which researcher's and articles' graphs always come with full contextual information and well-marked axes; and a theoretical domain in which graphs are merely abstract, content-free forms specifying that an undescribed behavior was measured by an undescribed process under some undescribed conditions over an unspecified length of time, and yielded the graph shown, much like the first graph presented in this chapter. The latter approach assumes that certain visual forms are stimulus controls for corresponding conclusions about the relationships between data and the conditions under which they were gathered—visual forms that *should* function as stimulus controls for certain conclusions no matter what the contextual information might be.

On reflection, it may seem that this approach is an attempt to convert graphic analysis, recommended here in part because it allows the researcher to exercise skilled personal judgment in deciding what an experiment shows, into the objective, supposedly judgment-free decision making put forward as the ideal outcome of statistical analysis. True, there are visual forms that tend to compel certain conclusions no matter what their content might be; the first graph of this chapter was constructed with one of those forms to accomplish exactly that. Thus, there are indeed such forms; in an earlier era, they would be referred to as *gestalts*. But the problem in relying exclusively on them is that doing so does not represent much of the real-world research and clinical practice under study. Researchers, clinicians, teachers, and literature readers never examine content-free graphs for very long; invariably, they see those visual forms only in context, and almost certainly, their final conclusions about those graphs result from an interaction between the form, the clarity with which the actual data fit the form, and the total context relevant to those data. Thus studies of the interpretation of content-free graphs are a crucial part of the analysis of graphical interpretation, but gravely incomplete as an analysis of the real-world process.

Second, many of these studies were group designs using statistical analysis to understand the use of graphic analysis with single-subject designs. In other words, tools and designs from one domain of inquiry were used to evaluate the tools and designs of another—tools and designs that are usually adopted systematically by those researchers who have found the alternatives inadequate for their purposes. This evaluation is formally possible, of course; we remark only on the irony of it. It would be interesting to discover how many journals devoted to the statistical analysis of data from group designs would publish a single-subject design using visual analysis to clarify *their* methodology.

Perhaps a chapter like this one should confront its readers directly with a rudimentary assessment of their own visual analysis skills, now that the readers have read about the variables controlling others' visual analysis skills. For that purpose, two sets of six graphs each have been prepared and are presented here (see Figs. 2.2 and 2.3).

The first graph of the first set was constructed by entering a random-number table at random and taking the first 40 digits (the integers between 0 and 9) that the table presented there. The first graph of the second set was constructed in the same way, subsequent to a second randomly chosen entry of the random-number table. Two sets were made only because even one replication conveys a great deal more generality than a single experience.

Each of these two groups of 40 digits was then divided into the first 10 digits, the second 10, the third 10, and the fourth 10, in the order in which they were found in the table. The first and third groups of 10 were considered as an A condition and its repetition; and the second and fourth were considered as a B condition and its repetition.

The first graph in each of these two six-graph sets is simply a graph of these 40 numbers as an ABAB design. The second graph adds a constant 1 to each number in the two B conditions; the third adds a constant 2 to each number in the two B conditions, the fourth a constant 3, the fifth a constant 4, and the sixth a constant 5. Beside each graph is printed the probability-level result of what is often called an independent-t test of the hypothesis that the 20 As are a sample from the same population as the 20 Bs. (In that these digits in fact are drawn from a random-number table, they should be totally independent of each other—free of autocorrelation—and thus quite suitable for that test.) No other context of any sort is specified; take them as pure forms.

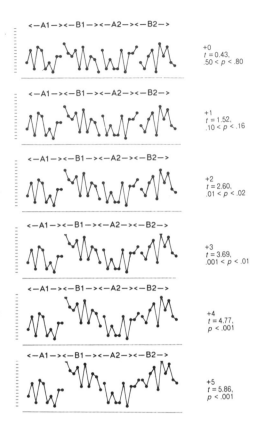

FIG. 2.2.   At the top, a graph of 40 successive digits drawn from a random-number table, arranged as if in an ABAB single-subject experimental design, and below it, five regraphings of those points. In the five regraphings (the second through sixth of these graphs), a constant has been added to each of the 20 points in the two B conditions; the value of the constant is shown at the right of each graph, along with the t statistic and probability level resulting from an independent-t test applied to these data.

These graphs create three very interesting questions for visual analysts. The first question is what magnitude of a simple additive effect you require to answer Yes to either of two questions about each of the six graphs in each set: (1) Speaking only to yourself, do you think that there is a systematic B effect? (2) Are you willing to publish these data under your name as an example of a systematic B effect? Many visual analysts may discover that there is a U-shaped interaction between the size of the additive effect and the similarity of their answers to these two questions (i.e., they answer similarly with No to both questions at the +0 and +1 levels, and similarly with Yes to both questions at the +5 level, but dissimilarly to the two questions at the intermediate +2, +3, and perhaps +4 levels). Some visual analysts may also be surprised to discover that given the variability of this simple distribution, the addition even of 5 to each point in B—which on the average should more than double the mean of the B conditions relative to the 4.5 mean generally characterizing A conditions of this distribution—does not always allow them an unequivocal Yes answer to the second question.

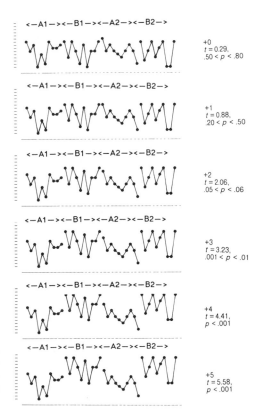

FIG. 2.3. A replication of Fig. 2.2, but with 40 successive digits drawn from another randomly selected part of the same random-number table.

The second question is whether you are as sensitive as the t test. Many visual analysts may find that while the addition of a constant 2 to the B points achieves (or virtually achieves) the conventional level of statistical significance via the t test, they are not willing to answer Yes to even the first question until the $+3$, and some only at the $+4$ level or $+5$ level. Baer (1977) has argued that visual analysts responding to data in single-subject designs probably display lower probabilities of Type-1 errors, and thereby correspondingly higher probabilities of Type-2 errors, than would many of the usual statistical analyses, and that doing so is an important component in developing an effective technology of behavior change. This tiny exercise is an example of the argument, but of course is not a proof of its generality.

The third question also cannot be answered by so tiny an exercise, but it can be suggested by it: If you are discovering that you cannot see the effects of some actually effective interventions as reliable—in particular, the adding of 1, 2, 3, or 4 to each observation in the B conditions—is that kind of discovery likely to change what you can see as an effect in the future? In other words, could you train yourself to detect such effects by exposing yourself to many, many graphs like these, one after another, some with an intervention of constant effectiveness, some without; then making your estimate of whether the Bs are different from the As; and then promptly being informed of exactly the extent to which the Bs are different from the As, if they are? Program your computer to present you with many such graphs of every kind of relevant effect (additive, multiplicative, autocorrelated, constant, variable, increasing, decreasing) in unknown and un-predictable order; to record your keyboarded answers to the two questions; and then to inform you of the truth. See if your standards are modifiable by this kind of feedback, which you will never encounter with the same certainty in real-life research and practice, yet which is exactly the appropriate reinforcer: knowledge of whether you were correct or incorrect. That is why graphs are made and read, is it not? Not to be rich, not to be liked, but to find out?

Third, the graphs of these studies often were devised by the researchers to display data characteristics prescribed by theories about the kinds of data that there should be, rather than representing actual data; they may have looked other worldly to many experienced viewers.

Fourth, in many instances (e.g., Rojahn & Schulze, 1985) only AB data formats were offered; these are not at all the typical designs of applied behavior-analytic research. True, the AB design is in principle the irreducible unit of single-subject research design, and some researchers under some conditions will consider it sufficient to allow a firm conclusion, when the data offer a perfect picture of experimental control. But much more of the field uses the AB design perhaps as a unit, but one so rarely offered alone as a form of proof that we could reasonably argue that for them, an ABA, BAB, or ABAB pattern is the func-tional unit controlling conclusions.

Fifth, at times the questions asked of the judges were ill defined, so that unmeasured, uncontrolled differences in interpretation may have accounted for low agreement. Many, many times the authors have found that students are willing to draw one conclusion in private, a somewhat different one if they expect their dissertation adviser to agree to it, yet a different one if they wish their dissertation oral-examination committee to agree, and a still different one for submission to a journal editor and, by presumption, their total professional audience. This point is not offered as an amusing picture of immature scientists at work, but as a realistic picture of virtually all scientists at work, who know not only what they think but also what other enthusiasts who like that conclusion will think, what scientists supportive of them but skeptical of their conclusion will think, and what unsupportive skeptics will think.

For example, Jones et al. (1978) asked if there was a "meaningful [reliable] change in level" across phases, but "reliable" was not defined: stable, durable, replicated? Nor was "change in level" defined (Is it the last data point in one phase compared with the first in the next, or mean shift across phases, or trend lines showing an overall change in phase level)?

Sixth, most studies included subjects with little or no knowledge or experience of visual analysis, and asked them to interpret the statistical or clinical significance of changes.

Seventh, in none of the studies were fine-grained analyses of within-phase variables investigated.

Eighth, in many studies a number of variables possibly relevant to visual analysis were confounded or manipulated simultaneously, making it difficult to identify the specific effects of any one variable on visual analysis.

Ninth, some studies used AB graphs in which a definite effect had been systematically programmed into the B conditions, and others in which no effect other than random variation distinguished the B condition from the A condition. In these studies, it was at least possible to ask how often visual analysis could detect the truth, which was that difference or lack of it, and to compare that rate of detecting that truth under various experimental conditions and to other methods of evaluating the same data, such as any of the numerous statistical models available and conceivably appropriate. But in many other studies, there was no known truth; the graphs had been chosen from the journals of the field, or had been constructed to display common or tricky patterns. In this latter case, when a certain statistical analysis says that there is a difference, and another statistical analysis says that there is not, and visual analysis says that there is or is not, which is correct? Indeed, does "correct" have any useful meaning in that context? The fact that these methods often generate different conclusions about the same data is an almost useless fact, unless we know which conclusion is somehow the better one.

As a consequence of these inadequacies, only tentative conclusions about the nature and effects of the variables influencing visual analysis seem justified so far. The differences from actual practice mean that it is impossible to know precisely how they affect the day-to-day judgments of persons making decisions from ongoing research or intervention data or from published research.

Future Developments

In addition to the areas of further research that have been suggested, there is a need for those interested in visual analysis to become familiar with developments in theory and research outside behavior analysis and to examine their applicability to the data-analysis problems we face. For example, in the areas of data presentation and information processing, Bertin (1981, 1983) and, as was recommended earlier, Tufte (1983, 1990) provide stimulating theoretical ideas and practical methods of evaluating and presenting data graphically. Some of the most significant contributions in the area of graphic discriminations have come through the careful parametric studies of Cleveland and his associates (Cleveland, 1984, 1985; Cleveland & McGill, 1984, 1986, 1987a; Cleveland et al., 1988). This work provides theoretical models founded in psychophysics and statistics that have been examined and developed thoroughly through research; consequently, they reflect a high standard of scientific inquiry and offer a conventionally sound platform for the further study of variables affecting visual analysis. We also may find ourselves shaped in our visual analyses by developments in the field of computer graphics, especially in the use of dynamic graphics (Cleveland & McGill, 1987b), to explore the effects of changing graphic formats and data-path characteristics, some of which may optimize data presentation and analysis. Finally, we can usefully explore the application of new designs and different types of graphing in our efforts to enhance communication and comprehension of the results of behavior-analytic research.

REFERENCES

Baer, D. M. (1977). Perhaps it would be better not to know everything. *Journal of Applied Behavior Analysis, 10*, 167–172.

Baer, D. M. (1988). An autocorrelated commentary on the need for a different debate. *Behavioral Assessment, 10*, 295–298.

Baer, D. M., & Parsonson, B. S. (1981). Applied changes from the steady state: Still a problem in the visual analysis of data. In C. M. Bradshaw, E. Szabadi, & C. F. Lowe (Eds.), *Quantification of steady-state operant behaviour* (pp. 273–285). Amsterdam: Elsevier/North Holland Biomedical Press.

Bailey, D. B., Jr. (1984). Effects of lines of progress and semilogarithmic charts on ratings of charted data. *Journal of Applied Behavior Analysis, 17*, 359–365.

Bertin, J. (1981). *Graphics and graphic information processing* (W. J. Berg & P. Scott, Trans.). New York: de Gruyter. (Original work published 1977)

Bertin, J. (1983). *Semiology of graphics.* (W. J. Berg, Trans.). Madison: University of Wisconsin Press. (Original work published 1973)

Busk, P. L., & Marascuilo, L. A. (1988). Autocorrelation in single-subject research: A counterargument to the myth of no autocorrelation. *Behavioral Assessment, 10*, 229–242.

Cleveland, W. S. (1984). Graphical methods for data presentation: Full scale breaks, dot charts, and multibased logging. *American Statistician, 38*(4), 270–280.

Cleveland, W. S. (1985). *Elements of graphing data.* Monterey, CA: Wadsworth.

Cleveland, W. S., & McGill, R. (1984). Graphical perception: Theory, experimentation, and application to the development of graphical methods. *Journal of the American Statistical Association, 79*(387), 531–554.

Cleveland, W. S., & McGill, R. (1986). An experiment in graphical perception. *International Journal of Man-Machine Studies, 25*, 491–500.

Cleveland, W. S., & McGill, R. (1987a). Graphical perception: The visual decoding of quantitative information on graphical displays of data. *Journal of the Royal Statistical Society, 150*(3), 192–229.

Cleveland, W. S., & McGill, R. (1987b). *Dynamic graphics for statistics.* Monterey, CA: Wadsworth.

Cleveland, W. S., McGill, M. E., & McGill, R. (1988). The shape parameter of a two-variable graph. *Journal of the American Statistical Association, 83*(402), 289–300.

Cooper, J. O., Heron, T. E., & Heward, W. L. (1986). *Applied behavior analysis.* Columbus, OH: Merrill.

De Prospero, A., & Cohen, S. (1979). Inconsistent visual analyses of intrasubject data. *Journal of Applied Behavior Analysis, 12*, 573–579.

Furlong, M. J., & Wampold, B. E. (1982). Intervention effects and relative variation as dimensions in experts' use of visual inference. *Journal of Applied Behavior Analysis, 15*, 415–421.

Gibson, G., & Ottenbacher, K. (1988). Characteristics influencing the visual analysis of single-subject data: An empirical analysis. *Journal of Applied Behavioral Science, 24*(3), 298–314.

Heshusius, L. (1982). At the heart of the advocacy dilemma: A mechanistic world view. *Exceptional Children, 49*(1), 6–13.

Hojem, M. A., & Ottenbacher, K. J. (1988). Empirical investigation of visual-inspection versus trend-line analysis of single-subject data. *Journal of the American Physical Therapy Association, 68*, 983–988.

Huitema, B. E. (1986). Autocorrelation in behavioral research: Wherefore art thou? In A. Poling, & R. W. Fuqua (Eds.), *Research methods in applied behavior analysis: Issues and advances* (pp. 187–208). New York: Plenum Press.

Huitema, B. E. (1988). Autocorrelation: 10 years of confusion. *Behavioral Assessment, 10*, 253–294.

Jones, R. R., Weinrott, M. R., & Vaught, R. S. (1978). Effects of serial dependency on the agreement between visual and statistical inference. *Journal of Applied Behavior Analysis, 11*, 277–283.

Kazdin, A. E. (1982). *Single-case research designs: Methods for clinical and applied settings.* New York: Oxford University Press.

Knapp, T. J. (1983). Behavior analysts' visual appraisal of behavior change in graphic display. *Behavioral Assessment, 5*, 155–164.

Lutz, R. R. (1949). *Graphic presentation simplified.* New York: Funk & Wagnalls.

Munger, G. F., Snell, M. E., & Loyd, B. H. (1989). A study of the effects of frequency of probe data collection and graph characteristics on teachers' visual analysis. *Research in Developmental Disabilities, 10*, 109–127.

Ottenbacher, K. J. (1986). Reliability and accuracy of visually analyzing graphed data from single-subject designs. *American Journal of Occupational Therapy, 40*, 464–469.

Parsonson, B. S., & Baer, D. M. (1978). The analysis and presentation of graphic data. In T. R. Kratochwill (Ed.), *Single-subject research: Strategies for evaluating change* (pp. 101–165). New York: Academic Press.

Parsonson, B. S., & Baer, D. M. (1986). The graphic analysis of data. In A. Poling & R. W. Fuqua (Eds.), *Research methods in applied behavior analysis: Issues and advances* (pp. 157–186). New York: Plenum Press.

Rojahn, J., & Schulze, H-H. (1985). The linear regression line as a judgmental aid in the visual analysis of serially dependent A–B time-series data. *Journal of Psychopathology and Behavioral Assessment, 7*, 191–206.

Sharpley, C. F., & Alavosius, M. P. (1988). Autocorrelation in behavioral data: An alternative perspective. *Behavioral Assessment, 10*, 243–251.

Shinn, M. R., Good, R. H., & Stein, S. (1989). Summarizing trend in student achievement: A comparison of methods. *School Psychology Review, 18*, 356–370.

Sidman, M. (1960). *Tactics of scientific research.* New York: Basic Books.

Skiba, R., Deno, S., Marston, D., & Casey, A. (1989). Influence of trend estimation and subject familiarity on practitioners' judgments of intervention effectiveness. *Journal of Special Education, 22*, 433–446.

Tawney, J. W., & Gast, D. L. (1984). *Single-subject research in special education.* Columbus, OH: Merrill.

Tufte, E. R. (1983). *The visual display of quantitative information.* Cheshire, CT: Graphics Press.

Tufte, E. R. (1990). *Envisioning information.* Cheshire, CT: Graphics Press.

Wampold, B. E., & Furlong, M. J. (1981). The heuristics of visual inference. *Behavioral Assessment, 3*, 71–92.

White, O. R. (1973). *A manual for the calculation of the median slope: A technique of progress estimation and prediction in the single case.* (Working paper No. 16). Eugene: University of Oregon, Regional Resource Center for Handicapped Children.

White, O. R. (1974). *The "split middle": A "quickie" method of trend estimation* (3rd revision). Unpublished manuscript, University of Washington, Experimental Education Unit, Child Development and Mental Retardation Center, Seattle.

White, O. R., & Haring, N. G. (1980) *Exceptional teaching* (2nd ed.). Columbus, OH: Merrill.

3 Philosophical and Statistical Foundations of Time-Series Experiments

Richard McCleary
University of California, Irvine

Wayne N. Welsh
Department of Criminal Justice, Temple University

Due to the influence of D. T. Campbell (1963, 1969; Campbell & Stanley, 1966; Cook & Campbell, 1979) and G. V. Glass (Glass, Willson, & Gottman, 1975), time-series "experiment" (or "quasi-experiment") has come to mean a simple contrast of pre- and postintervention levels of a dependent-variable time series. While this narrow definition simplifies the explication of validity and related design issues, it obscures the analytical problems common to all longitudinal analyses. From a statistical perspective, virtually all time-series analyses confront the same obstacle and strive for the same goal. Since this essay focuses on these statistical issues, we expand the definition of "time-series experiment" to include three variations. A few examples illustrate this broader, more realistic definition.

The time series in Fig. 3.1 illustrates the conventional type of time-series "experiment" which, for purposes of exposition, we call the *interrupted* time-series design (McDowall, McCleary, Hay, & Meidinger, 1980). These data are average monthly calls to Directory Assistance in Cincinnati (McSweeney, 1978). The series appears to trend upward until the 147th month, at which point the level of the series changes dramatically, dropping from a high of 90,000 to a low of 15,000 per month. Prior to March, 1974, the 147th month, Directory Assistance calls were free of charge. Thereafter, Cincinnati Bell initiated a 20-cent charge for each call. If the goal of an interrupted time-series experiment is to determine whether a treatment or intervention has had an impact on the dependent variable, in this case, there is little doubt. The visual impact of this intervention is striking.

Fig. 3.2 shows a more typical example of the interrupted time-series design.

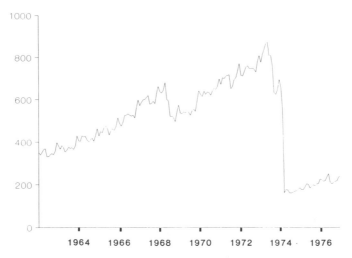

FIG. 3.1. Calls to Cincinnati directory assistance.

These data are weekly productivity measures for five workers in the first relay assembly room of the Hawthorne Western Electric plant near Chicago. From 1927 to 1933, Elton Mayo, Fritz Roethlisberger, and William Dickson examined the impact of rest pauses, shorter working days, and wage incentives on worker productivity (Gordon, 1983). Although the results of this famous experiment have been interpreted as evidence that improvements in social relations result in increases in productivity, analyses by Franke and Kaule (1978) suggest a more cynical interpretation.

On January 25, 1928, at the end of the 39th week, Workers 1 and 2 were replaced by Workers 1A and 2A, an effect Franke and Kaul called "managerial discipline" (labeled "A" in Fig. 3.2). These two workers, they suggest, were replaced by management "because of their unsatisfactory attitudes in response to requests for greater diligence and more output" (p. 627). If workers who performed inadequately were replaced, the productivity trends in Fig. 3.2 would be due mainly to simple managerial discipline and, to a lesser degree, economic adversity and scheduled rest time. On the other hand, Schlaifer (1980) argues that the two workers were replaced not for discipline, but because they threatened the integrity of the experiment. This is an empirical question, of course, which we will address at a later point.

The second "intervention" in Fig. 3.2 was the October 24, 1929, stock market crash at the end of the 130th week (labeled "B" in Fig. 3.2); Franke and Kaul suggested this created job insecurity and spurred workers to increase their productivity. Schlaifer (1980) suggests that little job insecurity was likely experienced by workers until May 5, 1930 (the 158th week), when layoffs began (labeled "C" in Fig. 3.2).

A – Workers 1 and 2 Are
      Replaced

B – Stock Market Crashes

C – Layoffs Begin

D – Worker 5 Leaves

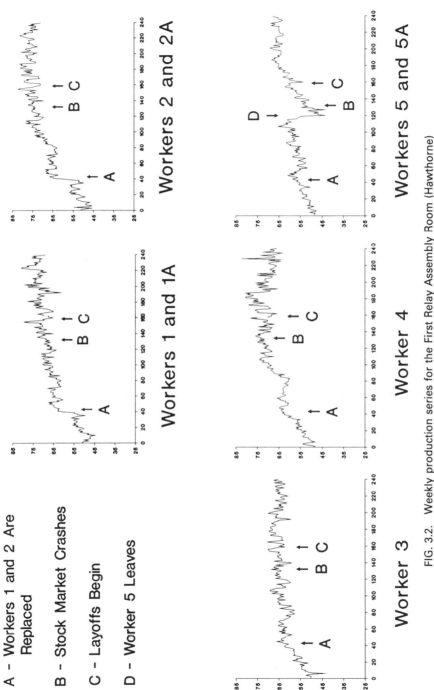

FIG. 3.2. Weekly production series for the First Relay Assembly Room (Hawthorne) experiment.

Finally, Franke and Kaul (1978) suggested that increases in rest time at different periods (not shown here) had the effect of increasing worker productivity (number of relay switches produced per hour per operator) by reducing fatigue. An additional incident that had a negative, rather than a positive impact on productivity was the temporary, voluntary replacement of Worker 5 by a less-experienced and less-skilled worker in the 120th week (labeled "D" in Fig. 3.2); she returned in the 160th week of the experiment. Franke and Kaul argued that managerial discipline had the strongest effect of these hypothetical explanatory variables on increased worker productivity. Overall, they suggested, these three variables (discipline, crash, and rest time) provided better explanations for improved productivity than "unmeasured changes in the human relations of workers" (p. 638), which, of course, was the conclusion of the original Hawthorne researchers.

The validity of this interpretation not withstanding, this series and the Directory Assistance series in Fig. 3.1 exhibit *trend,* a common property of longitudinal data. Trend complicates analyses of time-series experiments. In this particular case, since the series rises consistently from 1927 to 1932, literally any intervention will have an apparent impact on productivity. Comparing the productivity of these workers before and after the October, 1929, stock market crash, for example, will lead to the conclusion that this event had a profound impact on the workers' performance. In fact, this is the basis of an unresolved dispute between Franke (1980) and Schlaifer (1980) whose details will be addressed shortly.

In both the Hawthorne and Directory Assistance examples, an intervention occurs at a known point in time. In both cases, we hypothesize that the series level changes at the intervention point, so a null hypothesis of no impact is tested by comparing the series level before and after the intervention. The most obvious difference between these two examples is the magnitudes of the respective effects. In the Hawthorne experiment, there is a gradual upward trend throughout the time series and a slight shift in the level of the series at the point where two of the workers are replaced for disciplinary reasons. In the Directory Assistance example, the series trends upward until the point where a charge is implemented. In this case, however, the series level not only shifts dramatically at the point of intervention, but does so in a negative direction. Statistical analysis is not necessary to conclude that the intervention effect in the Directory Assistance example is stronger than the intervention effect in the Hawthorne series. Unfortunately, profound effects are rare. Smaller, gradual effects are the norm in social sciences applications and, for this reason, design of a time-series experiment is a crucial concern.

Threats to internal validity are the most common problems associated with the interrupted time-series design. For example, is it plausible that the productivity impacts observed in the Hawthorne experiment are not due to the hypothesized intervention but, rather, to some natural process, such as workers learning their jobs better (Pitcher, 1981)? Questions of this sort can only be answered by assessing the impact of alternative explanations, usually, by incorporating proxy variables for the threats to internal validity into the analytical model. Questions of internal validity do not concern us in this chapter, however.

To develop a statistical model for analysis of the interrupted time-series design, let Y_t denote the tth observation of a dependent variable time series— monthly calls to Directory Assistance or weekly productivity measures in our two examples—and let X_t be a binary variable corresponding to the intervention. That is

$$X_t = 0 \text{ prior to an intervention}$$
$$= 1 \text{ thereafter}$$

The expected impact of the intervention is then given by the model

$$Y_t = \beta_0 + \beta_1 X_t$$

Pre-intervention, that is, $X_t = 0$ and[1]

$$E(Y_t | X_t = 0) = \beta_0$$

Postintervention, on the other hand, $X_t = 1$ and

$$E(Y_t | X_t = 1) = \beta_0 + \beta_1$$

So β_1 is the *impact* of the intervention on the level of Y_t.

Ignoring the problem of estimating β_1, a generalization of this model suggests a second type of time-series experiment. If X_t is itself an integral ("real") time series, β_1 is the *effect* of X_t on Y_t. The resulting *concomitant* time-series experiment analyzes patterns of covariance in two or more series to determine whether the covariation is due to a causal relationship (Cook, Dintzer, & Mark, 1980; Mark, 1979). The data in Fig. 3.3, for example, are the cotton price and lynching time series used by Hovland and Sears (1940) to test the frustration–aggression hypothesis of Dollard, Doob, Miller, Mowrer, and Sears (1939). In simple terms, the frustration–aggression hypothesis holds that aggression results whenever goal-oriented behavior is frustrated. As Hovland and Sears state: "The strength of instigation to aggression varies with the amount of interference with the frustrated goal-response" (1940, p. 301). Hovland and Sears argue that aggressive acts will rise during economic depression and fall during years of prosperity. In general, bad economic conditions represent a greater interference with customary goal responses than good conditions.

This hypothesis was tested by correlating the number of lynchings during the years 1882 to 1930 with cotton prices (most lynchings occurred in the 14 Southern states where cotton was the basic commodity). Hovland and Sears argued that

---

[1]$E(Y_t)$ denotes the "expected value" of Y_t, in this case, the arithmetical mean or "level" of the dependent-variable time series. Expectation algebra is developed in an appendix to this chapter.

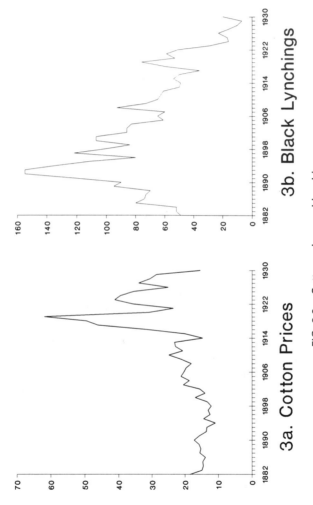

3a. Cotton Prices

3b. Black Lynchings

FIG. 3.3.   Cotton prices and lynchings.

a negative correlation between these measures indicated a displacement of aggression toward persons in a less-favorable and protected position in society. The study demonstrated that aggression resulted not only from psychological factors, but from a complex of social, psychological, political, and economic factors (Goldstein, 1986).

For another example, Fig. 3.4 shows the number of references to two personality tests, the Rorschach and MMPI, indexed in *Psychological Abstracts* for 1950–1985 (Polyson, Peterson, & Marshall, 1986). Prior research has demonstrated that the Rorschach and MMPI were the two most heavily researched psychological tests. Polyson et al. reported that research on both the MMPI and Rorschach declined from 1971 to 1975, but thereafter, Rorschach references leveled off at about 40–60 references per year, while the MMPI enjoyed a renewal in research interest. Averaging the yearly references for each test for the decades 1950–1959, 1960–1969, and 1970–1979, Polyson et al. suggest that an interesting trend appears: in the 1950s, Rorschach references far outnumbered those for the MMPI. In the 1960s, average references for the two tests did not differ significantly, while the average yearly references for the MMPI outstripped those of the Rorschach in the 1970s. This led Polyson et al. to suggest a "competition" hypothesis between the two tests. There may be a negative correlation between the yearly research levels for the two tests, such that productive years for one test tend to be relatively unproductive for the other. The basis of this hypothesis is a possible competition between the two schools of psychological thought that led to the development of each instrument: the rational–theoretical approach (Rorschach) versus the empirical approach (MMPI). The authors then test their hypothesis by computing a simple Pearson correlation coefficient, which failed to support the hypothesis.

While Polyson et al. formulate an interesting hypothesis, they did not adequately test it. They treat their longitudinal data in a cross-sectional manner, thereby losing much sensitivity in the data. They used simple *t*-tests to assess differences in citations of the two tests for each decade, and a simple correlation coefficient to assess the overall relationship between the two tests over a 36-year period. Consecutive observations of each series are not independent, however, and an appropriate statistical analysis must account for these problems of serial dependence. In addition, two time series will be correlated due to common patterns of drift or trend. Appropriate statistical analysis must separate the components of between-series correlation due to stochastic processes versus systematic variation.

From a design perspective, plausible alternative interpretations abound in the concomitant time-series design. Any observed relationship could be due to the influence of systematic but unmeasured sources of variation that the researcher can only speculate about, or an observed relationship could simply be due to common sources of error variance. It is unlikely that theoretical or logical concerns can eliminate the plausibility of alternative interpretation in the concomi-

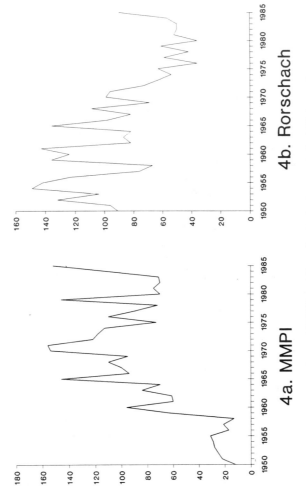

4a. MMPI   4b. Rorschach

FIG. 3.4.   Annual MMPI and Rorschach citation totals in APA journals.

FIG. 3.5.   Annual skirt width measurements.

tant time-series design, except in the most trivial examples (e.g., the correlation between temperature and air-conditioner usage). Therefore, the researcher must attempt to eliminate plausible alternative interpretations by designing the experiment in such a way that either suspected sources of influence can be measured and controlled for in the analysis, or common variance between two time series can be separated into deterministic versus stochastic components.

This introduces a third type of time-series experiment, more primitive than the interrupted and concomitant designs. The *descriptive* time-series experiment consists of decomposing the variance in a single time series into deterministic— trends and cycles, for example—and stochastic components. In most cases, social science research involves causal hypotheses and the examination of trends and cycles is the precursor to more sophisticated time-series experiments. In a few cases, however, trends or cycles can be substantively meaningful in their own right. Two examples illustrate this point.

Figure 3.5 shows annual skirt width measurements over a 150-year period recorded from museum fashion plates of women's dresses. Richardson and Kroeber (1940) argue that the pattern of change in these data is not trend but, rather, a cycle. Hypothesizing that change in fashion is due less to individual taste than to complex but stable sociocultural factors, they find remarkable stability in dress styles. Periods of cultural unsettlement, they suggest, including episodes such as wars and political crises, generate fashion cycles such as that shown in Fig. 3.5. More important for our purposes, however, these data illustrate another type of time-series experiment. If a pattern of change is not due to chance, then it must be caused in an empirically discoverable manner. And this, according to Kroeber (1969), distinguishes anthropology from history. In practice, unfortunately, purely random causes can appear to generate ostensibly nonrandom or deterministic patterns of change. A series of coin flips will always trend in the short run, for example, and may often exhibit mysterious cycles that suggest deterministic forces. Formal time-series analyses can shed some light on this issue, but random and nonrandom patterns of change in a single time series are often indistinguishable.

Figure 3.6 shows the annual percentage of homicides in Canada for 1961–1983 attributable to two offender/victim relationship categories (Silverman & Kennedy, 1987). Silverman and Kennedy argue that homicides by strangers exhibit patterns distinctly different from spouse/lover homicides. Homicide between intimates is easily viewed as the outgrowth of the emotionally charged atmosphere of an intimate relationship, while homicide by strangers is often viewed more as a threat to the prevailing social order, evidencing the general disintegration of society. In an analysis that relies exclusively upon visual interpretation of findings, the authors attempt to interpret the trends and patterns in both time series. They suggest, for example, that:

> The proportion of stranger homicide rose gradually to a rather dramatic peak in 1980 (29%), followed by an equally dramatic decline in 1982 and 1983 (18%) . . . while the proportion of spouse/lover homicide has been in steady decline sine the 1960s . . . . (p. 283)

While this study is purely descriptive in nature, the authors incorrectly assume trends by visually examining peaks and valleys in the data. Only statistical analysis can answer whether observed trends are significant or not and the problem of outliers in these data make even the authors' visual interpretations questionable (for example, their conclusions regarding percentages of stranger homicides). Indeed, the conclusion that the authors draw from their visual interpretation appears unsupported by even visual inspection: "The rate of spouse/lover homicide is relatively stable, even though the proportion has been falling; the rates of the other forms of homicide, however, are rising" (p. 304). While Fig. 3.6 may appear to display a weak, downward trend in spouse/lover homicide, the other series appears to remain fairly stable.

The analysis of trends and cycles is a descriptive enterprise at best. Although causal hypotheses are generally lurking in the background (e.g., Kroeber's "cultural unsettlement" and Silverman & Kennedy's explicit "social disintegration"), it is clear that each of these two examples attempts to make some conclusions about trends and fluctuations in time-series data. Neither study utilizes any independent variables, but discusses changes in the dependent variable over time based upon the visual inspection of plotted series. However, even descriptive analyses must use an appropriate technique to infer anything substantive about trends or cycles. For their stated purposes, the type of "eyeball analysis" used by these authors is unconvincing at best and misleading at worst.

The design problems of the univariate time-series analysis are somewhat analogous to those of the "one-shot case study" design described by Campbell

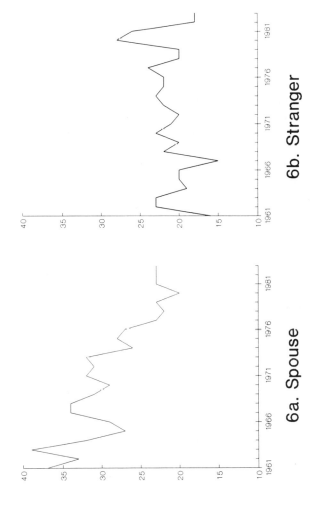

6a. Spouse   6b. Stranger

FIG. 3.6.   Proportions of total homicides by victim-offender relationship.

51

and Stanley (1966; Cook & Campbell, 1979). The basic problem with those designs is that no pre-intervention measures are collected, and no control group observations are available to rule out rival hypotheses. However, as Cook and Campbell note, "The case study is useful for purposes unrelated to inferring causation, such as assessing whether there was a treatment and how well it was delivered, or generating new hypotheses about the phenomenon under investigation" (p. 98). We agree with this perspective; descriptive studies can serve a valuable heuristic function. The problem with many such analyses, however, is that even basic questions about trend are assumed rather than proven, and that such interpretations seem too readily accepted as fact, even if only used to formulate further hypotheses and guide future research. If preliminary conclusions are unsubstantiated, then future research is not likely to uncover valid or meaningful relationships.

While interrupted time-series experiments, concomitant time-series experiments, and descriptive analyses are quite different in terms of design issues, they are nearly identical in terms of statistical issues. All three variations of the time-series experiment are subject to similar statistical problems. In the next section, we review these statistical problems. In subsequent sections, we develop statistical time-series models to deal with the problems common to all time-series experiments.

STATISTICAL PROBLEMS

The statistical problems common to all time-series experiments are best illustrated in the context of an ordinary least-squares (OLS) regression of Y_t on an independent variable time series, X_t. The OLS regression model is written as

$$Y_t = \beta_0 + \beta_1 X_t + U_t$$

In concomitant time-series experiments, X_t is a time series; β_1 is the causal effect of X_t on the dependent variable, Y_t. In interrupted time-series experiments, X_t is a dummy variable or step function; β_0 and β_1 are the dependent variable's pre- and postintervention levels, respectively, and their difference $(\beta_0 - \beta_1)$ is the intervention's effect or impact. Finally, in descriptive experiments, X_t is a trend or cycle count; β_1 is the magnitude of the trend or cycle.

In each case, analysis aims at estimating parameters β_0 and β_1 and testing their statistical significance. OLS estimates of β_0 and β_1 are

$$\hat{\beta}_0 = \bar{Y} - \hat{\beta}\bar{X}; \text{ and } \hat{\beta}_1 = 1/n \sum_{t=1}^{n} (X_t - \bar{X})(Y_t - \bar{Y})/s_Y^2$$

And if the model's error (or *disturbance* or *noise*) term is white noise—that is, if

$$U_t \sim NID(0, \sigma_U^2)$$

then the OLS parameter estimates have *all* of the most desirable statistical properties. If the error term is *not* white noise, however—and is often the case when
the dependent variable is a time series—OLS estimates of β_0 and β_1 may
seriously misstate the relationship between X_t and Y_t.

A complete development of this topic requires more space than is allotted
here. So, directing the interested reader to Kmenta (1986, pp. 260–345), Johnston (1984, pp. 291–329) or any comparable regression text, we note only that
OLS time-series regressions are a perilous exercise for even the most experienced
analyst. Instead, we recommend a set of regression-*like* models and methods
developed by Box and Jenkins (1976) expressly for time-series data. To initiate
these so-called Box–Jenkins (or ARIMA) models and methods, consider how
one might test the OLS white-noise assumption. First, since error terms are
unobserved, null hypotheses about their properties cannot be tested directly. If
the errors are white noise, however, the dependent variable (which is a simple
linear transformation of the errors) must be white noise, too. For white-noise
errors then

$$Y_t \sim NID(\mu_Y, \sigma_Y^2)$$

And of course, if the observed series is *different than* white noise, then the
unobserved errors are *not* white noise. For time series, unfortunately, tests of the
white-noise null hypothesis

$$H_0: U_t \sim NID(0, \sigma_U^2); \; Y_t \sim NID(\mu_Y, \sigma_Y^2)$$

are not as simple and straightforward as one might think; longitudinal data
violate the assumptions of all cross-sectional parametric tests.

In practice, H_0 is rejected on either of two necessary conditions. If the series
is *non*stationary—this term will be defined shortly—*or* if successive observations Y_t and Y_{t+k} are *not* independent, H_0 is rejected. Unfortunately, tests of
stationarity assume independence and tests of independence assume stationarity.
Breaking this vicious circle requires a simplifying assumption, which will be
introduced shortly.

Stationarity

At one level, the concept of stationarity is simple. Unlike other time-series
properties, for example, experienced analysts can spot a nonstationary series
from appearances alone. The Richardson–Kroeber series (Fig. 3.3) looks nonstationary because it drifts up and down in apparent cycles; the Hawthorne series
(Fig. 3.2) looks nonstationary because it trends systematically; in fact, most of
the time series introduced in this chapter (and indeed, most social and behavioral
science time series) *appear* to be and *are* nonstationary.

While eyeball inspections are often adequate for nominal null hypothesis
tests, the reader should be warned that appearances *can* be deceiving. In any

event, stationarity is one of the thorniest concepts in time-series analysis.[2] Confusion arises because there are many types of stationarity. A time series is stationary in the *strictest sense,* for example, if its probability density function is constant over time. Formally, that is, if

$$Prob(Y_1, Y_2, \ldots, Y_t) = Prob(Y_{1+k}, Y_{2+k}, \ldots, Y_{t+k})$$

then Y_t is strict-sense (or strictly) stationary. For a hypothetical example of a strictly stationary series, consider a continuing coin-flip experiment. The probability of a "head" is constant with respect to time, any particular sample of the series—say, HTTHHTTHT—is equally likely to occur today, tomorrow, or next year.

Strict-sense stationarity eliminates all formal sampling problems; one sample of n observations is as good as any other. Unless the analyst *knows* that a series is strictly stationary, however, strict-sense stationarity is not very useful. In the real world, even a coin-flip series might not satisfy this definition. One method of demonstrating strict-sense stationarity, for example, might be to demonstrate that the first n sample moments of the time series are constant. That is, to demonstrate that

First Moment: $E(Y_t) = E(Y_{t+k})$

Second Moment: $E(Y_t)^2 = E(Y_{t+k})^2$

$::$

nth Moment: $E(Y_t)^n = E(Y_{t+k})^n$

But even for moderately small k and $n,$ this method might require thousands of sample time series. While strict-sense stationarity is a good idea in theory, then, it is almost never used in practice.

Widest sense stationarity is somewhat more useful. If the series mean and variance are constant over time, then the series is said to be *wide-sense* (or *widely*) stationary. It is often possible to demonstrate that the first two sample moments of a series are constant over time. That is, to demonstrate that

$$E(Y_t) = E(Y_{t+k}) = \bar{Y}$$
$$E(Y_t - \bar{Y})^2 = E(Y_{t+k} - \bar{Y})^2 = s_Y^2$$

Two n-observation samples of widely stationary process can be different, so this definition leaves much to be desired. If a widely stationary series is Normal, however, its third through nth moments are constant and the strictest sense definition is satisfied. The common practice is to *demonstrate* that a time series is widely stationary and, then, to *assume* Normality. Left with no other choice, we

---

[2]See Parzen (1962, pp. 66–103) or Dhrymes (1974, p. 385) for formal definitions of stationarity. When we say "stationary" in this chapter, we mean stationary in the widest sense. This will be explained shortly.

adopt that convention here; *all* time series are assumed to be sampled from Normal processes.

Following this convention, it is convenient to think of stationary series as having both constant means and variances; a series may then be stationary, nonstationary in mean, nonstationary in variance, or nonstationary in both mean and variance. Although the Richardson–Kroeber series and the Hawthorne series do not look exactly alike—one series *drifts* while the other *trends*—both series are *nonstationary in mean* and, in this sense, pose the same statistical problem. Neither series has a time-invariant reference point for measuring deviations or changes; what would ordinarily be the natural reference point—the mean— changes over time.

One widely used solution to this problem involves *differencing* the series. This amounts to subtracting the first observation from the second, the second observation from the third, and so on. Denoting the differenced Y_t series by y_t, this is written as,

$$y_1 = Y_2 - Y_1$$
$$y_2 = Y_3 - Y_2$$
$$::$$
$$y_{n-1} = Y_n - Y_{n-1}$$

The y_t series is shorter than the Y_t series by one observation but, in exchange for this observation, the series is given a time-invariant reference point—a constant mean. This is illustrated by Figs. 3.7 and 3.8, which show the differenced Hawthorne and Richardson–Kroeber series. Instead of drifting and/or trending, the differenced series fluctuate noisily about their respective means; the dif- ferenced series are stationary in mean.

In substantive terms, each observation of the differenced series is interpreted as an observation-to-observation change in the level of the raw series. We are now analyzing changes and, if the differenced series is white noise, the OLS regression of y_t on X_t,

$$y_t = \beta_0 + \beta_1 X_t + U_t$$

estimates the effects of the *level* of X_t on *change* in the level of Y_t. To make this point explicit, substitute $Y_t - Y_{t-1}$ for y_t in the left-hand side of the model.

$$Y_t - Y_{t-1} = \beta_0 + \beta_1 X_t + U_t$$

Then adding Y_{t-1} to both sides,

$$Y_t = Y_{t-1} + \beta_0 + \beta_1 X_t + U_t$$

We call this the *difference equation* form of the OLS regression model. The parameter β_0 is no longer interpreted as an intercept but, instead, is interpreted as the constant change from observation to observation. When β_0 is nonzero, Y_t has

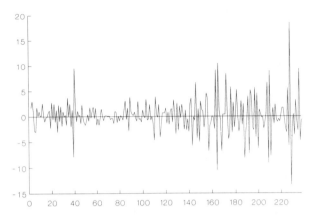

FIG. 3.7. Differenced mean productivity for the First Relay Assembly Room (Hawthorne) experiment.

a secular trend as in the Hawthorne series; when β_0 is zero, on the other hand, Y_t merely drifts as in the Richardson–Kroeber series.

Assuming that y_t is white noise, of course, parameters β_0 and β_1 can be estimated as the OLS regression of y_t on X_t. While y_t is stationary in mean by virtue of differencing, however, it is too early to assume white noise. On the contrary, since differencing has no effect on variance, y_t need not even be stationary. The differenced Richardson–Kroeber series look stationary in mean and variance; differencing is sufficient. (The apparent "blip" in 1917 may be an exception, but we will address this anomaly shortly.) The differenced Hawthorne

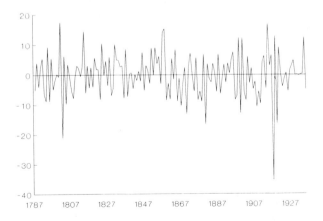

FIG. 3.8. Differenced annual skirt width measurements.

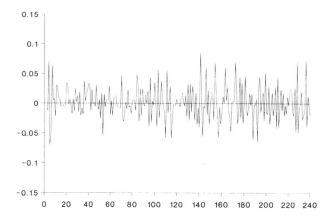

FIG. 3.9. Mean productivity, differenced logarithms.

series, on the other hand, looks nonstationary. Fluctuations grow systematically larger with time; series variance steadily increases, that is, so differencing is not sufficient.

When a time series is nonstationary in variance, as in this case, it must be transformed. Figure 3.9 shows the differenced natural logarithms of the Hawthorne series. This implies the model,

$$Z_t = Ln(Y_t)$$

$$Z_t = Z_{t-1} + \beta_0 + \beta_1 X_t + U_t \quad \text{or}$$

$$z_t = \beta_0 + \beta_1 X_t + U_t$$

Log transformation and differencing seem to do the trick; variations in the differenced logarithms are constant throughout the series, so we conclude that z_t is stationary.

Assuming that z_t is white noise again, parameters β_0 and β_1 can be estimated as the OLS regression of z_t on x_t. If z_t is *not* white noise, however—as we will soon demonstrate, it is not—OLS estimates of β_0 and β_1 will misstate the *XY* relationship. To generalize the model, let N_t denote a *general* error term. Substituting N_t for U_t,

$$z_t = \beta_0 + \beta_1 X_t + N_t$$

$$Z_t = Z_{t-1} + \beta_0 + \beta_1 X_t + N_t$$

Like white noise, the N_t disturbance term must be stationary; unlike white noise, however, N_t and its lagged values N_{t-k} need not be independent. We now address the problem identifying the structure of N_t and, then, incorporating that structure into the model to satisfy OLS regression assumptions.

Autocorrelation

After a series has been made stationary by differencing and/or transformation, it is tested for *autocorrelation*. The autocorrelation function (ACF) used for this purpose is approximately equal to the Pearson product–moment correlation coefficient of Y_t and Y_{t+k}.[3] For a series of n observations, the ACF is estimated as

$$r_k = \sum_{i=1}^{n} (Y_i - \bar{Y})(Y_{i+k} - \bar{Y})/s_Y^2 \qquad k = 0, 1, 2, \ldots$$

To see how this formula works, lag Y_t forward in time and examine the observation pairs between lag–0 and lag–n by going down the columns:

lag–0	Y_1	Y_2	Y_3	$\cdots$	$\cdots$	$\cdots$	Y_n		
lag–1		Y_1	Y_2	Y_3	$\cdots$		Y_{n-1}	Y_n	
lag–2			Y_1	Y_2	Y_3	$\cdots$	Y_{n-2}	Y_{n-1}	Y_n

and so forth. Arrayed in this way, we see that r_1 is the correlation of the series (lag–0) and its first lag (lag–1); r_2 is the correlation of the series (lag–0) and its second lag (lag–2); and in general, r_k is the correlation of the series (lag–0) and its kth lag (lag–k).

There are three nontechnical points to be noted about the ACF. First, by definition, Y_t is always perfectly correlated with itself. That is

$$r_0 = 1$$

Second, also by definition,

$$r_k = r_{-k}$$

We get the same ACF, in other words, whether we lag Y_t forward or backward. Because the ACF is symmetrical about lag–0, only its positive half need be used. Third, each time Y_t is lagged, a pair of observations is lost. Thus, r_1 is estimated from $n - 1$ pairs of observations, r_2 is estimated from $n - 2$ pairs of observations and so forth. As k increases, confidence in the estimate of r_k diminishes.

Assuming Normality, serial independence implies that Y_t and Y_{t+k} are uncorrelated. The white-noise null hypothesis then amounts to

$$H_0: r_k = 0$$

This null hypothesis is tested by comparing the value of r_k with its standard errors (SEs).[4] Figure 3.10a shows the ACF estimated from the stationary

---

[3]Since the numerator and denominator of r_k have different numbers of observations ($n - k$ and n respectively) r_k is only *approximately* equal to the Pearson product–moment correlation coefficient between Y_t and Y_{t-k}.

[4]Two technical points. First, the ACF is a *biased* estimate of the correlation between Y_t and Y_{t-k}; the degree of bias diminishes as the series grows longer, however. Second, exact standard errors of r_k are not generally available. See Kendall, Stuart, and Ord (1986, pp. 547–571) for details and approximate formulas.

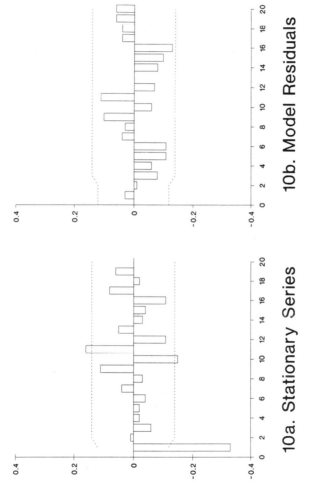

10a. Stationary Series   10b. Model Residuals

FIG. 3.10.   Hawthorne experiment ACFs.

Hawthorne series. The value of $r_1 = -.33$ lies outside the 95% confidence intervals (± 2 SE) and is thus statistically significant. The white-noise null hypothesis is rejected; this series is not white noise.

Autocorrelation has been likened to a disease that infects time-series data (Judd & Kenny, 1981). Accordingly, tests are run to determine if the data are infected and, when a series is infected as in this case, the exact *form* or *pattern* of the disease—and there are only two forms of autocorrelation—is identified from their ACFs. A first-order moving average (MA) disturbance term is characterized by a nonzero value of r_1 and zero values for all subsequent lags. That is, by

$$r_1 \neq 0$$

$$r_k > 1 = 0$$

Although the ACF in Fig. 3.10a is ambiguous in some respects, it is at least consistent with first-order MA disturbance term.[5] The MA disturbance term is written as

$$N_t = U_t - \theta U_{t-1}$$

where U_t is white noise and θ is an MA parameter. The value of the MA parameter is constrained in absolute value to unity. That is,

$$-1 < \theta < +1$$

The MA parameter is not interpreted literally as the correlation of successive time-series observations. It is a function of this correlation, nevertheless, so the greater the autocorrelation in a time series, given an MA disturbance, the larger the value of θ.

The only real check on the validity of this identification, of course, is to estimate the model. For this purpose only, the model is

$$Ln(Y_t) = Ln(Y_{t-1}) + \beta_0 + U_t - \theta U_{t-1}$$

Using a nonlinear software package (Liu & Hudak, 1986), parameters β_0 and θ of this model are estimated as

$$\hat{\beta}_0 = .001 \qquad \text{with } SE(\hat{\beta}_0) = .0010$$

$$\hat{\theta} = .448 \qquad \text{with } SE(\hat{\theta}) = .0584$$

Since this model has no independent variables, these estimates have no substantive meaning. If our identification of an MA disturbance is correct, however, the model residuals will be white noise. Figure 3.10b shows an ACF estimated from the model residuals. Since none of the first 20 lags of this ACF is statistically different than zero, we conclude that the model residuals are white noise.

---

[5]The marginally significant values of r_{10} and r_{11} are due to chance. Expected ACFs for first-order MA and AR processes are derived in an appendix. McCleary and Hay (1980, pp. 66–75) derive the general ARMA ACF.

Figure 3.11a shows an ACF estimated from the stationary Richardson–Kroeber series. The values of $r_1 = -.38$ and $r_2 = .23$ lie outside the 95% confidence intervals (± 2 SE), so the white-noise null hypothesis is rejected for this series, too. In this case, however, the ACF identifies an autoregressive (AR) disturbance term. We write this as

$$N_t = \varphi N_{t-1} + U_t$$

where φ is interpreted literally as the correlation between successive observations of the process. Using the same algebraic procedures, the AR ACF is expected to be

$$r_1 = \varphi, \, r_2 = \varphi^2, \, \ldots, \, r_k = \varphi^k$$

Since φ must be smaller than unity in absolute value, successive lags of the AR ACF grow smaller by geometrical increments. This is more or less what we see in Fig. 3.11a. If $\varphi \simeq -.4$, that is, then $\varphi^2 \simeq .2$, $\varphi^3 \simeq -.04$ and so forth. In short, this ACF is the classic signature of an AR process.

But again, to check the validity of this identification, we estimate the simple difference equation with an AR disturbance. Parameter estimates are

$$\hat{\beta}_0 = -.162 \qquad \text{with } SE(\hat{\beta}_0) = .5663$$

$$\hat{\varphi} = -.378 \qquad \text{with } SE(\hat{\varphi}) = .0761$$

Figure 3.11b shows an ACF estimated from this model's residuals. The 20th lag of this ACF is statistically significant but we expect 1 significant lag in 20 by chance alone.[6] More important, none of the earlier lags is different than zero, so these residuals are white noise. Therefore, our diagnosis of the noise processes in these two models is supported and we can now estimate the hypothesized causal parameters of the two models.

EXAMPLE ANALYSES

In preceding sections, we demonstrated that the Hawthorne and Richardson–Kroeber series violated crucial assumptions of OLS regression. Accordingly, in both cases, we developed model structures to account for nonstationarity in both mean and variance and for autocorrelation. The model proposed for the Hawthorne series is

$$Ln(Y_t) = Ln(Y_{t-1}) + \beta_0 + \beta_1 X_t + U_t - \theta U_{t-1}$$

For the Richardson–Kroeber series, on the other hand, we propose[7]

---

[6]In our analysis of the Hawthorne series, the value of $r_1 = -.33$ was sufficient to reject H_0. There is no double standard at work here. On the contrary, the first lag of the ACF is particularly important; the 20th lag is not. See McCleary and Hay (1980, p. 2.12) for a discussion of this issue.

[7]The AR model can be reduced by backward substitution to an infinite series of lagged white noise disturbances. To avoid this conceptual complication, we write here as two equations.

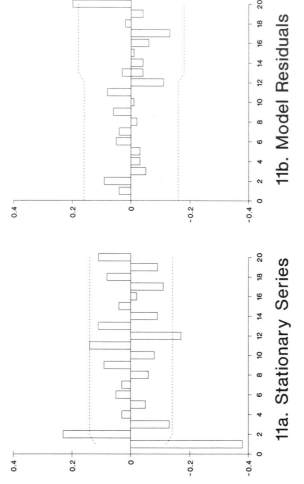

11a. Stationary Series   11b. Model Residuals

FIG. 3.11.   Annual skirt width ACFs.

$$Y_t = Y_{t-1} + \beta_0 + \beta_1 X_t + N_t \text{ where } N_t = \varphi N_{t-1} + U_t$$

The structures of these models account for nonstationarity and autocorrelation with the purpose of allowing us to estimate parameters β_0 and β_1. We now use these models (and the principles underlying these models) to demonstrate the uses of time-series analysis. The time-series data plotted in Figs. 3.1 through 3.6 are listed in Appendix B and we urge the reader to use these data to replicate our analyses. Our analyses are intended to demonstrate broad principles and in doing this, we necessarily underemphasize the finer, subtler principles that are best learned through hands-on experience.

Estimating a Trend

Nonstationary time series fall into one of two categories: series that *trend* and series that *drift*. In most cases, there is no need to distinguish between trend and drift because, in most cases, nonstationarity is nothing more than a statistical confound, an obstacle to estimating impacts, correlations, and the like. In some cases, however, the distinction is crucial. A major question we must ask of our data in these cases is: To what degree is any apparent trend in the series attributable to hypothesized causal forces? The homicide series in Fig. 3.4 are an example. Silverman and Kennedy (1987) state with no analysis that homicides of spouses *de*creased and homicides of strangers *in*creased since 1960. This is an empirical question, of course, which can be answered only by estimating trends for the series and testing the estimates for statistical significance.

Questions of trend cannot be answered absolutely, of course, for there are infinitely many types of trend. Invoking the rule of parsimony, however, the analysis is limited to *linear* trends. One method of estimating a linear trend is to regress Y_t on the index $t = 1, 2, \ldots, n$. That is,

$$Y_t = \beta_0 + \beta_1 t + N_t$$

If the usual assumptions are warranted, β_1 is interpreted as the mean *change* in Y_t for each unit change in t, the Y_t trend, in other words. The OLS estimate of the spouse homicide model is

$$Y_t = 36.461 - .654t \qquad \text{with } SE(\beta_1) = .086$$

As Silverman and Kennedy predict, the trend in spouse homicides is negative; the rate decreases by approximately .65 per year. The OLS estimate of the stranger homicide model is

$$Y_t = 19.634 + .122t \qquad \text{with } SE(\beta_1) = .091$$

Again, as Silverman and Kennedy predicted, the trend in stranger homicides is positive; the rate increases by approximately .12 per year.

Figure 3.12 shows the homicide series with OLS trends superimposed. The

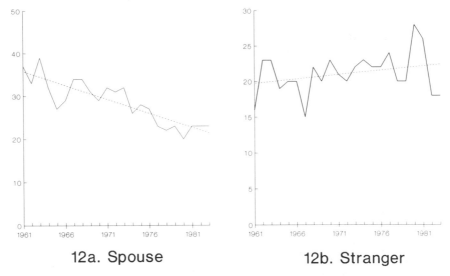

12a. Spouse   12b. Stranger

FIG. 3.12.   Predicted and observed homocide trends.

OLS trend is the predicted value of Y_t, represented as a straight line about which Y_t fluctuates. The line rises for values of $\beta_1 > 0$ and falls for values of $\beta_1 < 0$. When $\beta_1 = 0$, the series is trendless—which implies that it drifts—and this suggests a simple test to distinguish trend and drift. If Y_t follows a linear trend, then the null hypothesis,

$$H_0\colon Y_t \text{ drifts; } \beta_1 = 0$$

will be rejected. For the spouse homicide series, the OLS SE of β_1 is .086, *so this trend is statistically significant.*[8] For the stranger homicide series, however, the SE of β_1 is .091, so in this case, the trend is not statistically significant. On the contrary, while the trend is positive, it falls in the range expected of stochastic drift.

One problem with OLS trend models is that the parameter β_1 is difficult to estimate, especially in the presence of outliers. To demonstrate the basis of the problem, we computed Cook's Distances (Cook, 1977, 1979) for the trend lines in Fig. 3.13. Cook's Distances measure the influence of observations on the OLS estimate of β_1. Ideally, no single observation will be more influential than any other. But when the independent variable increases monotonically—in this case, the independent variable is t and $t = 1, 2, \ldots, n$-observations near the beginning and end of the series will be more influential than middle observations. Figure 3.13 makes this point. These Cook's Distances are standardized and can

---

[8]The ratio the parameter estimate $(-.65)$ to its standard error $(.086)$ is distributed as *Student's t* with 21 degrees of freedom. The *t*-value of $(-.65/.086=)$ -7.56 is significant with $P < .0001$.

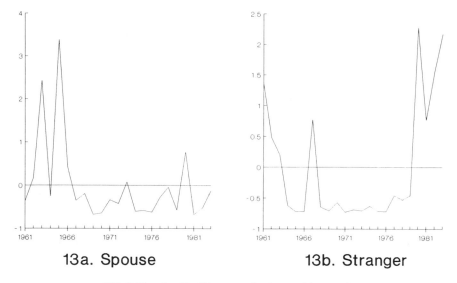

13a. Spouse   13b. Stranger

FIG. 3.13.   Cook's Distances for homocide trends.

be interpreted roughly as z-scores. A few statistically significant Distances are expected due to chance and, in fact, six (of 46) are significant at the .05 level. The statistically significant Distance scores are expected to be randomly scattered over time, however, and this is not what we see in Fig. 3.13. For spouse homicides, the third and fifth observations are significantly influential; for stranger homicides, the first, 20th, 22nd, and 23rd observations are significantly influential; in either case, none of the middle observations is significantly influential.

Estimating β_1 from a difference equation models avoids this particular problem. To introduce these method, we write regression trend models for consecutive observations Y_t and Y_{t-1},

$$Y_t = \beta_0 + \beta_1 t + N_t$$

$$Y_{t-1} = \beta_0 + \beta_1(t-1) + N_{t-1}$$

The difference of Y_t and Y_{t-1} is thus

$$Y_t - Y_{t-1} = \beta_0 + \beta_1 t + N_t - [\beta_0 + \beta_1(t-1) + N_{t-1}]$$

$$= \beta_1 + \eta_t \qquad \text{where } \eta_t = N_t - N_{t-1}$$

In this model, the OLS estimate of β_1 is the mean difference.

$$\hat{\beta}_1 = 1/(n-1) \sum_{i=1}^{n-1} y_i \qquad \text{where } y_i = Y_i - Y_{t-1}$$

Since this estimate does not involve t, the relative influence of an observation depends only on the magnitude of the observation, not on the order of the observation in the series. For spouse homicides, the difference equation model is

$$Y_t = Y_{t-1} - .636 \qquad \text{with } SE(\beta_1) = .731$$

For stranger homicides,

$$Y_t = Y_{t-1} + .091 \qquad \text{with } SE(\beta_1) = .827$$

While the signs of the estimates do not change, in both cases, trends estimated from difference equation models are smaller and not statistically significant. This is a typical result.

Difference equation trend models are not without problems. If the undifferenced N_t disturbance term is white noise, for example, η_t will *not* be white noise. Otherwise, the autocorrelation structure of η_t will at least be more complicated than the structure of N_t. This poses no real problem in the vast majority of cases but, in some cases, especially for short time series, the problem may be serious.[9] In this particular case, the series are too short and variant to support identification of either N_t or η_t, so we have little confidence in hypothesis tests based on either model. However, there is no evidence to support the claim by Silverman and Kennedy (1987) that stranger homicides are trending upward.

Estimating an Impact

It is almost always a fallacy to read substantive meaning into the structure of a disturbance term; there is ordinarily no substantive reason why a disturbance should be MA rather than AR and vice versa. Likewise, the distinction between trend and drift is substantively meaningless in most cases. One might conclude then that any statistically adequate time-series model is as good as any other and, indeed, this is true. A time-series model is nothing more than a *filter* that removes autocorrelation and nonstationarity from the series and every model that accomplishes this end is as good as any other. To reinforce the filter analogy, we diagram the time-series model as a "black box" that takes time series inputs and transforms them to white-noise outputs. That is,

$$\hat{Y}_t \rightarrow \boxed{} \rightarrow U_t$$

Due to such (desirable) properties as "parsimony" and "elegance," some models will look "better" than others but *any* model that removes autocorrelation and nonstationarity is statistically adequate. Assuming further that the filter leaves

---

[9]See Judd and Kenny (1981) for a statement of this problem in the context of time-series experiments.

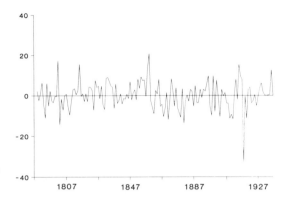

FIG. 3.14.   Richardson-Kroeber
residuals.

other properties of the series unchanged, the *prewhitened* output of the filter can
be used to test substantive hypotheses.

To illustrate, recall that the differenced Richardson–Kroeber time series (Fig.
3.5) was adequately fit by a first-order AR disturbance model, which we write as

$$(Y_t - Y_{t-1}) = -.162 - .378(Y_{t-1} - Y_{t-2}) + U_t$$

Residuals of this model (shown in Fig. 3.14)

$$U_t = (Y_t - Y_{t-1}) + .162 + .378(Y_{t-1} - Y_{t-2})$$

$$= .162 + Y_t - .622Y_{t-1} - .378Y_{t-2}$$

are white noise. Now Richardson and Kroeber argued that aesthetics change
during times of "cultural unsettlement" and, thus, that fashion changes could be
used as indicators (but not necessarily a cause or effect) of cultural change. In
particular, to the extent that periods of instability, such as political crises or wars,
reflect emerging cultural disruptions, temporal variability in fashion might suggest times of instability. High variability, then, indicates strain and/or resistance
in cultural styles.

For example, Richardson and Kroeber report sharp climaxes in shortness and
narrowness of skirt width during the Napoleonic period in France (circa 1799–
1814). The next 40 years showed a time of relative peace between the major
European states. Marked unsettlement began again about 1900, evidenced by
extreme variability in skirt width over the 14 years prior to World War I (achieving a high of 64 inches in 1901, and a low of 23 inches in 1911). Interestingly, for
the 150 years of this time series, skirt widths reached their all-time minimums in
1811 and 1926. Richardson and Kroeber noted that cultural strain might, in some
cases, manifest itself most highly during postwar years of readaptation.

Since "all things change," of course, statistical significance is the crux of this
issue. If indeed war is strongly related to cultural unsettlement, we would expect

to find larger residuals (unexplained variance in the series) during postwar periods than in prewar periods. And since the residuals of the first-order AR model are white-noise-independent, normally distributed, and homoscedastic—they can be sorted into time periods and compared with any parametric test statistic.[10] Two examples make this point.

Example 1.   Mean residuals for most active period of the Napoleonic wars (1805–1814) and the post-Napoleonic years (1815–1824) are -1.5 and 1.5 respectively. The t-statistic for this difference ($t = 1.26$ with 18 degrees of freedom) is not statistically significant ($p < .23$), so consideration of the mid- and postwar years adds nothing to the explanation of variance in skirt widths already predicted by drift and autocorrelation. It is not theoretically relevant to estimate the variance of skirt width in pre-Napoleonic years, however, because France (and Europe in general) could be considered nothing if not extremely unsettled during the years 1787–1799 (the French Revolution occurred in 1789; Napoleon declared himself Emperor in 1799).

Example 2.   Residuals for the pre- (1909–1913), mid- (1914–1918), and post-World War I (1919–1923) periods in France have the following means and standard deviations:

	N	Mean	S.D.	S.E.
Prewar	5	-4.7	8.7	3.9
Midwar	5	-0.4	19.1	8.6
Postwar	5	-1.6	6.1	2.8

Again, the F-statistic for this one-way ANOVA ($F = .15$ with 2 degrees and 12 degrees of freedom) is not statistically significant and this suggests that consideration of the onset, duration, and demise of the war adds little to the explanation of variance in skirt width already predicted by the passage of time and the autoregressive function.

The Richardson–Kroeber residuals could be broken down into infinite time periods and effects of numerous interventions—changes in political leadership, social movements, fads, and so on—could be tested. Put simply, once we have the properties of white noise in a set of observations, we can ignore the common problems of trend and autocorrelation and proceed directly to test any and all hypotheses that would ordinarily be complicated by autocorrelation, trend, and other violations of the classical assumptions.

In practice, however, residual contrasts are problematical for one simple reason. If the model parameters representing impact, trend and autocorrelation

---

[10]Recall that white noise meets the assumptions of parametric (Normal) statistical tests. That is, $U_t \sim \text{NID}(0,\sigma^2)$. Each U_t can be reviewed as the outcome of a distinct experiment.

are not independent, which is often the case, residual contrasts will be biased in favor of the null hypothesis. For an illustration of this point, we need look no further than the Hawthorne experiment. To analyze the Hawthorne time series, Franke and Kaul (1978) regressed "hourly productivity" on variables purporting to measure the onset of "managerial discipline" (X_{1t}), the onset of "economic depression" (X_{1t}), and "rest time" (X_{3t}). If these independent variables are defined as

$$X_{1t} = 0 \text{ prior to the 40th observation; } = 1 \text{ thereafter}$$

$$X_{2t} = 0 \text{ prior to the October 24, 1929; } = 1 \text{ thereafter}$$

$$X_{3t} = \text{Minutes of rest time}$$

then parameters of the OLS regression model

$$Y_t = \beta_0 + \beta_1 X_{1t} + \beta_2 X_{2t} + \beta_3 X_{3t} + U_t$$

are interpreted as change in the level of Y_t due to the onset of "managerial discipline" (β_1); change in the level of Y_t due to the onset of "economic depression" (β_2); and change in the level of Y_t due to a 1-minute change in "rest time" (β_3). This interpretation assumes that Y_t is stationary, however—or that the nonstationary part of Y_t has been modeled—and this is clearly not the case. As we have shown, this series is nonstationary in both mean and variance and, since lacking structures to accommodate these properties, estimates of model parameters are confounded with the unmodeled structures.

To illustrate the nature and consequences of this confound, we estimated the model in four steps. First, with no interventions,

$$\hat{Y}_t = 64.69$$

Second, with the effect of "managerial description,"

$$\hat{Y}_t = 52.98 + 13.98 \, X_{1t}$$

Third, with the effects of "managerial discipline" and "economic depression,"

$$\hat{Y}_t = 52.98 + 11.06 \, X_{1t} + 5.33 \, X_{2t}$$

And fourth, with all three effects entered,

$$\hat{Y}_t = 50.63 + 9.62 \, X_{1t} + 4.75 \, X_{2t} + .18 \, X_{3t}$$

Figures 3.15a–d plot the predicted series ($\hat{Y}_t$) corresponding to these models against the observed series (Y_t). Careful comparisons of $\hat{Y}_t$ and Y_t reveal an important lesson.

In Fig. 3.15a, $\hat{Y}_t$ is a simple straight line, running parallel to the time axis, representing the time-invariant level if Y_t. Since Y_t is nonstationary, which is to say that it has no time-invariant level, this model is wholly implausible, conceptually and visually. In Figs. 3.15b and 3.15c, the observed series have two and

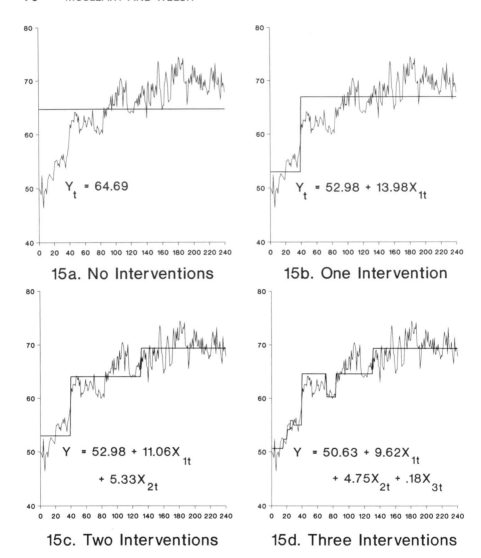

15a. No Interventions

15b. One Intervention

15c. Two Interventions

15d. Three Interventions

FIG. 3.15.   Stepwise intervention models.

three levels, representing respectively the before/after effects of "managerial discipline" and "economic depression." These models are not so obviously implausible, at least visually, and that is the kernel of the problem. Effect contrasts tend to mimic the systematic rise and/or fall of a nonstationary series; in effect, model parameter estimates and trend or drift are confounded. This is most apparent in Fig. 3.15d. Here "rest time" (X_{3t}) has entered the model to complete the confound. Since the series is nonstationary, this model too is implausible.

Based on visual appearances, however, unlike the first three models, this model is not obviously implausible.

This argument extends to questions of cause and effect. Although Franke and Kaul (1978) report statistically significant effects for all three variables, statistical confounding is a simpler explanation. Segments of a nonstationary series have different means by definition and, so, *any* before/after contrast tends to be significant. Figures 3.15a–d reinforce this point and the conclusion would be the same whether this problem is analyzed as a uncontrolled threat to internal validity (*"History,"* see Campbell & Stanley, 1963; Cook & Campbell, 1979) or as a purely statistical concern. Models that fail to account for any and all nonstationary properties of a time series are uninterpretable.

Using a difference equation to model the nonstationary mean of this time series and an empirically identified MA1 noise component, the effects of "managerial discipline," "economic depression," and "rest time" on "productivity" are estimated as

$$\hat{\beta}_1 = 3.55; \quad \text{with } SE(\hat{\beta}_1) = 1.49$$

$$\hat{\beta}_2 = -.23; \quad \text{with } SE(\hat{\beta}_2) = 1.48$$

$$\hat{\beta}_3 = 0.095; \quad \text{with } SE(\hat{\beta}_3) = 0.037$$

Controlling for trend, then, the effect of economic depression is substantively and statistically insignificant; but just as Franke and Kaul report, the effects of managerial discipline and rest time are significant.

Of course, this managerial discipline effect was estimated from the mean performance of all five workers. But since Workers 1 and 2 were replaced with the onset of managerial discipline, this amounts to comparing the *pre*-intervention performance of Workers 1 and 2 with the *post*-intervention performance of Workers 1A and 2B and this makes no sense. Schlaifer (1980) argues—and we concur—that if the managerial discipline effect exists, it will be found by comparing the productivity of Workers 3, 4, and 5 *before* and *after* the start of the 40th week. We leave this exercise to the reader. The reader should remember to log-transform the series prior to differencing (see Fig. 3.9), of course, and the series should be analyzed individually.

Estimating a Correlation

While it is generally true that "correlation does not imply causality," *under very limited circumstances,* time series correlations can be used to test causal hypotheses.[11] The ideal circumstances require a unidirectional lagged causal relationship, which we write as

---

[11]Reflecting the contribution of Granger (1969), these "limited circumstances" are called "Granger causality." The philosophical foundations of Granger causality are outside the scope of this chapter. Enlightening discussions are found in Granger and Newbold (1977), Madalla (1988), Newbold (1982), and Zellner (1979). See Simon (1952, 1957) for a general discussion of this issue.

$$X_{t-k} \rightarrow Y_t$$

and more important, that X_t and Y_t be white noise. Under these ideal circumstances, the Pearson product–moment correlation coefficient of X_{t-k} and Y_t

$$r_k = \sum_{t=1}^{n-k} (X_{t-k} - \bar{X})(Y_t - \bar{Y})/s_X s_Y$$

gives an unbiased estimate of the causal relationship. Nonzero values of r_k reject the causal null hypothesis at a known level of confidence. Circumstances are rarely ideal in practice, unfortunately. Causal relationships are seldom as simple as $X_{t-k} \rightarrow Y_t$, for example, and worse, there are very few white-noise time series. When the series are not white noise, r_k misstates their causal relationship. Unbiased estimates of the relationship are still possible (though difficult) but that topic is too detailed and technical for this essay.[12] Instead, we concentrate on those aspects of the problem that relate to nonstationarity and autocorrelation.

Returning to Fig. 3.4, recall that Polyson et al. (1986) hypothesized a "competition" between the MMPI and Rorschach tests that would leave a negative correlation between annual citations for the two tests. The causal null hypothesis in this case is

H_0: MMPI and Rorschach series are independent; $r_k = 0$

Bartlett (1935) gives the SE of r_k as

$$SE(r_k) = 1/\sqrt{n - k}$$

For time series of 36 years, then

$$SE(r_0) = 1/\sqrt{36} \approx .167$$
$$SE(r_{\pm 1}) = 1/\sqrt{35} \approx .169$$
$$SE(r_{\pm 2}) = 1/\sqrt{35} \approx .171$$

and so forth. Polyson et al. consider only the unlagged relationship measured by r_0. By a $\pm 2SE$ criterion, the value of $r_0 = -.23$ reported by Polyson et al. is not statistically significant, so the null hypothesis cannot be rejected in favor of the "competition" hypothesis. There are at least two flaws in this logic, however.

The first flaw occurs when Polyson et al. rule out all hypothetical lags except zero. Given the nature of scientific publishing, "competition" between the MMPI and Rorschach tests would more likely result in a correlation lagged by 1 or 2 years. Figure 3.16a plots the so-called *cross-correlation function* (CCF)

---

[12]For analyses of these specific data, see O'Grady (1988). More generally, Cook, Dintzer, and Mark (1980; Mark, 1979) discuss the problems of interpreting r_k when one or both series are not white noise. McCleary and Hay (1980, pp. 227–273) develop the same material from a slightly different perspective. Technical treatments are found in Haugh (1976) and Haugh and Box (1977).

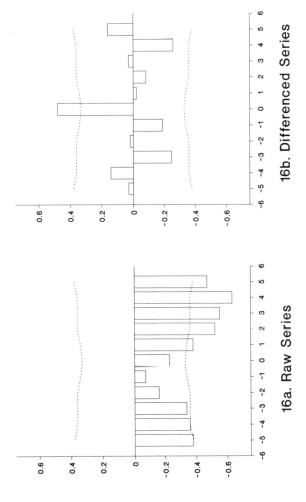

16a. Raw Series

16b. Differenced Series

FIG. 3.16.   CCFs for MMPI and Rorschach series.

73

between the MMPI and Rorschach series. The left-hand side of this CCF is computed from the lagged Rorschach series, so negative lags measure the causal effects of Rorschach on MMPI. The right-hand side is computed from the lagged MMPI series, so positive lags measure the causal effects of MMPI on Rorschach. Judging from this CCF, then, contrary to the conclusions of Polyson et al., the causal null hypothesis must be rejected. The evidence suggests that there is indeed a competition between MMPI and Rorschach proponents, albeit a lopsided one. When MMPI citations rise, Rorschach citations rise in subsequent years. The causal effect peaks 4 years after the initial rise and, presumably, returns to a steady-state.

Before making too much of this CCF, however, note that neither the MMPI series nor the Rorschach series is white noise. In fact, judging from Fig. 3.4, neither series is stationary and this invalidates any conclusions one might draw from the CCF. Since nonstationary series lack either constant mean and/or constant variance, correlations are undefined. On the other hand, due to common trend, *all nonstationary series will be highly correlated*. Responding to Polyson et al., O'Grady (1988) makes this point and draws very different conclusions about the relationship between these series. Figure 3.16b shows a CCF estimated from differenced MMPI and Rorschach series. When the series are made stationary, the CCF has only one significant value; $r_0 = .48$. Since this value is positive, moreover—not negative as the "competition" hypothesis predicts—it supports a very different conclusion. Rather than expand on this technical subject, we direct the reader to O'Grady (1988) for a more complete analysis of this issue.

CONCLUSION

In this chapter, we broadened the definition of time-series experiment to include at least three types of analyses: (1) examination of the impact of a before/after intervention on a single time series; (2) examination of correlated (concomitant) time series for possible causal relationships; and (3) univariate analyses of trends and cycles in a single time series. Two examples of each type of design were presented.

Although each type of analysis presents unique design and validity issues, as we briefly discussed, each raises common statistical problems which must be diagnosed and controlled in time-series analysis: (1) nonstationarity, (2) autocorrelation, and (3) trend. Most social science time series appear to be and are nonstationary. Before we can analyze such data, however, we must make them stationary by either differencing and transforming the series. Otherwise, parameter estimates will be unreliable, as we illustrated with the Hawthorne productivity series.

Autocorrelation is a major contribution of noise to time-series data. Even if the analyst has controlled for nonstationarity, the presence and form of autocorrelation (serial dependence) must be correctly assessed, modeled, and tested. Once we have identified the correct form of the "noise" component of time-series data, we can model its presence in the time-series equation in order to estimate properly the substantive parameters of a time-series model.

Trend is another problem common to time-series observations. Although time series appear to trend upwards or downwards, the analyst must assess the degree to which such trend is due to deterministic (systematic) forces versus stochastic (random) processes. Apparent trends are often deceiving (especially so-called linear trends, which we limited our discussion to) and upon statistical inspection, may turn out to be simply random drift. In the Silverman and Kennedy homicide data, for example, one hypothesized trend (decrease in spouse homicides) was supported by statistical analysis; the other (increase in stranger homicides) was not.

The message by now should be clear: When statistical problems in time-series analyses are not adequately diagnosed and controlled, erroneous or unsubstantiated conclusions are inevitable. We reanalyzed several time series to illustrate these problems.

In their analysis of the Hawthorne data, Franke and Kaul (1978) failed to detrend their data before subjecting it to OLS time-series regression. We further identified the structure of the error term in this time series as a first-order, moving average process. We found small, barely significant treatment effects for the hypothesized "managerial discipline" and "scheduled rest time" interventions, and a nonsignificant effect for the "economic depression" variable, in marked contrast to Franke and Kaul's results.

Problems of nonstationarity and unanalyzed trend also led to unsubstantiated conclusions by Polyson et al. regarding the hypothesized "competition" between the Rorschach and MMPI personality tests. Treating the time series of citations for the two tests as if they were stationary, Polyson et al. calculated a simple Pearson zero-order correlation of $-.23$. However, as we illustrated, due to common trend, all nonstationary time series will be highly correlated. When the time series were made stationary, and the appropriate (CCF) was calculated, we found a positive correlation of .48. In other words, rather than the hypothesized "competition" effect, we found evidence for a relatively trivial "support" effect, which suggests that increased interest in personality testing results in increased citations of both tests.

While design issues remain crucial to time-series experiments and to the validity of experiments in general, the time-series analyst must be particularly sensitive to the common statistical problems illustrated in this chapter. Otherwise, results will be misleading at best, and, at worst, totally invalid.

REFERENCES

Bartlett, M. S. (1935). Some aspects of the time-correlation problem in regard to tests of significance. *Journal of the Royal Statistical Society, 98,* 536–543.

Berkowitz, L. (1982). Aversive conditions as stimuli to aggression. In L. Berkowitz (Ed.), *Advances in experimental social psychology* (Vol. 15, pp. 249–288). New York: Academic Press.

Box, G. E. P., Jenkins, G. M. (1976). *Time series analysis: Forecasting and control* (2nd Rev. Ed.). San Francisco: Holden–Day.

Box, G. E. P., & Cox, D. R. (1964). An analysis of transformations. *Journal of the Royal Statistical Society, B, 26,* 211–243.

Campbell, D. T. (1963). From description to experimentation: Interpreting trends as quasi-experiments. In C. W. Harris (Ed.), *Problems in measuring change.* Madison: University of Wisconsin Press.

Campbell, D. T. (1969). Reforms as experiments. *American Psychologist, 24,* 409–429.

Cook, R. D. (1977). Detection of influential observations in linear regression. *Technometrics, 19,* 15–18.

Cook, R. D. (1979). Influential observations in linear regression. *Journal of the American Statistical Association, 74,* 169–174.

Cook, T. D., & Campbell, D. T. (1979). *Quasi-experimentation: Design and analysis issues for field settings.* Boston: Houghton–Mifflin.

Cook,, T. D., Dintzer, L., & Mark, M. M. (1980). The causal analysis of concommitant time series. In L. Bickman (Ed.), *Applied social psychology annual* (Vol. 1). Beverly Hills, CA: Sage, pp. 93–135.

Dhrymes, P. J. (1974). *Econometrics: Statistical foundations and applications.* New York: Springer-Verlag.

Dollard, J., Doob, L., Miller, N., Mowrer, O., & Sears, R. L. (1939). *Frustration and aggression.* New Haven, CT: Yale University Press.

Franke, H. F. (1980). Comment: Worker productivity at Hawthorne (Reply to Schlaifer). *American Sociological Review, 45,* 1006–1027.

Franke, H. F., & Kaul, J. D. (1978). The Hawthorne experiments: First statistical interpretation. *American Sociological Review, 43,* 623–643.

Glass, G. V., Willson, V. L., & Gottman, J. M. (1975). *Design and analysis of time series experiments.* Boulder: Colorado Associated University Press.

Goldstein, J. H. (1986). *Aggression and crimes of violence.* New York: Oxford University Press.

Gordon, J. R. (1983). *A diagnostic approach to organizational behavior.* Boston: Allyn & Bacon.

Granger, C. W. J. (1969). Investigating causal relations by econometric models and cross-spectral methods. *Econometrica, 37,* 424–438.

Granger, C. W. J., & Newbold, P. (1977). *Forecasting economic time series.* New York: Academic Press.

Haugh, L. D. (1976). Checking the independence of two covariance stationary time series: A univariate residual cross correlation approach. *Journal of the American Statistical Association, 71,* 378–385.

Haugh, L. D., & Box, G. E. P. (1977). Identification of dynamic regression (distributed lag) models connecting two time series. *Journal of the American Statistical Association, 72,* 121–130.

Hepworth, J. T., & West, S. G. (1940). Lynchings and the economy: A time-series reanalysis of Hovland and Sears. *Journal of Personality and Social and Psychology, 55,* 239–247.

Hovland, C. I., & Sears, R. R. (1940). Minor studies of aggression: IV. Correlation of lynchings with economic indicies. *Journal of Psychology, 9,* 30–310.

Johnston, J. (1984). *Econometric methods* (3rd Ed.). New York: McGraw–Hill.

Judd, C. M., & Kenny, D. A. (1981). *Estimating the effects of social interventions.* New York: Cambridge University Press.

Kendall, M., Stuart, A., & Ord, J. K. (1983). *The advanced theory of statistics* (Vol. 3, 4th Ed.). London: Charles Griffin and Co.

Kmenta, J. (1986). *Elements of econometrics* (2nd Ed.). New York: Macmillan.

Kroeber, A. L. (1969). *Configurations of cultural growth.* Berkeley: University of California Press.

Land, K. C., & Spilerman, S. (1975). *Social indicator models*. New York: Russell Sage Foundation.

Liu, L. M., & Hudak, G. B. with G. E. P. Box, M. E. Muller, & G. C. Tiao. (1985). *The SCA Statistical System Reference Manual*. DeKalb, IL: Scientific Computing Associates.

Ljung, G. M., & Box, G. E. P. (1978). On a measure of lack of fit in time series models. *Biometrika, 65*, 297–303.

McCleary, R., & Hay, R. A., Jr. (1980). *Applied time series analysis for the social sciences*. Beverly Hills, CA: Sage.

McDowall, D., & Loftin, C. (1981). ARIMA causal models: An introduction and an application to deterrence research. In J. Hagan (Ed.), *Deterrence reconsidered: Methodological innovations* (pp. 135–148). Beverly Hills, CA: Sage.

McDowall, D., McCleary, R., Hay, R. A., Jr., & Meidinger, E. E. (1980). *Interrupted time series analysis*. Vol. 21, University Papers Series: Quantitative Applications in the Social Sciences. Beverly Hills and London: Sage.

McSweeney, A. J. (1978). The effects of response cost on the behavior of a million persons: Charging for directory assistance in Cincinnati. *Journal of Applied Behavioral Analysis, 11*, 47–51.

Madalla, G. S. (1988). *Introduction to econometrics*. New York: Macmillan.

Mark, M. M. (1979). The causal analysis of concomitancies in time series. In T. D. Cook & D. T. Campbell (Eds.), *Quasi-experimentation: Design and analysis issues for field settings*. (pp. 321–339). Boston: Houghton Mifflin.

Mintz, A. (1946). A re-examination of the correlations between lynchings and economic indices. *Journal of Abnormal and Social and Psychology, 41*, 54–160.

Newbold, P. (1982). Causality testing in economics. In O. D. Anderson (Ed.), *Time series analysis: Theory and Practice* (pp. 701–716). New York: North–Holland.

O'Grady, K. E. (1988). "MMPI and Rohrschach: Three decades of research": A time series re-analysis. *Professional Psychology: Research and Practice, 19*, 132–133.

Parzen, E. (1962). *Stochastic processes*. San Francisco: Holden-Day.

Pierce, D. A., & Haugh, L. D. (1977). Causality in temporal systems: Characterizations and a survey. *Journal of Economics, 5*, 265–293.

Pitcher, B. L. (1981). The Hawthorne experiments: Statistical evidence for a learning hypothesis. *Social Forces, 60*, 133–149.

Polyson, P., Peterson, R., & Marshall, C. (1986). MMPI and Rorschach: Three decades of research. *Professional Psychology: Research and Practice, 17*, 476–478.

Reed, J. S., Doss, G. E., & Hurlbert, J. S. (1987). Too good to be false: An essay in the folklore of social science. *Sociological Inquiry, 57*, 1–11.

Richardson, J., & Kroeber, A. L. (1940). Three centuries of women's dress fashions: a quantitative analysis. *Anthropological Records, 5*(2), 111–154.

Ross, H. L. (1982). *Deterring the drinking driver: Legal policy and social control*. Lexington, MA: Lexington Books.

Schlaifer, R. (1980). The relay assembly test room: An alternative statistical interpretation (Comment on Franke and Kaul, ASR, October, 1978). *American Sociological Review, 45*, 995–1005.

Schwert, G. W. (1979). Tests of causality: The message in the innovations. In K. Brunner & A. H. Meltzer (Eds.), *Three aspects of policy and policymaking: Knowledge, data, and institutions* (pp. 55–96). New York: North–Holland.

Silverman, R. A., & Kennedy, L. W. (1987). Relational distance and homicide: The role of the stranger. *Journal of Criminal Law and Criminology, 78*(2), 272–308.

Simon, H. A. (1952). On the definition of the causal relation. *Journal of Philosophy, 49*, 517–528.

Simon, H. A. (1957). *Models of man*. New York: Wiley.

Spitzer, J. J. (1982). A fast and efficient algorithm for the estimation of parameters in models with the Box-and-Cox transformation. *Journal of the American Statistical Association, 77*, 760–766.

Zellner, A. (1979). Causality and econometrics. In K. Brunner & A. H. Meltzer (Eds.), *Three aspects of policy and policymaking: Knowledge, data, and institutions* (pp. 9–54). New York: North–Holland.

APPENDIX A—EXPECTED VALUES

The *expected value* of the random variable X, denoted $E(X)$, is interpreted as the arithmetic mean. For discrete X, that is

$$E(X) = \sum_{i=1}^{n} X_i p(X_i)$$

where $p(X_i)$ is probability $\text{Prob}(X = X_i)$. For continuous X, on the other hand,

$$E(X) = \int_{-\infty}^{+\infty} X_i f(X_i)\ dx$$

where $f(X_i)$ probability density function of X. Although these definitions seem formidable—especially in the continuous case—the expected value can be interpreted simply as the arithmetical mean of a variable.

Expected values are first encountered in the definition of white noise. The white noise process has a zero-mean and constant variance. That is,

$$EU_t = 0 \text{ and } EU_t^2 = \sigma_u^2$$

Realizations of the white-noise process, furthermore, are *independent,* which is to say that

$$E(U_t U_{t-k}) = 0 \text{ for any lag-}k$$

Realizations of *AR* and *MA* processes, on the other hand, are *not* independent. That is,

$$E(N_t N_{t-k}) \neq 0$$

It is this serial dependence of *AR* and *MA* realizations that motivates time-series analysis.

In practice, expected values are calculated directly by summing or integrating a random variable, depending on whether it is discrete or continuous. In many cases, however, expected values can be manipulated algebraically to yield expressions of axiomatic expected values, such as

$$EU_t = 0;\ EU_t^2 = \sigma_u^2;\ E(U_t U_{t-k}) = 0$$

which can be evaluated directly. Expected value algebra has three simple rules following from definitions. First, *the expected value of a constant is equal to n times the constant.* That is,

$$E(K) = n\text{K}$$

Second, *the expected value of a constant times X is equal to the constant times the expected value of X*. That is,

$$(E(KX) = KE(X)$$

Third, *the expected value of a sum of random variables is equal to the sum of the expected values*. That is,

$$E(X + Y + Z) = E(X) + E(Y) + E(Z)$$

The most important properties of *ARMA* time-series processes are derived by straightforward application of these three rules. We begin with derivations of the first-order *MA* and *AR* processes.

ARMA Variances. The variance of a first-order *MA* process

$$N_t = U_t - \theta U_{t-1}$$

is defined as

$$VAR(N_t) = E[N_t - E(N_t)]^2$$

Assuming without loss of generality that N_t has a zero mean,

$$\begin{aligned} VAR(N_t) = &= E(U_t - \theta U_{t-1})(U_t - \theta U_{t-1}) \\ &= E(U_t^2 - 2\theta U_t U_{t-1} + \theta^2 U_{t-1}^2) \\ &= EU_t^2 - E(2\theta U_t U_{t-1}) + E(\theta^2 U_{t-1}^2) \end{aligned}$$

Since θ is a constant, this can be rewritten as

$$Var(N_t) = EU_t^2 - 2\theta E(U_t U_{t-1}) + \theta^2 EU_{t-1}^2$$

The first and last terms of this expression are σ_U^2 and $\theta^2 \sigma_U^2$.

$$Var(N_t) = \sigma_U^2 - 2\theta E(U_t U_{t-1}) + \theta^2 \sigma_U^2$$

Since U_t is white noise, furthermore, U_t and U_{t-1} are independent, so the middle term is zero. Thus,

$$VAR(N_t) = \sigma_U^2 + \theta^2 \sigma_U^2 = \sigma_U^2(1 + \theta^2)$$

which shows that the variance of a first-order *MA* process is a function of the variance of the underlying white-noise process and the *MA* parameter.

Although the variance of a first-order *AR* process has a somewhat more complicated derivation, it too uses the same three rules.

$$\begin{aligned} VAR(N_t) &= E(\varphi N_{t-1} + U_t)^2 \\ &= E(\varphi N_{t-1} + U_t)(\varphi N_{t-1} + U_t) \\ &= E(\varphi^2 N_{t-1}^2 + 2\varphi N_{t-1} U_t + U_t^2) \\ &= E(\varphi^2 N_{t-1}^2) + E(2\varphi N_{t-1} U_t) + EU_t^2 \\ &= \varphi^2 EN_{t-1}^2 + 2\varphi E(N_{t-1} U_t) + EU_t^2 \end{aligned}$$

Since the first-order *AR* process is stationary, its variance is constant over time. That is,

$$EN_{t-1}^2 = EN_{t-k}^2 = VAR(N_t)$$

The first and last terms of this expression are $VAR(N_t)$ and σ_U^2 then and by substitution,

$$Var(N_t) = \varphi^2 Var(N_t) + 2\varphi E(N_{t-1}U_t) + \sigma_U^2$$

$$Var(N_t) - \varphi^2 Var(N_t) = 2\varphi E(N_{t-1}U_t) + \sigma_U^2$$

$$Var(N_t)(1 - \varphi^2) = 2\varphi E(N_{t-1}U_t) + \sigma_U^2$$

The derivation would be simplified greatly if $E(N_{t-1}U_t)$ were zero—and it is but this is not obvious. To show that $E(N_{t-1}U_t)$ is, in fact, zero, note that N_{t-2} can be written as,

$$N_{t-2} = \varphi N_{t-3} + U_{t-2}$$

Substituting $(\varphi N_{t-3} + U_{t-2})$ for N_{t-2},

$$N_{t-1} = \varphi N_{t-2} + U_{t-1}$$
$$= \varphi(\varphi N_{t-3} + U_{t-2}) + U_{t-1}$$
$$= \varphi^2 N_{t-3} + \varphi U_{t-2} + U_{t-1}$$

Of course, N_{t-3} can be written as,

$$N_{t-3} = \varphi N_{t-4} + U_{t-3}$$

So by substitution again

$$N_{t-1} = \varphi^2 N_{t-3} + \varphi U_{t-2} + U_{t-1}$$
$$= \varphi^2(\varphi N_{t-4} + U_{t-3}) + \varphi U_{t-2} + U_{t-1}$$
$$= \varphi^3 N_{t-4} + \varphi^2 U_{t-3} + \varphi U_{t-2} + U_{t-1}$$

Continuing this backward substitution indefinitely,

$$N_{t-1} = U_{t-1} + \varphi U_{t-2} + \varphi^2 U_{t-3} + \varphi^3 U_{t-4} + \ldots + \varphi^k U_{t-1-k}$$

Multiplying both sides by U_t,

$$N_{t-1}U_t = U_t(U_{t-1} + \varphi U_{t-2} + \varphi^2 U_{t-3} + \varphi^3 U_{t-4} + \ldots + \varphi^k U_{t-1-k})$$
$$= U_t U_{t-1} + \varphi U_t U_{t-2} + \varphi^2 U_t U_{t-3} + \varphi^3 U_t U_{t-4}$$
$$+ \ldots + \varphi^k U_t U_{t-1-k}$$

From the definition of white noise, the expected value of each term on the right-hand side is zero, so

$$E(N_{t-1}U_t) = 0$$

With this result, the variance of the first-order *AR* process simplifies to

$$\mathrm{Var}(N_t) = \sigma_U^2/(1 - \varphi^2) \qquad -1 < \varphi < 1$$

Again, the variance of a first-order *AR* process is a function of the variance of the underlying white-noise process and the *AR* parameter.

ARMA Covariances. The covariance of two *ARMA* realizations, N_t and N_{t-k}, is defined as

$$\mathrm{COV}(N_tN_{t-k}) = \mathrm{E}(N_tN_{t-k})$$

For the first-order *MA* process then, let $k = 1$ and

$$\begin{aligned}
\mathrm{COV}(N_tN_{t-1}) &= \mathrm{E}(N_tN_{t-1}) \\
&= \mathrm{E}(U_t - \theta U_{t-1})(U_{t-1} - \theta U_{t-2}) \\
&= \mathrm{E}(U_tU_{t-1} - \theta U_tU_{t-2} - \theta U_{t-1}^2 + \theta U_{t-1}U_{t-2}) \\
&= \mathrm{E}U_tU_{t-1} - \theta \mathrm{E}U_tU_{t-2} - \theta \mathrm{E}U_{t-1}^2 + \theta \mathrm{E}U_{t-1}U_{t-2}
\end{aligned}$$

Since U_t, U_{t-1} and U_{t-2} are independent, only the third term of this expression is nonzero. Thus

$$\mathrm{COV}(N_tN_{t-1}) = -\theta\sigma_U^2$$

At the second lag, $k = 2$ and

$$\begin{aligned}
\mathrm{COV}(N_tN_{t-2}) &= \mathrm{E}(N_tN_{t-2}) \\
&= \mathrm{E}(U_t - \theta U_{t-1})(U_{t-2} - \theta U_{t-3}) \\
&= \mathrm{E}(U_tU_{t-2} - \theta U_tU_{t-3} - \theta U_{t-1}U_{t-2} + \theta U_{t-1}U_{t-2}) \\
&= \mathrm{E}U_tU_{t-2} - \theta \mathrm{E}U_tU_{t-3} - \theta \mathrm{E}U_{t-1}U_{t-2} + \theta \mathrm{E}U_{t-1}U_{t-2} \\
&= 0
\end{aligned}$$

For the same reason, covariances for all lags $k > 2$ are zero.

The covariance function of the first-order *AR* process is derived iteratively. For $k = 1$.

$$\begin{aligned}
\mathrm{COV}(N_tN_{t-1}) &= \mathrm{E}[(N_t)(N_{t-1})] \\
&= \mathrm{E}[(\varphi N_{t-1} + U_t)(N_{t-1})] \\
&= \mathrm{E}(\varphi N_{t-1}^2 + U_tN_{t-1}) \\
&= \varphi \mathrm{E}N_{t-1}^2 + \mathrm{E}U_tN_{t-1} \\
&= \varphi \mathrm{VAR}(N_t)
\end{aligned}$$

For $k = 2$

$$\mathrm{COV}(N_tN_{t-2}) = \mathrm{E}[(N_t)(N_{t-2})]$$

$$= E[(\varphi N_{t-1} + U_t)(N_{t-2})]$$
$$= E(\varphi N_{t-1} N_{t-2} + U_t N_{t-2})$$
$$= \varphi E N_{t-1} N_{t-2} + E U_t N_{t-2}$$
$$= \varphi COV(N_{t-1} N_{t-2})$$

Since the first-order *AR* process is stationary,

$$COV(N_{t-1} N_{t-2}) = COV(N_t N_{t-1}) = \varphi VAR(N_t)$$

So by substitution,

$$COV(N_t N_{t-2}) = \varphi[\varphi VAR(N_t)] = \varphi^2 VAR(N_t)$$

Continuing this procedure, we show that, in general,

$$COV(N_t N_{t-k}) = \varphi^k VAR(N_t)$$

for any lag k.

ARMA ACFs. The *standardized* covariance function, or *ACF,* is defined as the ratio of covariance to variance. For the first-order *MA* process then,

$$\rho_I = -\theta \sigma_U^2 / \sigma_U^2 (1 + \theta^2)$$
$$= -\theta/(1 + \theta^2)$$
$$\rho_{k>1} = 0$$

Accordingly, the first-order *MA ACF* has a significant "spike" at the first lag and nothing at subsequent lages. For the first-order *AR* process, on the other hand,

$$\rho_I = \varphi^k VAR(N_t)/VAR(N_t)$$
$$= \varphi^k$$

The first-order *AR ACF* decays exponentially, or geometrically, to zero. The *ACF*s in Figs. 3.10 and 3.11 are typical *MA* and *AR ACF*s.

B1—Cincinnati Directory Assistance (McSweeney, 1978)

	Jan	Feb	Mar	Apr	May	Jun	Jul	Aug	Sep	Oct	Nov	Dec
62	350	339	351	364	369	331	331	340	346	341	357	398
63	381	367	383	375	353	361	375	371	373	366	382	429
64	406	403	429	425	427	409	402	409	419	404	429	463
65	428	449	444	467	474	463	432	453	462	456	474	514
66	489	475	492	525	527	533	527	522	526	513	564	599
67	572	587	599	601	611	620	579	582	592	581	630	663
68	638	631	645	682	601	595	521	521	516	496	538	575
69	537	534	542	538	547	540	526	548	555	545	594	643

	Jan	Feb	Mar	Apr	May	Jun	Jul	Aug	Sep	Oct	Nov	Dec
70	625	616	640	625	637	634	621	641	654	649	662	699
71	672	704	700	711	715	718	652	664	695	704	733	772
72	716	712	732	755	761	748	748	750	744	731	782	810
73	777	816	840	868	872	811	810	762	634	626	649	697
74	657	549	162	177	175	162	161	165	170	172	178	186
75	178	178	189	205	202	185	193	200	196	204	206	227
76	225	217	219	236	253	213	205	210	216	218	235	241

B2—The Hawthorne Experiment (Franke, 1980)

	Wrkr 1	Wrkr 2	Wrkr 3	Wrkr 4	Wrkr 5	Rest
001	51.1	51.3	50.4	48.2	48.3	00
002	50.5	48.1	50.0	49.9	48.7	00
003	47.6	45.6	50.2	52.9	48.0	00
004	50.2	54.5	52.6	54.0	50.8	00
005	48.1	47.0	50.3	51.1	47.8	00
006	46.7	45.7	43.7	48.1	47.7	00
007	47.2	48.9	51.0	49.9	50.1	00
008	47.4	48.9	51.6	50.0	50.4	00
009	46.4	48.1	52.9	51.0	51.8	00
010	44.4	46.6	52.5	51.1	50.1	00
011	48.8	49.5	54.4	51.2	48.7	00
012	47.5	51.2	54.5	53.8	52.1	00
013	50.3	52.4	54.4	53.9	50.4	00
014	52.1	53.3	54.3	52.9	50.9	00
015	50.7	53.4	54.8	52.7	50.4	00
016	52.9	51.1	53.1	52.6	51.0	10
017	52.1	48.9	55.2	53.3	50.4	10
018	49.9	50.6	53.3	54.5	50.2	10
019	50.6	51.6	51.4	52.2	51.6	10
020	51.8	51.7	54.9	55.0	52.9	10
021	54.2	56.4	56.0	54.4	54.2	20
022	52.8	53.0	58.7	56.9	53.2	20
023	55.8	56.8	56.1	55.8	51.9	20
024	53.7	55.6	57.0	57.1	52.6	20
025	55.2	55.9	54.1	54.0	51.8	30
026	53.9	54.6	54.4	56.2	54.2	30
027	53.2	51.4	55.9	55.3	53.7	30
028	54.0	52.7	58.3	57.3	54.3	30
029	55.2	54.9	57.4	55.4	54.3	25

(*continued*)

B2—The Hawthorne Experiment (Franke, 1980) (*Continued*)

	Wrkr 1	Wrkr 2	Wrkr 3	Wrkr 4	Wrkr 5	Rest
030	54.9	56.0	57.8	56.4	55.6	25
031	52.2	55.4	57.9	56.3	54.5	25
032	56.4	56.6	57.8	56.6	54.6	25
033	54.7	55.2	57.7	54.9	53.4	25
034	53.3	52.9	58.6	58.6	50.4	25
035	49.4	49.7	57.7	58.6	53.2	25
036	53.2	52.5	58.5	61.1	53.7	25
037	53.2	52.0	59.7	59.1	55.8	25
038	55.0	51.9	61.8	60.4	55.4	25
039	54.5	56.3	62.6	62.5	55.0	25
040	60.7	59.9	62.1	62.0	56.0	25
041	63.0	64.7	61.6	63.5	56.8	25
042	62.4	64.6	60.4	62.5	55.9	25
043	62.8	66.7	62.8	63.6	57.3	25
044	62.0	64.5	63.8	63.7	58.8	25
045	64.0	62.2	66.2	64.0	56.7	25
046	64.8	65.1	62.6	62.6	56.2	25
047	64.8	68.5	63.7	64.9	59.1	25
048	64.5	67.0	63.8	64.5	61.0	25
049	65.3	68.1	62.8	63.3	57.6	25
050	67.3	68.5	61.9	61.6	60.2	25
051	65.3	66.9	61.6	60.7	56.6	25
052	67.7	69.0	61.4	61.1	58.0	25
053	62.2	62.9	58.8	60.2	56.5	25
054	63.5	63.8	60.5	62.0	55.7	25
055	60.1	62.9	64.0	61.7	54.9	25
056	61.3	63.3	61.9	62.7	55.7	25
057	62.0	63.6	65.1	64.6	51.6	25
058	64.6	64.9	61.8	64.2	53.2	25
059	65.8	67.1	63.6	65.9	55.4	25
060	63.9	64.4	62.3	64.2	56.7	25
061	64.9	65.7	62.9	63.8	55.7	25
062	65.5	64.5	61.2	62.1	53.3	25
063	65.2	66.7	62.7	61.7	52.4	25
064	64.7	65.6	65.4	63.2	53.2	25
065	66.5	67.3	65.0	63.4	53.9	25
066	66.4	67.5	62.7	62.6	56.0	25
067	65.6	66.2	63.5	62.7	54.8	25
068	64.7	64.9	64.3	62.9	53.6	25

B2—The Hawthorne Experiment (Franke, 1980) (*Continued*)

	Wrkr 1	Wrkr 2	Wrkr 3	Wrkr 4	Wrkr 5	Rest
069	63.7	63.5	65.1	63.0	52.4	25
070	68.0	68.5	64.4	63.1	58.9	25
071	64.7	66.1	62.3	63.2	58.4	25
072	61.1	62.6	62.1	62.6	56.5	00
073	61.7	62.9	60.7	62.3	55.7	00
074	62.6	63.9	60.1	61.9	55.2	00
075	61.9	63.4	59.4	60.5	55.7	00
076	63.0	64.4	61.8	61.5	57.3	00
077	62.9	64.0	60.4	62.4	56.2	00
078	63.3	64.5	57.7	61.2	57.9	00
079	61.8	63.3	58.0	61.3	55.2	00
080	61.0	62.8	59.6	60.4	57.3	00
081	62.9	63.8	60.1	60.6	55.2	00
092	63.9	65.2	58.3	60.6	56.4	00
083	63.2	65.1	57.7	59.9	54.6	00
084	65.6	67.0	61.7	61.3	60.1	25
085	67.6	69.0	64.7	64.4	59.4	25
086	61.6	67.3	61.5	63.8	60.8	25
087	67.1	68.7	60.5	65.5	61.5	25
088	65.9	67.9	58.8	62.2	61.6	25
089	67.0	69.8	63.3	66.4	58.4	25
090	66.5	68.8	65.1	67.3	57.1	25
091	65.0	67.7	64.2	67.7	58.6	25
092	66.6	70.3	65.6	67.9	57.6	25
093	66.9	68.8	65.5	68.8	58.2	25
094	69.6	73.3	65.2	68.4	59.1	25
095	66.3	71.1	61.8	67.5	55.2	25
096	67.4	74.1	65.8	70.5	59.6	25
097	65.2	69.5	65.1	69.9	56.8	25
098	65.2	69.8	64.4	69.5	59.0	25
099	65.6	71.8	62.6	68.4	58.4	25
100	70.1	74.1	64.6	69.7	60.2	25
101	70.3	73.9	64.1	69.8	61.1	25
102	65.5	70.9	62.7	69.5	57.1	25
103	70.0	73.5	68.5	72.9	60.1	25
104	67.2	73.1	66.6	72.2	57.3	25
105	67.1	73.5	65.3	71.7	59.3	25
106	69.1	75.6	69.1	74.1	61.8	25
107	69.5	75.0	69.1	73.4	65.5	25

(*continued*)

B2—The Hawthorne Experiment (Franke, 1980) (*Continued*)

	Wrkr 1	Wrkr 2	Wrkr 3	Wrkr 4	Wrkr 5	Rest
108	70.3	74.8	67.6	73.4	63.4	25
109	69.5	74.2	66.5	72.0	62.6	25
110	64.4	71.0	62.1	67.3	60.6	25
111	70.9	78.6	61.8	71.2	62.0	25
112	68.9	75.8	63.6	71.6	59.3	25
113	68.8	76.8	63.3	71.4	60.3	25
114	71.2	78.4	66.2	73.8	60.9	25
115	66.4	71.9	61.2	69.7	61.2	25
116	66.7	71.3	59.5	68.1	56.5	25
117	65.6	70.7	60.1	68.8	56.0	25
118	64.5	70.1	60.7	69.5	55.5	25
119	63.5	69.5	61.3	70.2	55.0	25
120	68.5	74.3	63.5	71.9	43.5	25
121	65.6	71.9	66.7	70.5	47.1	25
122	66.7	72.4	64.4	71.4	46.7	25
123	65.5	71.0	64.3	69.8	49.1	25
124	68.3	72.9	65.6	70.7	46.5	25
125	66.7	73.8	66.9	72.3	50.1	25
126	68.1	75.6	64.6	71.1	51.5	25
127	69.8	75.1	66.3	74.4	43.4	25
128	67.9	75.4	66.2	75.0	49.2	25
129	66.5	73.8	65.5	71.5	48.9	25
130	69.3	75.0	63.8	74.2	54.7	25
131	66.8	73.5	64.2	71.4	51.6	25
132	68.8	74.6	68.8	73.5	53.0	25
133	68.3	74.2	65.0	73.2	53.1	25
134	69.8	76.9	67.4	75.6	54.1	25
135	73.0	77.2	67.0	76.1	52.3	25
136	72.0	74.6	62.5	73.5	53.4	25
137	70.9	75.5	66.6	74.8	54.9	25
138	69.0	74.1	63.9	72.2	51.2	25
139	70.6	75.1	60.0	71.6	51.0	25
140	64.9	69.4	59.0	68.6	53.0	25
141	73.4	76.5	64.4	71.1	57.8	25
142	73.1	77.2	67.3	74.7	57.3	25
143	69.9	73.0	63.4	68.9	55.1	25
144	69.5	72.1	64.0	68.8	54.3	25
145	68.1	72.7	63.6	68.0	53.9	25

B2—The Hawthorne Experiment (Franke, 1980) (*Continued*)

	Wrkr 1	Wrkr 2	Wrkr 3	Wrkr 4	Wrkr 5	Rest
146	72.1	78.0	65.4	74.7	56.6	25
147	70.7	76.7	65.1	70.4	56.9	25
148	74.6	78.8	65.9	71.9	56.6	25
149	70.2	76.3	64.4	66.9	57.6	25
150	70.4	73.3	64.1	69.9	56.7	25
151	70.5	75.3	65.3	71.2	58.5	25
152	71.9	76.5	65.5	72.3	59.7	25
153	70.7	73.0	64.6	70.1	58.1	25
154	78.4	80.7	69.2	70.1	62.0	25
155	79.6	82.4	69.6	74.7	62.1	25
156	75.6	79.5	70.1	78.3	59.8	25
157	69.4	74.8	67.6	71.5	59.7	25
158	70.3	74.4	66.2	69.6	60.7	25
159	67.8	71.7	62.0	68.4	59.6	25
160	64.9	71.0	65.1	68.5	53.4	25
161	67.7	71.3	63.4	68.3	56.2	25
162	67.4	71.3	62.4	65.8	59.9	25
163	69.8	78.2	63.7	75.0	60.7	25
164	70.5	79.3	66.4	74.5	58.2	25
165	72.8	79.1	70.5	75.0	61.1	25
166	70.2	76.9	67.2	76.2	63.3	25
167	68.2	78.2	62.9	75.6	61.4	25
168	64.8	71.6	63.6	68.8	61.2	25
169	65.7	71.8	63.6	69.2	60.8	25
170	66.6	72.0	63.5	69.6	60.4	25
171	67.6	72.1	63.5	70.0	60.0	25
172	70.6	80.1	64.8	78.5	63.1	25
173	73.8	80.7	69.0	79.1	63.2	25
174	72.2	76.5	68.5	74.6	61.9	25
175	69.8	75.2	66.3	71.6	63.4	25
176	74.8	78.6	66.6	77.4	65.4	25
177	71.4	75.4	69.2	74.2	63.6	25
178	74.5	79.6	69.7	77.0	65.6	25
179	70.7	74.9	68.2	74.8	65.4	25
180	71.7	75.8	67.8	75.2	65.1	25
181	77.6	80.8	68.5	80.5	65.1	25
182	74.0	81.0	69.0	80.6	65.0	25
183	70.6	78.8	68.8	77.6	66.3	25

(*continued*)

B2—The Hawthorne Experiment (Franke, 1980) (*Continued*)

	Wrkr 1	Wrkr 2	Wrkr 3	Wrkr 4	Wrkr 5	Rest
184	71.5	77.8	67.1	76.8	67.0	25
185	73.2	80.7	66.4	79.9	66.1	25
186	72.3	80.1	66.7	78.2	67.7	25
187	71.8	81.6	68.5	80.7	68.5	25
188	69.3	73.5	67.4	72.5	66.6	25
189	71.4	73.3	66.9	69.3	67.4	25
190	72.8	74.5	65.3	68.7	66.1	25
191	70.5	76.7	65.3	72.7	64.7	25
192	61.0	76.0	59.4	65.4	65.7	25
193	65.4	75.2	61.7	70.6	64.1	25
194	69.4	77.7	66.8	74.6	64.0	25
195	66.7	78.1	65.9	72.4	64.3	25
196	72.1	77.2	66.5	69.7	64.1	25
197	72.2	78.6	66.2	75.4	63.9	25
198	66.9	78.4	65.3	71.3	64.2	25
199	76.9	74.3	70.0	75.9	67.6	25
200	77.5	74.9	69.0	69.6	68.1	25
201	72.0	72.5	67.6	71.0	69.4	25
202	79.1	81.0	65.9	71.6	65.3	25
203	74.8	77.0	63.1	71.4	64.4	25
204	70.2	75.8	36.1	71.4	67.7	25
205	74.9	78.7	67.6	69.0	64.7	25
206	73.4	78.4	64.3	68.0	63.2	25
207	74.2	76.3	62.8	68.5	64.7	25
208	74.2	74.9	65.1	75.2	66.7	25
209	73.0	72.6	63.9	66.1	65.6	25
210	75.4	74.7	65.1	75.1	66.6	25
211	71.3	74.8	63.3	67.3	66.0	25
212	71.3	75.1	61.2	66.5	66.7	25
213	72.6	77.8	63.9	68.2	66.5	25
214	70.1	76.4	65.4	66.7	66.0	25
215	72.9	76.5	66.8	69.1	65.7	25
216	72.4	76.9	62.4	68.6	63.2	25
217	72.1	77.2	62.5	67.5	63.1	25
218	68.1	74.1	64.3	67.0	63.0	25
219	71.6	74.3	64.0	66.0	64.5	25
220	69.8	77.4	60.6	66.4	64.8	25
221	72.5	78.7	62.3	68.1	64.9	25
222	76.2	80.0	64.0	69.8	65.0	25

B2—The Hawthorne Experiment (Franke, 1980) *(Continued)*

	Wrkr 1	Wrkr 2	Wrkr 3	Wrkr 4	Wrkr 5	Rest
223	80.8	81.4	65.8	69.5	65.0	25
224	80.0	80.2	64.3	67.2	65.1	25
225	76.8	78.1	65.5	64.0	65.1	25
226	78.0	79.5	66.6	69.9	65.0	25
227	73.0	74.9	64.8	63.8	64.9	25
228	74.3	74.9	66.4	82.4	68.7	25
229	72.4	74.9	65.0	69.0	67.5	25
230	74.5	76.7	62.5	66.7	66.7	25
231	71.1	72.3	66.6	67.2	68.9	25
232	71.8	75.6	66.7	73.5	65.7	25
233	71.6	76.1	64.7	66.8	64.9	25
234	72.0	73.3	62.4	65.9	63.6	25
235	70.4	73.4	62.1	63.1	63.3	25
236	75.8	77.0	67.3	72.5	65.2	25
237	73.2	73.9	63.4	67.7	65.5	25
238	75.2	76.0	64.3	67.1	65.4	25
239	70.0	71.7	67.4	69.1	67.5	25
240	68.8	71.1	65.4	66.0	68.0	25

B3—Per-acre Cotton Prices (Hovland & Sears, 1940)

	0	1	2	3	4	5	6	7	8	9
188			18.46	14.96	14.56	14.75	13.94	15.61	15.33	15.80
189	17.34	15.77	13.61	13.54	10.94	14.50	12.54	13.12	12.21	13.39
190	17.02	14.01	15.65	20.58	18.77	21.32	20.41	19.76	18.18	21.18
191	24.99	20.80	22.95	23.27	14.79	20.09	31.82	46.20	49.60	62.00
192	31.10	23.60	35.68	41.30	39.60	35.55	25.15	34.08	30.69	28.79
193	15.52									

B3—Black Lynchings (Hovland & Sears, 1940)

	0	1	2	3	4	5	6	7	8	9
188			49	52	52	80	74	73	70	95
189	90	121	155	155	134	112	80	122	102	84
190	107	107	86	86	83	61	65	60	93	73
191	65	63	61	50	49	54	50	36	60	76
192	53	59	51	29	16	17	23	16	10	7
193	20									

B4—MMPI Citations (O'Grady, 1988)

Year	0	1	2	3	4	5	6	7	8	9
195_	12	22	25	28	29	31	17	21	13	63
196_	96	60	61	84	70	146	94	100	110	95
197_	154	156	122	118	113	73	110	90	72	146
198_	70	75	70	71	112	152				

B4—Rorschach Citations (O'Grady, 1988)

Year	0	1	2	3	4	5	6	7	8	9
195_	91	96	132	104	149	142	123	76	67	136
196_	124	143	82	87	82	136	98	82	109	69
197_	99	96	73	63	54	63	36	59	42	61
198_	36	52	50	50	57	90				

B5—Skirt Widths (Richardson & Kroeber, 1940)

Year	0	1	2	3	4	5	6	7	8	9
178_								56.3	51.1	55.1
179_	51.0	53.2	58.6	52.1	43.3	52.6	43.8	49.3	44.4	42.7
180_	42.9	42.2	59.6	38.5	44.7	35.0	38.5	37.8	32.6	24.8
181_	24.2	27.2	29.4	28.9	31.3	45.8	39.8	42.9	38.6	41.1
182_	37.0	42.7	44.5	46.3	38.1	48.6	48.5	53.2	49.6	55.6
183_	48.7	44.2	54.4	59.4	64.3	67.0	70.0	62.3	70.9	63.6
184_	63.9	64.6	60.0	60.1	58.2	59.4	57.3	64.8	59.6	62.7
185_	64.2	61.3	70.3	70.2	79.3	83.0	89.2	86.2	100.3	115.6
186_	107.1	104.3	96.1	101.6	100.1	108.6	99.8	98.7	88.4	85.5
187_	88.0	74.9	77.6	84.8	84.5	79.0	84.8	76.4	70.9	62.0
188_	68.8	52.3	56.0	54.7	52.2	56.0	56.6	50.9	57.8	51.5
189_	50.2	53.7	51.1	55.0	55.5	60.7	68.3	60.0	53.0	65.3
190_	52.5	64.8	58.9	50.4	56.5	53.7	56.0	51.2	49.0	38.4
191_	32.9	23.2	27.4	33.7	29.1	46.1	49.1	55.7	20.3	33.2
192_	16.8	26.0	26.4	22.4	21.3	22.0	16.5	18.0	21.2	26.0
193_	25.9	26.0	25.8	25.9	26.2	38.7	33.8			

B6—Spouse Homicides (Silverman & Kennedy, 1987)

Year	0	1	2	3	4	5	6	7	8	9
196_		37	33	39	32	27	29	34	34	31
197_	29	32	31	32	26	28	27	23	22	23
198_	20	23	23	23						

B6—Spouse Homicides (Silverman & Kennedy, 1987)

Year	0	1	2	3	4	5	6	7	8	9
196_		16	23	23	19	20	20	15	22	20
197_	23	21	20	22	23	22	22	24	20	20
198_	28	26	18	18						

4 The Intensive Examination of Social Interactions

Bruce E. Wampold
University of Wisconsin–Madison

Traditionally, the focus of single-case research has been on the behavior of single individuals. Although some designs, such as multiple-baseline designs, examine the behavior of more than one individual, rarely do single-case designs focus on the interactions among individuals. That is to say, the *case* in single-case designs is the individual rather than a social system. Nevertheless, scientists in a number of areas of psychology, education, and related areas have been increasingly interested in the intensive examination of social interactions. There is no doubt that social behavior is bidirectional in that an individual's behavior is both a response to another's previous behavior as well as a stimulus for the other's behavior. A child's tantrum may be a response to a denied request as well as the stimulus to the parent to acquiesce to the request. It is this unfolding of behavior over time between two or more individuals that is the focus of this chapter.

Although the methods described in this chapter are not applicable to traditional single-case designs, they contain the sine qua non of single-case research—the intensive analysis of behavior. To understand the sequence of behaviors generated in a social interaction it is necessary to examine the timing of the behaviors in the interaction. That a parent acquiesces to a child is interesting; that a parent increases his or her probability of acquiescence after a tantrum provides the information that is vital to understanding the contingencies that maintain tantrums.

In the simplest case, the methods in this chapter will answer the question of whether one behavior follows another behavior more often than would be expected by chance. Does a tantrum increase the probability of acquiescence? For a marital couple, does a positive behavior increase the probability that the spouse will reciprocate with a positive behavior? In psychotherapy, does a therapist's minimal encourager increase the probability that the client will continue telling a story? Other methods will be presented that will detect more complex patterns in social interactions, such as bidirectional behavior patterns and dominance.

Although the methods presented are designed to study intensively the interactions among a single system, variations of the method allow for the examination of several interactions by the same system (e.g., the interactions of a marital couple over the course of therapy) as well as for the comparison of several interactions (e.g., the interactions of distressed and nondistressed couples). Moreover, the relation between various patterns of behavior in the interaction can be linked to global measures (e.g., what is the relation between dominance in a mother/child interaction and the psychosocial functioning of the mother?).

It should be noted that as a relatively new area, the methods for analyzing social interactions are diffuse and paradigms are just beginning to emerge. The purpose of this chapter is to present one such approach to the analysis of social interactions. This approach fits nicely in this book because it is conceptually similar to several other approaches presented earlier. Although several terms have been used to describe generically the analysis of the sequence of behaviors generated by a social interaction, the term *sequential analysis* seems to have been most widely adopted.

It should be noted that other methods have been proposed for analyzing sequential categorical data, the most comprehensive of which are those based on log-linear methods (Allison & Liker, 1982; Budescu, 1984; Feick & Novak, 1985; Iacobucci & Wasserman, 1988). In those instances where various paradigms test functionally equivalent hypotheses, the respective tests are identical or require a trivial correction. For instance, the unidirectional z-test discussed later is similar to the Allison and Liker (1982) z-test.

This chapter contains three major sections. First, the mathematical model and the resulting methods for analyzing sequences of behavior are presented. Second, examples of research that have relied on these methods are discussed. These examples illustrate how the methods can be used, and help to establish the utility of the methods. Finally, issues and limitations related to the use of these methods are raised.

BASIC PROCEDURES

The Model

Although the focus of this discussion is on the analysis of the data generated by a social interaction, it is helpful to understand how those data are collected. Typically, the interaction between two or more persons is recorded. From the recording, the stream of behaviors of the participants is coded yielding a sequence of categorical codes. There are several issues in the coding of the behaviors that need to be considered.

First, because the coding system reduces the richness of the interaction to a finite set of behavioral codes, choice of a coding system that is sensitive to the hypothesized constructs in the interaction is critical. For example, systems exist that reflect power and involvement (Penman, 1980), control and support (Pett, Vaughan–Cole, Egger, & Dorsey, 1988), emotion (based on facial expressions; Ekman & Friesen, 1978), and marital behavior (Weiss & Summers, 1983), among others. Bakeman and Gottman (1986) have discussed extensively the issues of coding systems.

A second issue related to data collection is the reduction of a continuous stream of behaviors to discrete units. Generally, the units can be one of two types: events or time intervals. Many hybrid unitization systems exist. The unitization system selected should be sensitive to the phenomena being investigated, as well as to the mathematical assumptions of the statistical tests used subsequently (Bakeman & Gottman, 1986; Gottman, 1979; Wampold & Margolin, 1982).

A final concern in coding interactions is the reliability of the coding. Although much has been written about the reliability of coding in general, reliability in the context of social interactions raises unique issues (Bakeman & Gottman, 1986; Gottman, 1980; Wampold & Holloway, 1983). For example, one troublesome aspect is the reliability of the unitization (Bakeman & Gottman, 1986). Present solutions to the reliability problem are unsatisfactory in many respects and this issue will be revisited later in this chapter.

As the discussion turns to statistical tests, it should be kept in mind that decisions about generation of the data (viz., coding systems, unitization, and reliability) are critical to the validity of the study and to the statistical analyses. The assumptions of the methods to be presented here are discussed toward the end of the chapter.

To illustrate the procedures discussed in this chapter, suppose that an interaction between a husband and wife is recorded and coded using a system that classifies the behavior of each spouse into three mutually exclusive categories: positive, negative, and neutral. In this presentation, the sequence of behaviors generated in the social interaction will be assumed to be a single sequence of behaviors, where any behavior is allowed to follow itself. (Although these restrictions are limiting, procedures that allow for their relaxation are discussed later.) According to this model, the social interaction yields a sequence of n behaviors $b_1, b_2, b_3, \ldots, b_n$. For the husband-and-wife example, the sequence might be

$$H(+) \; H(0) \; W(-) \; H(-) \; W(-) \; W(-) \; H(0) \; \bullet \bullet \bullet \; H(-) \; W(0).$$

Frequencies of the behaviors of an interacting system may provide important information about the interaction. An analysis of the frequencies of the behaviors, however, is insensitive to the pattern of the behaviors. Two couples could express negative behaviors with the same frequency but use those negative behaviors very differently. For one couple, the negative behaviors may be dispersed randomly throughout the interaction whereas for the other couple the negative behaviors may tend to follow each other. In the latter case, a quid pro quo is established in that a negative behavior elicits a negative behavior by the spouse. Indeed, Margolin and Wampold (1981) found that distressed and nondistressed couples do not significantly differ with regard to the frequency of negative behaviors. However, distressed couples reciprocated negative behavior, whereas nondistressed couples tended to emit negative behaviors randomly throughout the interaction.

The purpose of the statistical analyses discussed in this chapter is to detect various nonrandom aspects of the sequence of behaviors generated in a social interaction. In all cases, the null hypothesis is that the order of the behaviors is random. If the null hypothesis is true, the probability that a behavior will follow another behavior will be equal to the probability that the behavior will occur at any point in the sequence. That is, the conditional probability of behavior j occurring given i occurred immediately before will be equal to the unconditional probability that j will occur. For example, suppose that of a sequence of 200 behaviors, 60 behaviors were husband-positive; thus, the unconditional probability of husband-positive is $60/200 = 0.30$. Further, suppose that the wife displayed 50 positive behaviors during the interaction. Under the null hypothesis of randomness, it would be expected that 0.30 of these 50 behaviors would be followed by husband-positive. Thus the expected number of times husband reciprocates wife's positive behavior would be $50(.30) = .15$. Finally, suppose that the number of times the wife's positive behavior was reciprocated in this interaction was 21. Clearly the obtained number of times the husband reciprocated the wife's positive behavior was greater than the expected value under the null hypothesis of randomness. The question is whether or not 21 instances of this pattern is sufficiently large to reject the null hypothesis. If the null hypothesis is rejected, there is said to be *unidirectional dependence* from wife-positive to husband-positive. Statistical tests for unidirectional as well as several other patterns will be presented in this chapter. Moreover, other indexes that measure the degree to which a pattern is displayed in interactions will be discussed.

Before discussing particular tests, additional notation and background are needed. Let n_i be the number of behaviors in the sequence that are classified as behavior i.[1] Further, let T_{ij} be the number of transitions from behavior i to behavior j; that is, T_{ij} is the number of times that behavior j followed behavior i in the sequence. Typically, the number of transitions from one behavior to another is displayed in a transition frequency matrix, where the entry in row i and column j is the number of transitions from behavior i to behavior j, T_{ij}. An example of a transition frequency matrix is presented in Table 4.1 for the marital dyad dis-

---

[1] In previous discussions of these methods, the term "behavioral state" was used. Here, the term "behavior" is used to be consistent with others (e.g., Bakeman & Gottman, 1986).

TABLE 4.1
Hypothetical Transition Frequency Matrix for a Marital Pair

	Subsequent State						
Antecedent State	1	2	3	4	5	6	Total
1. Husband -positive	17	12	6	16	7	2	$n_1 = 60$
2. Husband-neutral	3	13	6	13	3	2	$n_2 = 40$
3. Husband negative	5	4	2	6	1	2	$n_3 = 20$
4. Wife-positive	21	6	3	10	8	2	$n_4 = 50$
5. Wife-neutral	6	4	2	5	1	1	$n_5 - 1 = 19$
6. Wife-negative	8	1	1	0	0	0	$n_6 = 10$
Total							$N - 1 = 199$

Note. The final (200th) behavior observed was wife-neutral, and theefore $n_5 = 20$. The total number of transitions is one less than the number of behaviors, and this $N = 200$. From "Tests of Dominance in Sequential Categorical Data" by B. E. Wampold (1984). *Psychological Bulletin, 96*, p. 426. Copyright (1984) by the American Psychological Association. Reprinted by permission.

cussed previously. The entries in the table represent the number of transitions from one behavior to another. For example, the 21 in row 4 and column 1 indicates that the husband followed the wife's positive behavior with a positive behavior 21 times (i.e., $T_{41} = 21$). Although the transition frequency matrix parsimoniously summarizes the interaction, the statistics presented in this chapter are based on the properties of the sequence of the categorically coded behaviors.

Basis for Statistical Tests

Recall that the null hypothesis for the various statistical tests discussed here is that the behaviors in the sequence are random. The alternative hypothesis is that a particular type of nonrandomness exists in the sequence. Each type of nonrandomness reflects a pattern in the data that may be of interest to the investigator, and statistics that are sensitive to particular nonrandom patterns will be presented. In this section, the statistical basis for the tests are presented; however, a complete understanding of this material is not necessary to use the statistical tests presented later.

The degree to which a particular type of nonrandomness is manifest in the sequence is determined by applying the quadratic assignment (QA) paradigm. The QA paradigm is a randomization type procedure for examining structures in various types of matrices (Hubert, 1987; Hubert & Baker, 1977; Hubert & Levin, 1976; Hubert & Schultz, 1976). Briefly, the QA paradigm involves a data matrix Q and a structure matrix C. The data matrix Q represents the outcome of a study such that each entry uv in the matrix reflects the similarities between the objects u and v. The entries in the structure matrix C are chosen by the researcher to reflect a particular arrangement to be tested. A cross-product statistic Γ indicates the degree to which the data matrix Q is reflected in the hypothesized structure in the matrix C. To evaluate the size of Γ, Q is held constant and the rows and columns of C are simultaneously permuted to obtain $r!$ Γ indexes, where r is the order of Q and C. In the present case, reference to the randomization distribution of Γ is impractical; fortunately, formulas for the mean and variance of Γ have been derived (Hubert & Schultz, 1976) and will be used in the present case to calculate a standardized test statistic.

In the context of sequential categorical data, the data matrix Q is an $N \times N$ matrix that represents each of the $N - 1$ transitions.[2] The structure matrix C is selected to reflect the various types of nonrandomness in the sequence. Designed in this way, the index Γ is equal to the number of transitions of various designated behaviors that are of interest to the researcher. The appropriate choice of the structure matrix C yields tests of important phenomena in the social interaction. The intricacies of defining the structure matrix C and derivation of the formulas for the mean and variance of the number of transitions are described elsewhere (Wampold, 1984; Wampold & Margolin, 1982). To assign statistical significance, the z-score

$$z = \frac{\Gamma - E(\Gamma)}{\sqrt{Var(\Gamma)}} \tag{1}$$

(where Γ is the index that reflects the nonrandomness of interest) is compared with the standard normal distribution.[3] If the value of z is sufficiently large, the null hypothesis of randomness is rejected in favor of the alternative that the hypothesized interactional pattern is present.

STATISTICAL TESTS FOR VARIOUS INTERACTIVE PHENOMENA

Unidirectional Dependence

Unidirectional dependence refers to the case where behavior j follows behavior i more (or less) than would be expected by chance. Recall that the husband followed the wife's positive behavior with a positive behavior 21 times, whereas

---

[2]Although the entries in the data matrix Q are transitions, this matrix is not the frequency transition matrix. The frequency transition matrix is a $K \times K$ matrix (where K is the number of different behaviors in the coding system) and the entries are the number of transitions from one behavior to another. The data matrix Q is an $N \times N$ matrix and the entries are 1s or 0s, depending on whether or not a transition occurred. See Wampold and Margolin (1982) for the details of the data matrix.

[3]Comparison to a normal distribution for the statistics discussed here appears to be justified, but raises some issues that are discussed toward the end of this chapter.

the expected value was 15. Whether 21 is sufficiently greater than 15 to reject the null hypothesis of randomness in favor of unidirectional dependence can be gauged by using the formulas derived from the QA paradigm. Specifically, T_{ij} indexes the number of transitions from behavior i to behavior j; as well

$$E(T_{ij}) = \frac{n_i n_j}{N} \tag{2}$$

and

$$\text{Var}(T_{ij}) = \frac{n_i n_j (N - n_i)(N - n_j)}{N^2(N - 1)} \tag{3}$$

(Wampold & Margolin, 1982). For the present example of the husband reciprocating the wife's positive behavior

$$E(T_{41}) = \frac{50(60)}{200} = 15$$

(as was calculated previously) and

$$\text{Var}(T_{41}) - \frac{(50)(60)(200 - 50)(200 - 60)}{(200)^2(199)} = 7.91$$

Therefore,

$$z = \frac{21 - 15}{\sqrt{7.91}} = 2.13,$$

which is sufficiently large, given an alpha of .05, to reject the null hypothesis in favor of the alternative that the husband reciprocated the wife's positive behavior with a positive behavior. That is, the husband responded positively to his wife's positive behavior more often than would be expected by chance.

Bidirectional Dependence

Bidirectional dependence refers to transitions from behavior i to behavior j and simultaneously from behavior j to behavior i. Bidirectional dependence is applicable when the researcher wishes to determine whether or not a dyad manifests a particular pattern in a circular fashion; for example, does the husband reciprocate the wife's positive behavior *and* does the wife reciprocate the husband's positive behavior? This interactive pattern has been referred to as a "circuit" (Holloway, Freund, Gardner, Nelson, & Walker, 1989) and is illustrated in Fig. 4.1.

It is important to note that bidirectional dependence tests the two unidirectional tests simultaneously. A bidirectional test is valuable because it can be used to test a research hypothesis directly (Wampold, Davis, & Good, 1990). If the

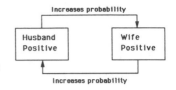

FIG. 4.1.   Bidirectional   circuit
involving positive reciprocity.

research question does not refer to the participants so much as the phenomenon (i.e., reciprocity of positive behaviors), then the bidirectional test provides a single test of the hypothesis. It should be noted that the two unidirectional tests contained in a bidirectional test are not independent (Wampold & Margolin, 1982).

Bidirectional dependence is judged by examining the number of transitions from behavior i to behavior j and from behavior j to behavior i [i.e., $(T_{ij} + T_{ji})$]. The formulas

$$E(T_{ij} + T_{ji}) = \frac{2n_i n_j}{N} \tag{4}$$

and

$$\text{Var}(T_{ij} + T_{ji}) = \frac{2n_i n_j [n_i n_j + (N - n_i)(N - n_j) - N]}{N^2(N - 1)} \tag{5}$$

are used to standardize $(T_{ij} + T_{ji})$. To illustrate the bidirectional test, the positive reciprocity for the interaction summarized in Table 4.1 is conducted. Note that the number of transition from husband-positive to wife-positive, T_{14}, is equal to 16 (vis-à-vis the expected value of 15). Therefore, the total number of transitions related to positive reciprocity $(T_{14} + T_{41})$ is equal to 37. The expected value is

$$E(T_{14} + T_{41}) = \frac{2(60)(50)}{200} = 30.$$

Application of Equation 5 yields $\text{Var}(T_{14} + T_{41}) = 17.94$. Thus

$$z = \frac{37 - 30}{\sqrt{17.94}} = 1.65,$$

which is sufficiently large (barely) to reject the null hypothesis of randomness in favor of the alternative that positive reciprocity was exhibited by this couple.

Other Questions Involving the Sum of Transitions from More Than 2 Cells

The QA paradigm can be used to derive formulas for testing hypotheses involving the sum of the transitions from any two or more cells (Wampold & Margolin,

1982). An interesting pattern in marital interaction is the tendency for partners to follow negative behaviors with positive behaviors less often than would be expected by chance. To determine whether that pattern was exhibited, the sum T_{61} + T_{34} would be compared with the expected value of this sum via a z-statistic. In general, to test simultaneously the unidirectional independence of i to j and the unidirectional independence of k to l ($j \neq k$, $i \neq l$, $i \neq k$, and $j \neq l$), a z-score is calculated by using the following formulas:

$$E(T_{ij} + T_{kl}) = \frac{n_i n_j + n_k n_l}{N} \tag{6}$$

and

$$\mathrm{Var}(T_{ij} + T_{kl}) =$$
$$\frac{n_i n_j (N - n_i)(N - n_j) + n_k n_l (N - n_k)(N - n_l) + 2 n_i n_j n_k n_l}{N^2(N - 1)} \tag{7}$$

Other multicell tests also have been derived (Wampold & Margolin, 1982).

Dominance

One of the more interesting constructs related to social interactions is dominance. Although dominance has been operationalized in various ways, in the context of the probabilistic relations among behavior in an interaction, dominance is characterized as an inequality in the influence between the participants in the interaction. Specifically, Gottman and Ringland (1981) defined dominance "as an *asymmetry in predictability*; that is, if B's behavior is more predictable from A's past than conversely, A is said to be dominant" (p. 395). If the wife is dominant, then the husband's behavior is more predictable from the wife's than the wife's is from the husband. It should be noted that dominance defined in this way refers to the consequences of behavior rather than on the nature of the behavior. An interactant can express a very powerful behavior, yet it might have little impact on the other person's behavior; similarly, a seemingly innocuous behavior may be quite influential. For example, a particular facial expression of a child may get the parent to acquiesce to a request because prior conditioning indicates that the facial expression is the precursor of a tantrum given noncompliance with the request. The difference between expressed and achieved power is discussed by Holloway et al. (1989).

To illustrate the concept of dominance, consider again the transition frequency matrix presented in Table 4.1. With regard to positive reciprocity, recall that the husband's positive behavior was predictable from the wife's [$T_{41} = 21$, $E(T_{41}) = 15$, $z = 2.13$). However, the wife's positive behavior was nonsignificantly predictable from the husband's [$T_{14} = 16$, $E(T_{14}) = 15$, $z = 0.36$). It appears that the wife is dominant because the husband's positive behavior is more predictable from the wife's than conversely. However, a statistical test of the asymmetry in predictability is needed and is presented below. Two types of dominance are considered: parallel dominance (i to j versus j to i) and nonparallel dominance (i to j versus k to l).

Parallel Case The simplest test of dominance involves the asymmetry in predictability of i to j and j to i. If the predictabilities are in the same direction (i.e., i increased the probability of j and j increases the probability of i or i decreases the probability of j and j decreases the probability of i), dominance is gauged by examining the difference of T_{ij} and T_{ji} (Wampold, 1984).[4] Specifically, the formula for the z-score in this case is given by

$$z = \frac{(T_{ij} - T_{ji}) - E(T_{ij} - T_{ji})}{\sqrt{\text{Var}(T_{ij} - T_{ji})}} \tag{8}$$

where $E(T_{ij} - T_{ji}) = 0$ and

$$\text{Var}(T_{ij} - T_{ji}) = \frac{2n_i n_j(N - n_i - n_j + 1)}{N(N - 1)} \tag{9}$$

In the marital example involving dominance related to positive reciprocity, $T_{41} - T_{14} = 5$, indicating that the husband reciprocated his wife's positive behavior with a positive behavior more frequently than conversely. By Equation 9, $\text{Var}(T_{41} - T_{14}) = 13.72$. To test for dominance with regard to this interactive pattern, the value of z is calculated using Equation 8. In this case $z = 1.35$. The positive value of z indicates that there was a tendency for the wife to be dominant [because the difference $(T_{41} - T_{14})$ was used]; however, the size of z was insufficiently large to reject the null hypothesis that there was no dominance. In this case, if the husband were dominant, a negative z-score would be expected.

If the predictabilities are not in the same direction (i increases the probability of j and j decreases the probability of i, or vice versa), then dominance is gauged by

$$z = \frac{(T_{ij} + T_{ji}) - E(T_{ij} + T_{ji})}{\sqrt{\text{Var}(T_{ij} + T_{ji})}} \tag{10}$$

where $E(T_{ij} + T_{ji}) = 2n_i n_j/N$ and

$$\text{Var}(T_{ij} + T_{ji}) = \frac{2n_i n_j[n_i n_j + (N - n_i)(N - n_j) - N]}{N^2(N - 1)} \tag{11}$$

---

[4]The rationale for taking the difference between T_{ij} and T_{ji} seems logical because dominance refers to the difference in predictability. However, calculation of dominance becomes complicated in several instances and the reader is referred to Wampold (1984).

Nonparallel case. In the nonparallel case, the predictability of i to j and k to l ($j \neq k$, $i \neq l$, $i \neq k$, and $j \neq l$) is considered. When predictabilities are in the same direction,

$$z = \frac{(n_k n_l T_{ij} - n_i n_j T_{kl}) - E(n_k n_l T_{ij} - n_i n_j T_{kl})}{\sqrt{\mathrm{Var}(n_k n_l T_{ij} - n_i n_j T_{kl})}} \tag{12}$$

where $E(n_k n_l T_{ij} - n_i n_j T_{kl}) = 0$ and

$$\mathrm{Var}(n_k n_l T_{ij} - n_i n_j T_{kl}) =$$

$$\frac{n_i n_j n_k n_l (N n_i n_j + N n_k n_l - n_i n_j n_k - n_i n_j n_l - n_i n_k n_l - n_j n_k n_l)}{N(N-1)} \tag{13}$$

When the predictabilities are in opposite directions,

$$z = \frac{(n_k n_l T_{ij} + n_i n_j T_{kl}) - E(n_k n_l T_{ij} + n_i n_j T_{kl})}{\sqrt{\mathrm{Var}(n_k n_l T_{ij} + n_i n_j T_{kl})}} \tag{14}$$

where $E(n_k n_l T_{ij} + n_i n_j T_{kl}) = 2 n_i n_j n_k n_l / N$ and

$$\mathrm{Var}(n_k n_l T_{ij} + n_i n_j T_{kl}) =$$

$$\frac{n_i n_j n_k n_l (4 n_i n_j n_k n_l + N^2 n_i n_j + N^2 n_k n_l - N n_i n_j n_k - N n_i n_j n_l - N n_i n_k n_l - N n_j n_k n_l)}{N(N^2 - 1)}$$

$$\tag{15}$$

MEASURES OF PATTERN

To this point, statistical tests of various nonrandom aspects of a single interaction have been presented. There are two important limitations of this approach that can be addressed by examining a measure of pattern. The first limitation is that a statistically significant result does not provide information about the size of the effect. So, although the z-score may be sufficiently large to reject the null hypothesis of randomness in favor of some alternative (say, that there is unidirectional dependence from wife-positive to husband-positive), the degree to which this pattern is manifest is not known. Given fixed-base rates, as the number of behaviors in the sequence increases, so does the magnitude of the z-score (Wampold, 1989). As is the case of most statistical tests, depending on the sample size, two results with identical significance levels may reflect very different effect sizes.

The second problem with statistical tests of a single interaction is that the information gained is limited to that particular interaction. To increase generalizability, patterns of several interactions need to be examined. One might want to observe the same interactants over time, to sample many different interactions from the same population (e.g., many distressed couples), or to compare samples from different populations (e.g., distressed couples versus nondistressed couples).

To solve the two problems with statistical tests, Wampold (1989) adapted the kappa statistic to measure pattern in social interactions.[5] Kappa is a statistic that compares the obtained value of a statistic with its maximum (Hubert, 1977). In general,

$$\kappa = \frac{X - E(X)}{\text{Max}(X) - E(X)} \tag{16}$$

When applied to specific nonrandom patterns in social interactional data, kappa has several desirable properties. First, kappa is independent of the length of the sequence. Second, kappa is sensitive to the degree to which the obtained number of transitions is different from the expected value. When the number of transitions equals the expected value, kappa is equal to zero; if the number of transitions is greater than the expected value, kappa is positive; if the number of transitions is less than the expected value, kappa is negative. Third, kappa is bounded above by 1; that is, when the obtained number of transitions is equal to its maximum, kappa is equal to 1. However, kappa is not bounded below by -1, a problem that is remedied by transforming kappa. The resulting transformed kappa ranges from -1 to 1 (Wampold, 1989).

Unlike some measures of effect size, transformed kappa cannot be interpreted as a proportion of variance accounted for. Nevertheless, it does reflect the degree to which a pattern is manifest in an interaction. Larger transformed kappas indicate that the pattern occurs to a greater extent.

There is another use of kappa that holds promise of the analysis of social interactions. Because kappa and transformed kappa reflect the degree to which a pattern occurs, they can be used as observations to be analyzed in their own right (Wampold, 1989). For example, if transformed kappas were obtained for several distressed and for several nondistressed couples, then a two independent sample t-test could be conducted on the transformed kappa scores to test whether there were differences in the degree to which distressed and nondistressed couples display the interactive pattern under investigation. As indicants of the degree to which some interactive phenomenon is being displayed, transformed kappas could be subjected to more sophisticated analyses involving other phenomena, such as covariance structures analysis. One problem with using kappas as observations is that the distribution of these indexes are unknown; furthermore, it is unclear whether kappa or transformed kappa is the index of choice for this

---

[5]Although kappa used to index the degree to which a sequential pattern is manifest is similar to the kappa used for assessing interobserver reliability (Cohen, 1960), the contexts are different and it is best to keep them distinct.

purpose. Transformed kappa has the desirable property of being bounded by -1 and 1, eliminating the skewness that results from the bounds on kappa.

Kappa for Various Patterns

Unidirectional Dependence.   Because $E(T_{ij}) = n_i n_j/N$, the general formula for kappa in the unidirectional case reduces to

$$\kappa = \frac{T_{ij} - n_i n_j/N}{\max(T_{ij}) - n_i n_j/N} \qquad (17)$$

To find $\max(T_{ij})$, note that the maximum number of transition from i to j will occur when i is always followed by j. However, the number of transitions from i to j is limited by the number of is and js in the sequence. For example, if there are only 50 is in the sequence (i.e., $n_i = 50$), then there can be at most 50 transitions from i to j. Therefore,

$$\max(T_{ij}) = \min(n_i, n_j).$$

Thus

$$\kappa = \frac{T_{ij} - n_i n_j/N}{\min(n_i, n_j) - n_i n_j/N} \qquad (18)$$

Before illustrating kappa for the continuing marital interaction, transformed kappa will be discussed. Note that kappa is minimized when $T_{ij} = 0$, in which case

$$\kappa = \frac{-E(T_{ij})}{\min(n_i, n_j) - E(T_{ij})} \qquad (19)$$

If negative values of kappa are divided by the absolute value of this lower bound, the resulting transformed kappa, designated by κ', will range from -1 to 1. After simplification, transformed kappa reduces to the following:

$$\kappa' = \begin{cases} \dfrac{T_{ij} - n_i n_j/N}{\min(n_i, n_j) - n_i n_j/N} & \text{when } T_{ij} \geq E(T_{ij}) \\[2em] \dfrac{T_{ij} - n_i n_j/N}{n_i n_j/N} & \text{otherwise} \end{cases} \qquad (20)$$

To illustrate the use of transformed kappa, consider again reciprocity of the wife's positive behavior by the husband's. Recall that $T_{41} = 21$, $E(T_{41}) = 15$, $n_4 = 50$, and $n_1 = 60$ and therefore $T_{ij} > E(T_{ij})$. The maximum number of transitions possible is equal to $\min(n_4, n_1) = \min(50, 60) = 50$ and therefore

$$\kappa' = \frac{21 - 15}{50 - 15} = 0.17$$

The value of transformed kappa in this case is a measure of the degree to which the husband reciprocated the wife's positive behavior. That the value was positive indicates that husband followed the wife's positive behavior more often than would be expected by chance. In fact, vis-à-vis the expected value, the wife's positive behavior was reciprocated 17% of the maximum possible.

Bidirectional Dependence.   Recall that bidirectional independence involved examining of $(T_{ij} + T_{ji})$. When $n_i \neq n_j$

$$\kappa' = \begin{cases} \dfrac{(T_{ij} + T_{ji}) - 2n_in_j/N}{2\min(n_i, n_j) - 2n_in_j/N} & \text{when } (T_{ij} + T_{ji}) \geq E(T_{ij} + T_{ji}) \\[2ex] \dfrac{(T_{ij} + T_{ji}) - 2n_in_j/N}{2n_in_j/N} & \text{otherwise} \end{cases} \tag{21}$$

When $n_i = n_j$, $\min(n_i, n_j)$ needs to be replaced by $2n_i - 1 = 2n_j - 1$. For bidirectional reciprocity for the marital pair, $\kappa' = 0.10$.

Other Patterns.   As mentioned previously, several other multicell analyses are possible. Of particular relevance is the simultaneous test of the transition from i to j and k to l ($j \neq k$, $i \neq l$, $i \neq k$, and $j \neq l$). In this case

$$\kappa' = \begin{cases} \dfrac{(T_{ij} + T_{kl}) - (n_in_j + n_kn_l)/N}{\min(n_i, n_j) + \min(n_k, n_l) - (n_in_j + n_kn_l)/N} & \text{when } (T_{ij} + T_{kl}) \geq \\ & \quad E(T_{ij} + T_{kl}) \\[2ex] \dfrac{(T_{ij} + T_{kl}) - (n_in_j + n_kn_l)/N}{(n_in_j + n_kn_l)/N} & \text{otherwise} \end{cases} \tag{22}$$

Dominance.   Derivation of formulas for kappa for parallel and nonparallel dominance become complicated by the fact that predictability of for each behavior can be in one or two directions; thus, there are four cases for each type of dominance. Although this is cumbersome, it presents no special problems.

For parallel dominance, four transformed kappas will be given, one for each of the four cases.[6] For the first case in which $T_{ij} > E(T_{ij})$ and $T_{ji} \geq E(T_{ji})$,

$$\kappa' = \frac{T_{ij} - T_{ji}}{\min(n_i, n_j) - n_in_j/N} \tag{23}$$

---

[6]The careful reader will note that the four cases are not mutually exclusive or exhaustive. However, when the cases are not exclusive, either case will result in the same value for transformed kappa. Further, transformed kappa is zero for those instances not covered by one of the four cases.

In the second case in which $T_{ij} < E(T_{ij})$ and $T_{ji} \leq E(T_{ji})$

$$\kappa' = \frac{T_{ij} - T_{ji}}{-n_{nj}/N} \tag{24}$$

In the third case in which $T_{ij} > E(T_{ij})$ and $T_{ji} \leq E(T_{ji})$,

$$\kappa' = \begin{cases} \dfrac{(T_{ij} + T_{ji}) - 2n_i n_j/N}{\min(n_i, n_j) - n_i n_j/N} & \text{when } T_{ij} - E(T_{ij}) \geq E(T_{ji}) - T_{ji} \\[2ex] \dfrac{(T_{ij} + T_{ji}) - 2n_i n_j/N}{n_i n_j/N} & \text{otherwise} \end{cases} \tag{25}$$

And finally in the fourth case where $T_{ij} < E(T_{ij})$ and $T_{ji} \geq E(T_{ji})$,

$$\kappa' = \begin{cases} \dfrac{(T_{ij} + T_{ji}) - 2n_i n_j/N}{-n_i n_j/N} & \text{when } E(T_{ij}) - T_{ij} \geq T_{ji} - E(T_{ji}) \\[2ex] \dfrac{(T_{ij} + T_{ji}) - 2n_i n_j/N}{n_i n_j/N - \min(n_i, n_j)} & \text{otherwise} \end{cases} \tag{26}$$

To illustrate the use of kappa for the dominance pattern related to positive reciprocity discussed earlier, recall that husband's positive behavior was more predictable from the wife's than conversely, although the difference was not statistically significant (z-score for parallel dominance was 1.35, $n_1 = 60$, $n_4 = 50$, $T_{41} = 21$, $T_{14} = 16$, $E(T_{41}) = E(T_{14}) = 15$, $N = 200$). These data meet the criteria for case 1 and thus

$$\kappa' = \frac{T_{ij} - T_{ji}}{\min(n_i, n_j) - n_i n_j/N} = \frac{21 - 16}{\min(60, 50) - 60(50)/200} = 0.143$$

The formulas for kappa for the nonparallel case are similar to those for the parallel case. Again, four cases will be examined. For the first case where $T_{ij} > E(T_{ij})$ and $T_{kl} > E(T_{kl})$,

$$\kappa' = \begin{cases} \dfrac{n_k n_l T_{ij} - n_i n_j T_{kl}}{n_k n_l \min(n_i, n_j) - n_i n_j n_k n_l/N} & \text{when } n_k n_l T_{ij} - E(n_k n_l T_{ij}) \geq \\ & \quad n_i n_j T_{kl} - E(n_i n_j T_{kl}) \\[2ex] \dfrac{n_k n_l T_{ij} - n_i n_j T_{kl}}{n_i n_j \min(n_k, n_l) - n_i n_j n_k n_l/N} & \text{otherwise} \end{cases} \tag{27}$$

In the second case where $T_{ij} < E(T_{ij})$ and $T_{kl} \leq E(T_{kl})$,

$$\kappa' = \frac{n_k n_l T_{ij} - n_i n_j T_{kl}}{-n_i n_j n_k n_l/N} \tag{28}$$

In the third case where $T_{ij} > E(T_{ij})$ and $T_{kl} \leq E(T_{kl})$,

$$\kappa' = \begin{cases} \dfrac{n_k n_l T_{ij} + n_i n_j T_{kl} - 2n_i n_j n_k n_l/N}{n_k n_l \min(n_i, n_j) - n_i n_j n_k n_l/N} & \text{when } n_k n_l T_{ij} - E(n_k n_l T_{ij}) \geq \\ & \qquad E(\mathrm{n_i n_j T_{kl}}) - n_i n_j T_{kl} \\[2ex] \dfrac{n_k n_l T_{ij} + n_i n_j T_{kl} - 2n_i n_j n_k n_l/N}{n_i n_j n_k n_l/N} & \text{otherwise} \end{cases} \qquad (29)$$

In the fourth case where $T_{ij} < E(T_{ij})$ and $T_{kl} \geq E(T_{kl})$,

$$\kappa' = \begin{cases} \dfrac{n_k n_l T_{ij} + n_i n_j T_{kl} - 2n_i n_j n_k n_l/N}{-n_i n_j n_k n_l/N} & \text{when } E(n_k n_l T_{ij}) - n_k n_l T_{ij} \geq \\ & \qquad n_i n_j T_{kl} - E(n_i n_j T_{kl}) \\[2ex] \dfrac{n_k n_l T_{ij} + n_i n_j T_{kl} - 2n_i n_j n_k n_l/N}{n_i n_j n_k n_l/N - n_i n_j \min(n_k, n_l)} & \text{otherwise} \end{cases} \qquad (30)$$

Kappa and Significance Tests

Two alternatives have been presented so far: significance tests and kappa scores. For a single interaction, the significance of the test based on the z-score indicates whether the null hypothesis of randomness for that interaction is rejected. Rejection of the null leads to the conclusion that a certain interactive pattern is present. Transformed kappa indicates the degree to which the pattern occurred. Thus, for a single interaction, reporting significance level and the transformed kappa is informative. For example, reporting "$\kappa' = .35$, $p < .05$" indicates that the pattern occurred reliably and that it occurred, relative to the expected value under the null model, 35% of the maximum extent possible. Keep in mind that a fairly large transformed kappa may not be significant if the sequence is short or if the frequencies of the behaviors involved are few.

When several interactions are analyzed and the kappas are themselves subjected to statistical tests (such as a t-test), then the significance levels for individual interactions are not of interest. For example, if it was determined that distressed couples reciprocated negative behaviors to a greater extent than nondistressed couples, the significance level of negative reciprocity for each couple would not be consequential.

APPLICATIONS

The statistical tests and measures of pattern discussed herein can be used in a number of ways to understand social interactions. The purpose of this section is to review several studies that have applied these methods and to demonstrate how the results of the studies reveal the essence of an interaction.

Power and Involvement in Supervision—The Intensive Analysis of a Few Interactions

One of the primary uses of sequential analysis methods is to understand in depth one or a few social interactions. Holloway et al. (1989) used these methods to understand the nature of power and involvement in clinical supervision by portraying the nature of the social interaction between supervisors and a supervisee.

In 1982, Goodyear produced a series of videotapes of supervision. One videotape presents a counseling session between a counselor, Dr. Harold Hackney, and an actress, who takes the role of a client. The remaining five tapes present supervision of Dr. Hackney with regard to this counseling session by five master supervisors of various theoretical orientations, Drs. Norman Kagan (Interpersonal Process Recall), Erving Polster (*Gestalt*), Carl Rogers (Client-centered), Albert Ellis (Rational–emotive), and Rudolph Ekstein (Psychoanalytic). Although several attempts have been made to analyze these supervision sessions (Abadie, 1985; Friedlander & Ward, 1984; Goodyear, Abadie, & Efros, 1984), Holloway et al. (1989) applied the methods discussed earlier and discovered many interesting phenomena not detectable by the macroanalytical techniques used previously.

Holloway, Freund, Gardner, Nelson, and Walker (1989) coded transcripts of the supervision sessions using the Penman (1980) scheme, which is structured around the constructs of power and involvement at the manifest level and at the latent level of communication. The manifest level refers to the explicit report of the participants, whereas the latent level refers to the command information in the particular context of the manifest level. There are nine codes at the manifest level, where each code varies in the degree to which it reflects power and involvement in the relationship. Figure 4.2 organizes the manifest codes around these two dimensions as a 3×3 matrix such that degree of involvement is represented by the horizontal axis and degree of power is represented by the vertical axis. Similarly, the latent level contains 16 codes and is represented as a 4×4 matrix along the same dimensions of power and involvement, as illustrated in Fig. 4.3. Based on the transcripts of the supervisory sessions, each utterance was coded independently at the manifest and at the latent level.

The congruence of communication at the manifest and latent levels is assessed by comparing the respective levels of power and involvement of a particular utterance; if the relative degree of power and involvement for a particular utterance are similar, then the two levels of communication for that utterance are said to be congruent. Congruence of the manifest and latent levels of communication can be illustrated by superimposing the matrix for the manifest level onto the matrix for the latent level, as shown in Fig. 4.4. In this way, each cell at the manifest level overlaps with four cells at the latent level. The codes for any particular utterance are said to be congruent when they overlap. For example, the manifest code support is congruent with the latent codes initiate, share, offer, and collaborate.

POWER	AGGRESS AS • Asserts self • Shows aggression • Justifies behavior • Disapproves	ADVISE AD • Gives solutions • Gives guidance • Gives explanation • Gives summary	SUPPORT SP • Shows understanding • Reassures • Shows trust, confidence • Amuses
	DISAGREE DS • Differs • Corrects • Criticizes • Contradicts	EXCHANGE EX • Gives information • Gives suggestions • Asks for information • Asks for suggestions	AGREE AG • Confirms • Reconciles • Conciliates • Willingly agrees
	AVOID AV • Hesitates • Withdraws • Non-committal • Shows uncertainty	REQUEST RQ • Asks for decision • Asks for approval • Asks for evaluation • Asks for direction	CONCEDE CD • Passively accepts • Passively supports • Complies • Acquiesces

INVOLVEMENT

FIG. 4.2.   The manifest level codes for the Penman classification scheme. From *Communication Processes and Relationships,* p. 64, by R. Penman, 1980, London: Academic Press. Copyright 1980 by Academic Press. Adapted by permission.

POWER	REJECT RJ • Shows hostility • Discredits other • Denigrates task/other	CONTROL CN • Manoeuvres to gain control • Forceful challenges • Takes over, directs	INITIATE IN • Influences other • Leads without control • Stands for self while inviting other	SHARE SH • Joins forces • Openly confronts • Affirms self and other
	COUNTER CT • Defies, refuses • Defends self • Stands for self at expense of other	RESIST RS • Counteracts • Is cynical, skeptical • Sets up obstacles	OFFER OF • Tentatively suggests • Informs other • Is task orientated	COLLABORATE CB • Reciprocates other • Consents to co-operate • Expands on other
	EVADE EV • Vague and wordy abstracting • Does not respond directly • Manoeuvres out of situation	ABSTAIN AB • Is indecisive • Uses delaying tactics • Is unwilling to commit self	SEEK SK • Seeks confirmation • Requests information • Allows other to start	OBLIGE OB • Willingly accepts • Concurs with other • Endorses other
	REMOVE RM • Refuses to participate • Ignores other totally • Disassociates self	RELINQUISH RL • Concedes defeat • Backs away • Abandons previous position	SUBMIT SB • Defers to other • Gives responsibility to other • Takes path of least resistance	CLING CL • Seeks control by other • Accepts any directive • Mutually excludes

INVOLVEMENT

FIG. 4.3.   The latent level codes for the Penman classification scheme. From *Communication Processes and Relationships,* p. 66, by R. Penman, 1980, London: Academic Press. Copyright 1980 by Academic Press. Adapted by permission.

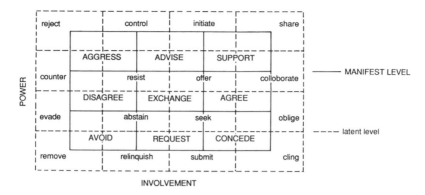

FIG. 4.4. The integration of the manifest and latent levels of the Penman scheme. From *Communication Processes and Relationships,* p. 67, by R. Penman, 1980, London: Academic Press. Copyright 1980 by Academic Press. Adapted by permission.

Various unidirectional patterns were selected by Holloway et al. (1989) because they were theoretically interesting, represented shifts in power and/or involvement, or because they occurred frequently or very infrequently. Holloway et al. represented those interactions that occurred more often than would be expected by chance graphically to portray the intricacies of supervisor and supervisee interactions. Figure 4.5 shows these representations for supervisors Rogers and Polster. Each arrow in Fig. 4.5 indicates a statistically significant and positive unidirectional z-score in the direction indicated. For instance, the arrow from AD for Rogers to CD for Hackney indicates that Hackney responded to Rogers's advise with a concede more often than would be expected by chance.

A cursory glance at the diagrams reveals that the interview between Polster and Hackney was much more reactive than that of the interview between Rogers and Hackney. That is, Polster and Hackney dramatically altered their rates of responding, given various antecedent behaviors, whereas for Rogers and Hackney, the rates of responding were not affected much by preceding behaviors. In the context of supervision, Holloway et al. observed the following with regard to Polster:

There was also a great diversity in the types of predictable interchanges in this interview and those interchanges presented a rather distinct picture of the Gestalt approach to supervision. All the significant patterns occurring more than expected by chance were interconnected at the manifest level and with the exception of one pattern . . . all were interconnected at the latent level. Within these complex routines there is some congruence between the manifest and latent levels; however, the patterns at the latent level of communication diverged from the manifest level at important junctures. . . . Polster exerted a powerful influence at the latent level not

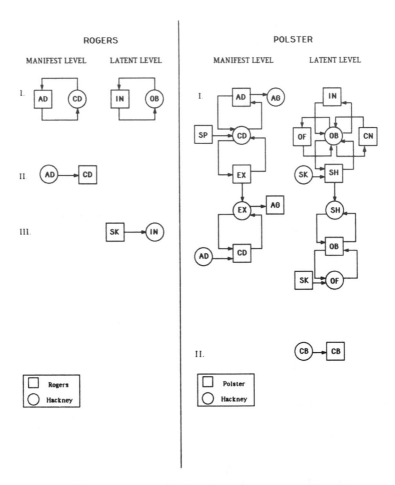

FIG. 4.5. Schematic for Rogers and Polster's supervision interviews with Hackney. From "The Relation of Power and Involvement to Theoretical Orientation in Supervision: An Analysis of Discourse," by E. L. Holloway, R. D. Freund, S. L. Gardner, M. L. Nelson, & B. R. Walker, 1989, *Journal of Counseling Psychology, 36,* pp. 97, 99. Copyright 1989 by the American Psychological Association. Adapted by permission.

only through his more obvious use of initiate and control messages (not evident in Hackney's discourse) but also in the manner in which Hackney must join with Polster (share message) to disengage from the minimal low-power response of oblige. . . . Overall, Polster and Hackney appeared to join each other in a very powerful way that was unique in comparison with the other interviews. If in fact Polster's goal in supervision was to engage the supervisee in a very powerful and intimate discussion, then the discourse analysis demonstrated his success. Polster and Hackney together created a very complex and interconnected system of discourse, in which there appeared a number of high-probability behaviors that might occur given a very simple message of encouragement. . . . The irony of the results in this study was the discovery that much of what occurs with regard to the use of power and involvement in the interaction is implicit, not explicit, in spite of the Gestalt tenet to make what is implicit explicit. (pp. 98–99)

In contrast, the Rogers's interview was described by Holloway et al. as follows:

It is also evident that in comparison with the other interviews, Hackney's work with Rogers resulted in the least number of predictable transitions. Rogers's primary strategy at the manifest level and latent level was a circuit in which Rogers offered to Hackney opinions and conceptualizations regarding the client to which Hackney responded with minimal encouragement. Perhaps, the most surprising finding in this interview is the rare expression of high positive involvement messages at the manifest or latent level (support or share, respectively) by Rogers or by Hackney and their exclusion from predictable routines of discourse. . . . Thus both the base-rate findings and sequential patterns described an interview that stayed in the world of ideas. (pp. 97–98)

The Use of Reinforcers in Psychotherapy

The intensive analysis of social interactions often involves examining more than one interaction. For instance, a social system could be observed over time, as is the case in the study reported in this section. Eleven sessions of a psychotherapy case were analyzed by Wampold and Kim (1989) to determine the probabilistic relationship among various client and counselor behaviors. Tests of unidirectionality, bidirectionality, and dominance were conducted. The use of transformed kappa is also illustrated.

In 1983, Hill, Carter, and O'Farrell studied mechanisms of psychotherapy by intensively analyzing a time-limited therapy with a female college student. The presenting problems were relationship difficulties, anxiety, and somatization. The orientation of the counselor focused on the relationship and experiencing within the session and the style of the counselor was described as interpretive and confrontive with a supportive atmosphere. Although the counseling resulted in therapeutic changes upon termination and at a 2-month follow-up, the client relapsed 7 months following termination. Hill et al. stated that brief therapy was not appropriate for this client because the client persisted in storytelling and avoided experiencing; according to Hill et al. "the client began treatment with a communication style which is not 'good' client behavior . . . [and] had very little awareness of her behavior or its impact on others, let alone an ability to understand why she behaved as she did" (p. 14). However, Hill et al. maintained that confrontation decreased client storytelling.

Hill et al. (1983) coded the stream of verbal behavior between counselor and client, using the Counselor and Client Verbal Response Category System (Hill et al., 1983). Each counselor behavior was classified as one and only one of 14 categories: minimal encourager, silence, approval-reassurance, information, direct guidance, closed question, open question, restatement, reflection, interpretation, confrontation, nonverbal referent, self-disclosure, and other. Similarly, each client behavior was classified as one and only one of 9 categories: simple responses, requests, description, experiencing, insight, discussion of plans, discussion of client–counselor relationship, silence, and other. Also, for each session, several outcome measures for each session were obtained. After each session, evaluations of the session by the counselor, client, and observers were obtained by completion of the short form of the Therapy Session Report (Elliott, 1980; Orlinsky & Howard, 1975) after the end of the session. The instrument was scaled such that larger scores indicated greater effectiveness. Satisfaction with counseling by counselor, client, and observers was measured, using a Likert-type scale where higher scores indicated greater satisfaction with the session.

Although Hill et al. (1983) used available methodology, Wampold and Kim (1989) analyzed further the data from this psychotherapy case, using the methods described in this chapter. Wampold and Kim's objective, in part, was to determine the antecedents and consequences of the code description, which involves the problematic behavior storytelling. The first of the 12 sessions was not analyzed because the recorder malfunctioned during the session and because the preponderance of client behaviors were coded as description.

To analyze the stimulus conditions for the description code, unidirectional tests as well as transformed kappas for transitions from several counselor codes to description were calculated across the 11 sessions. The top panel of Table 4.2 presents the transformed kappas for each session as well as the significance levels derived from the z-scores for unidirectional independence. Substantively, it is clear that the rate at which the client described increased significantly in response to counselor minimal encouragers (all kappas are positive and highly significant) and decreased in response to several other antecedent behaviors (e.g., silence, interpretation, and confrontation).

The second panel of Table 4.2 presents the transformed kappas for transitions from client description to several counselor codes. Substantively interesting here is that the frequency of counselor minimal encouragers increased in response to client description (all transformed kappas were positive and statistically significant).

From the two panels, it appears that there was a circuit involving minimal encouragers and description. Minimal encouragers increased the probability of description and description increased the probability of minimal encouragers. This bidirectional pattern can be tested directly. For instance, for Session 2, the z-score for this circuit was 13.03. This bidirectional pattern was prevalent across all 11 sessions. The substantive importance of bidirectional tests is established if one considers a social learning perspective where each response in an interaction is also a stimulus for the next behavior.

TABLE 4.2
Transformed Kappas for Various Patterns

					Session						
Pattern	2	3	4	5	6	7	8	9	10	11	12
				Counselor to Client							
ME to DE	.31**	.28**	.48**	.28**	.21**	.41**	.16**	.18**	.26**	.31**	.13**
IF to DE	-.67	-.90**	-.84**	-.80**	-.90**	-.80**	-.90**	-.67	.77**	-.84**	-.79**
RS to DE	-.78	-.81*	-1.00**	-.76**	-.09	-1.00**	-.71*	-.67**	.79**	-.60	-.75**
RF to DE	-.70	-.83*	-.65**	-.79**	-.67*	-.72*	-.77**	-.51	.77**	-.69*	-1.00**
IT to DE	-.77**	-.86**	-.93**	-.76**	-.73**	-.93**	-.95**	-.84**	.74**	-.92**	-.86**
CF to DE	-.84**	-.81*	-.76**	-.60**	-1.00**	-.67*	-.87**	-.83**	-.23	-.34	-.70**
				Client to Counselor							
DE to ME	.45**	.37**	.49**	.34**	.40**	.44**	.26**	.24**	.35**	.44**	.20**
DE to IF	-.18	-.80**	-.69**	-.41**	-.80**	-.72**	-.90**	-.67	-.66**	-.62**	-.57**
DE to RS	-.78	-.81*	-.43	-.63**	-.89**	-.62**	-.12	-.12	-.14	-1.00**	-.50**
DE to RF	-.70	-.66	-.39	-.58**	-.89**	-.58*	-1.00**	-.50	-.43	-.85**	-.86**
DE to IT	-.54**	-.91**	-.43**	-.69**	-.95**	-.80**	-.95**	-.92**	-.91**	-.70**	-.93**
DE to CF	-.54	-.61	-.76**	-.19**	-.73	-.67*	-.73*	-.66**	-.04	-.34	-1.00**

Note. CF = Counselor Confrontation, DE = Client Description, IF = Counselor Information, IT = Counselor Interpretation, ME = Counselor Minimal Encourager, RF = Counselor Reflection, RS = Counselor Restatement. From "Sequential Analysis Applied to Counseling Process and Outcome: A Case Study Revisited" by B. E. Wampold and K. H. Kim (1989). *Journal of Counseling Psychology, 36*, p. 360. Copyright (1989) by the American Psychological Association. Adapted by Permission.

*$p < .05$.
**$p < .01$.

Other aspects of sequential analysis methods can be demonstrated by exploring further the connection between minimal encouragers and description. Recall that, according to Hill et al., client description was a troublesome behavior in that it interfered with the psychotherapeutic process and that this behavior was attributed to person variables (viz., the communication style of the client). However, Wampold and Kim (1989) demonstrated that the counselor reinforced the client's description. According to behavioral principles, a reinforcer is a "consequential stimulus occurring contingent on a behavior that increases or maintains the strength . . . of the behavior . . . and is defined solely by the fact that it increases or maintains the behavior on which it is contingent" (Sulzer–Azaroff & Mayer, 1986, p. 400). Minimal encouragers were a consequential stimulus contingent on description because minimal encouragers occurred after description more often than would be expected by chance. That minimal encouragers increased or maintained the description was shown in three ways. First, description occurred after minimal encouragers more often than would be expected by chance. Second, when the rate at which description was reinforced was high, the frequency of the description was high. This finding was established by correlating across the 11 sessions transformed kappa for the pattern of minimal encourager to description with the base rate of minimal encourager; the correlation was equal to .49. Finally, in data that did not appear in Wampold and Kim, it was found that in the final third of each session, the degree to which the counselor reinforced client description decreased vis-à-vis the first two-thirds of the session (i.e., transformed kappa for this pattern was always less in the final third than in the first two-thirds of the session) and concomitantly, the base rate of description also decreased from the first two-thirds to the last third of the session.

The substantive use of tests of dominance can also be illustrated by this psychotherapy case. In the bidirectional pattern involving minimal encourager and description, it is not clear who, the counselor or the client, was driving this circuit. Indeed, a case could have been made that the client was reinforcing the counselor's use of minimal encouragers with description. To determine the relative strength of the directionality in this interaction, dominance tests were used. For example, in Session 2 recall that the transformed kappa from minimal encourager to description was .31 and the transformed kappa for description to minimal encourager was .45. Thus, it appears that the client was dominant because the counselor's use of minimal encourager was more predictable from the client's use of description than was the client's use of description from the counselor's use of minimal encouragers. Indeed, the test for dominance was statistically significant ($z = 2.44$), a pattern that was evident across the 11 sessions. This is substantively interesting because successful psychotherapy is typically characterized by patterns in which the counselor is dominant (Tracey, 1985).

A final illustration with this psychotherapy case involves demonstrating how sequential indexes can be linked with outcome measures. Because description was a troublesome client behavior that interfered with more psychotherapeutically strategic behaviors, such as experiencing, Wampold and Kim (1989) correlated the transformed kappa for patterns involving description and experiencing with the reinforcer minimal encourager as well as the base rates of description and experiencing with the outcome measures for each sessions. These correlations are found in Table 4.3. Wampold and Kim interpreted these correlations in the following way:

> That the correlations between the base rate of description and the client's satisfaction with and evaluation of the session were positive and the correlations between the base rate of experiencing and the client's satisfaction with and evaluation of the session were negative is understandable. Description typically is comfortable, non-threatening, and innocuous, whereas experiencing can be intimidating, threatening, and risky. The positive correlations between the degree to which experiencing is followed by a minimal encourager and the client's satisfaction with and evaluation of the session might indicate that even though experiencing is threatening, support for this important client activity is very much valued by the client (and by the counselor and observers). The interpretation of the negative correlations between

TABLE 4.3
Correlations of Outcome Variables and Process Variables Related to Client Description, Client
Description, and Counselor Minimal Encouragers

	Process Variables			
Outcome Variables	Base Rate of DE	Base Rate of EX	Transformed Kappa for DE to ME	Transformed Kappa for EX to ME
Client satisfaction	.27	-.40	-.41	.42
Client evaluation	.18	-.41	-.31	.74
Counselor satisfaction	-.68	.48	-.28	.21
Counselor evaluation	-.23	.06	-.48	.43
Observer satisfaction	-.49	.37	-.23	.23
Observer evaluation	-.37	.17	-.26	.40

Note. DE = Client Description, ME = Counselor Minimal Encourager. From "Sequential Analysis Applied to Counseling Process and Outcome: Ease Study Revisited" by B. E. Wampold and L. H. Kim (1989). *Journal of Counseling Psychology, 36*, p. 361. Copyright (1989) by the American Psychological Association. Reprinted by permission.

the degree to which the counselor follows a description with a minimal encourager and the clients' satisfaction with and evaluation of the sessions is more complex. Why is it that the client values description but does not value the reinforcement of description? A child may enjoy engaging in an inappropriate behavior, but reinforcement of this behavior by the parent indicates to the child that the parent is not concerned about the best interests of the child. In the context of this case, the client may have felt comfortable telling stories but interpreted the counselor's reinforcement of this behavior as an unwillingness by the counselor to engage in more efficacious interactions. (p. 362)

The Use of Control and Support by Mothers and Their Children

Although the psychotherapy case discussed earlier illustrated the linkage of microanalytical variables (viz., transformed kappas) with outcome variables, the analysis was limited to a case study. Pett, Vaughan–Cole, Wampold, Egger, and East (1987) examined 56 divorced mothers and their families to describe the relation between interactions of the mother and a target child with person and demographic variables. Pett et al. recorded the interactions between the mother and the child during dinner preparation and consumption and coded these interactions using an empirically derived system (Pett et al., 1988) that is sensitive to Patterson's (1976) notion of control and support.

Four interactive patterns were of interest: reciprocity of control, reciprocity of support, control dominance, and control/support dominance. Reciprocity of control and support refer to the bidirectional dependence of control and support, respectively. Reciprocity is said to be present if the bidirectional test for the behavior is statistically significant in the positive direction. Control dominance refers to an asymmetry in predictability with regard to controlling behaviors. If the mother's controlling behavior is more predictable from the child's controlling behavior than conversely, the child is said to be dominant. With regard to control/support dominance, the child is said to be dominant if he or she were more successful than the mother in using controlling behaviors to obtain supportive responses.

Several demographic and person variables were obtained for each family, including months since separation, family social status, level of mother psychosocial functioning, level of target child psychosocial functioning, sex of the target child, age of the target child, and number of children in the household.

Of interest in Pett et al.'s (1987) analysis was the relation between the interactive patterns (viz., reciprocity of control, reciprocity of support, control dominance, and control/support dominance) and the demographic and person variables. The simplest exploration of this relationship is to correlate the kappas for each pattern with the other variables. These correlations are presented in Table 4.4.

Care must be taken in the interpretation of these correlations. First, examine the negative correlation between age of the child and reciprocity of control. This correlation indicates that younger target children are involved to a greater degree in reciprocal patterns of control. Because boys were coded as zero and girls as one, the negative correlation between sex of the child and control dominance indicates that boys relative to girls are more dominant with regard to control. The negative correlations between psychosocial functioning and control/support

TABLE 4.4
Correlations of Interactional Patterns with Demographic and Person Variables

Demographic and Person Variables	Kappa[a] for Patterns			
	Reciprocity of Control	Reciprocity of Support	Control Dominance	Control/Support Dominance
Months since separation	.00	-.28*	.03	.12
Family social status[b]	.08	.30*	.07	.06
Level of mother functioning[c]	.01	-.09	-.01	-.26*
Level of child functioning[c]	.04	-.03	.04	-.36**
Sex of child[d]	-.23	.10	-.35**	-.20
Age of child	-.27*	-.07	.00	-.16
Number of children	.05	-.32*	.06	.12

[a]Kappa is formed such that positive scores indicate that the child is dominant and negative scores indicate that the mother is dominant.

[b]Higher scores indicate higher level of social status.

[c]Higher scores indicate higher levels of psychosocial functioning.

[d]Sex was dummy-coded, 0 = males, 1 = females.

*p < .05.
**p < .01.

dominance indicates that healthier mothers and children are involved in patterns in which the child displays a lesser degree of dominance with regard to using controlling behaviors to obtain supportive behaviors. On the other hand, for families with more dysfunctional mothers and children, children relative to their mothers, tend to be successful in using control to obtain support.

Although perusing a series of correlations is not the most sophisticated manner to understand relations, the Pett et al. (1987) study was a precursor to a more comprehensive study in which samples of families headed by divorced mothers and intact families are being obtained. Interactions are being recorded around dinnertime and in a structured play situation. This design will permit comparison of the interactive patterns involving married and divorced mothers to ascertain how divorce impacts child-rearing practices. In the comprehensive study, transformed kappas between the two samples will be compared to identify differences. A similar strategy was used to show differences in interactive patterns between distressed and nondistressed marital dyads, although that study was conducted prior to the development of kappa (Margolin & Wampold, 1981).

An Intervention That Altered Interactive Patterns

An interesting and potentially strategic use of sequential analysis involves examining interactive patterns before and after an intervention has been administered. A case-study by the family therapist Gerald Weeks afforded that possibility. Holloway, Wampold, and Nelson (1989) obtained the transcript of a psychotherapy session involving Weeks and a couple. In this session, Weeks delivered a discrete intervention, which made it possible to compare the interactive patterns before, during, and after the intervention.

The session analyzed was the 18th interview with a couple who had a long-standing monogamous relationship but who were unable to agree whether or not to marry. Moreover, the woman had persistent insomnia. Earlier, Weeks had unsuccessfully used symptom prescription (Weeks & L'Abate, 1982) with the woman to attempt to resolve the insomnia. In the session analyzed, based on comments made by the couple, Weeks realized that the symptom prescription had not been successful because the insomnia served the couple's system in that it made it possible to avoid issues related to sexuality and marriage. That is, the insomnia maintained the status quo of the relationship. Hence, at this point in the session, Weeks intervened with both the man and the woman. He reframed the symptom prescription to involve both members of the couple and engaged the man actively in the intervention.

Symptom prescription has been criticized because it removes a symptom but does not change the context and because it is a manipulative technique (Asher & Turner, 1980; Cottone, 1981; Rohrbaugh, Tennen, Press, & White, 1981). However, systems theorists claim that paradoxical interventions, of which symptom prescription is one, force the family systems to change and therefore the results of such procedures are not superficial (Frankl, 1985; Haley, 1976; Watzlawick, Beavin, & Jackson, 1967; Weeks & L'Abate, 1982). If the family systems theorists are correct, then an intervention, such as the one used by Weeks, should change the dynamics among members of a system. If this theory is so, then changes in the interactive patterns of the couple should be noticeable after the intervention. The purpose of Holloway, Wampold, and Nelson's (1989) study was to examine the interactive patterns of the couple before, during, and after Weeks's intervention.

The session analyzed was coded with the Penman (1980) system utilized in a study described earlier (see Figs. 4.2–4.4). Weeks identified the beginning and the end of the intervention and the interview was divided in three segments accordingly. A sequential analysis of the three segments was conducted to determine whether interactive patterns were different in the three segments.

As expected by the family theorists, there were a number of patterns that changed from preintervention to postintervention. With regard to the manifest level, Holloway, Wampold, and Nelson (1989) made the following conclusions:

> An examination of the significant patterns from male to female revealed that the incidence of negative involvement patterns reduced after the intervention whereas more neutral informational exchanges increased significantly during and after the intervention. Further it appeared that the female significantly reduced her behavior of conceding to the male's advice after the intervention.

Substantively interesting changes were also noted for the latent level:

> The male's response to the female appeared more symmetrical and engaging after the intervention and at the same time the male's rejection of the female's positive involvement responses decreased. However, the female's responses to the male did not reflect this same quality of positive reciprocity. She decreased exchanging of information responses whereas the complementary behavior of responding with a low power questioning response to his controlling behavior increased after the intervention.

ISSUES AND LIMITATIONS

The methods discussed here have shown promise for understanding the nature of social interactions. Specific hypotheses about social interactions can be tested against the null hypothesis of randomness in the sequence of behaviors. The methods can be used to study intensively one or a few interactions (e.g., Holloway, Freund, Gardner, Nelson, & Walker, 1989), one system over time (e.g., Wampold & Kim, 1989), relate interactive patterns to global measures (e.g., Pett et al., 1987; Wampold & Kim, 1989), compare different populations (Margolin & Wampold, 1981), and to identify changes in patterns due to interventions

(Holloway, Wampold, & Nelson, 1989). Studies are under way to examine whether teachers respond differently to accepted and rejected children, to determine the effect of the gender of supervisors and trainees on interactive patterns in clinical supervision, to discern patterns that characterize psychotherapy conducted where the working alliance between the counselor and the client is high and where it is low, and to identify the antecedents and consequences of withdrawal in marital interaction. Notwithstanding the modest success of several studies using the methods described in this chapter, there are a number of issues and limitations to these methods.

Reliability

Although the focus of this chapter has been on the analysis of sequential data and not on the collection and coding of the data, reliability in the context of sequential analysis raises some unique issues. Typically for behavioral data, interobserver agreement is used to indicate reliability in a generic sense. Interobserver agreement is based on the agreement of two or more observers about the frequencies or durations of behavior. However, Johnston and Bolstad (1973) argued that the analysis of social interactions involves the sequential nature of the system and interobserver agreement should focus on the position in the sequence. That is, an agreement is scored if the same behavior is observed at the same point (or within a small window) in the sequence. This stringent criterion became known as point-by-point reliability.

A number of problems with point-by-point reliability have been noted (Gottman, 1980; Wampold & Holloway, 1983), the most important of which is that it is too stringent:

> Since the goal of sequential analysis is the detection of sequential connections, the criterion for assessing reliability between observers should not be based on point-for-point (within time-window) agreement between observers, but rather, on the extent to which two independent observers produce data that yields similar sequential structure. (Gottman, 1980, p. 362)

Similarly, Hartmann (1977) noted that "as a general principle, reliability assessments should be conducted on the unit of behaviors subject to visual or statistical analysis" (p. 104).

Following the lead of Gottman (1980) and Hartmann (1977), Wampold and Holloway (1983) suggested that reliability be based on the degree to which two observers agree about the number of transitions from one behavior to another. This strategy seemed logical because statistical analyses are based on the frequencies of transitions. However, this approach is flawed for two reasons. First, the statistical analyses actually are based on the degree to which the observed number of transitions depart from the expected number of transitions rather than

TABLE 4.5
Interobserver Agreement Based on transformed Kappas

	Transformed Kappa			
Interaction	Positive Reciprocity		Dominance for Positive Behaviors	
	Observer 1	Observer 2	Observer 1	Observer 2
1	.32	.25	-.15	-.10
2	.06	.18	.13	-.02
3	.79	.52	-.47	-.33
4	.09	.03	.22	.12
5	.51	.83	-.07	.09
6	-.11	.15	.33	.58
7	.27	.12	.28	.12
8	.26	.38	-.14	-.05
9	.44	.21	-.56	-.46
10	.14	.21	-.12	.03
	$r = .67$		$r = .88$	

solely on the number of transitions. Second, and more fundamentally, reliability should be tied to the construct being measured, rather than on some intermediate statistic.

An alternative approach that is linked more closely to psychological constructs is suggested here. The goal of an analysis of social interactions is to assess the degree to which the interacting system relies on various patterns of interaction. These patterns should be reflective of some construct related to the particular context of the social interaction (for instance, dominance). The question then becomes "How well has this construct been measured?" If two observers are reliably coding an interaction with regard to the components of dominance, then the resulting transformed kappas for these two observers should be similar. Across a number of interactions, the transformed kappas should be similar, resulting in a sizable positive correlation, as suggested in the hypothetical data in Table 4.5. For these data, the observers exhibited a moderate level of agreement for positive reciprocity and a high level of agreement for dominance related to positive behaviors. More sophisticatedly, the transformed kappas for each observer could be a facet in a generalizability study (Cronbach, Gleser, Nanda, & Rajaratnam, 1972) or could represent an observed variable in a covariance structures analysis (Jöreskog & Sörbom, 1988).

The suggested method has the desirable property that it is tied to a particular construct such as dominance. As such, a different index of reliability would be obtained for each construct measured (e.g., control dominance, positive bidirectional reciprocity).

One disadvantage of the suggested reliability method is that it can only be calculated after the data are analyzed, which precludes using it in training. A useful training procedure is to form a confusion matrix using the point-by-point method (Bakeman & Gottman, 1986). From this confusion matrix, the most frequently miscoded behaviors are easily identified. Furthermore, requiring coders to meet a criterion based on percentage agreements corrected for chance (viz., the kappa of Cohen, 1960; Hartmann, 1977) on this stringent type of reliability assures, to an extent, the reliability of the constructs to be measured in the study.

Causality

In the methods described in this chapter, the primary question has been whether or not a behavior, say behavior j, follows another behavior, say behavior i, more or less often than would be expected by chance. If the frequency of j is sufficiently different from that expected by chance, then there is unidirectional dependence from i to j. Whether or not i *causes* j is an appropriate epistemological question.

Criteria for determining causation have interested philosphers, social scientists, and statisticians since at least the 1700s, and no definition has been (or likely ever will be) universally accepted. Nevertheless, at least one model of causation fits the model of social interactions discussed in this chapter. Suppes (1970) modified Hume's criterion of constant conjunction to include probabilistic relations between events:

> Roughly speaking, the modification of Hume's analysis I propose is to say that one event is the cause of another if the appearance of the first event is followed with a high probability by the appearance of the second, and there is no third event that we can use to factor out the probability relationship between the first and the second events. (p. 10)

According to Suppes's model, if there is unidirectional independence from i to j, then i is the cause of j provided that other causes of j are ruled out. The other causes should be on the same level of reduction (Cook & Campbell, 1979), which would tend to rule out factors such as intervening cognitions between the emission of i and the emission of j. Accordingly, potential causes of j other than would be other behaviors in the sequence or other aspects of the sequence. Two other potential causes involve autodependence and behaviors that do not immediately precede j, two issues that we will discuss.

It should be noted that Suppes's model deviates from those models of causation that require manipulation of an independent variable (see Holland, 1986, for a statistical analysis of these issues). In the context of social interactions, manipulation of behaviors is difficult but not impossible. Recall that the conjecture was made that minimal encouragers were reinforcing description in the Hill et al.

(1983) case analyzed by Wampold and Kim (1989). It would be possible to manipulate the probability with which a therapist used minimal encouragers in response to description and note the concomitant change in description.

Lags Other Than 1

To this point, only the immediate succession of a behavior by another behavior has been considered. That is, the analysis has focused on adjacent behaviors in the sequence. It is conceivable, even reasonable, that a behavior may be affected as well by behaviors that occurred earlier in the sequence. For instance, a husband might end a talking turn with a neutral behavior, which then is followed by the wife's emission of a negative behavior. However, the wife's negative behavior might have been motivated not by the immediately preceding neutral behavior but by the husband's negative behavior that occurred before he emitted the neutral behavior:

$$\ldots \text{H}(-) \ \text{H}(0) \ \text{W}(-) \ldots$$

Dependencies on the immediately preceding behavior are said to occur at lag 1, dependencies on a previous behavior two positions removed in the sequence are said to occur at lag 2, dependencies on a previous behavior three positions removed are said to occur at lag 3, and so on.

Statistical tests of lags other than 1 are conducted in a similar manner to those described in this chapter, with the exception that transitions are calculated at the lag of interest.[7] For example, if one were considering lag 2, then the entries in the transition frequency matrix would be the number of transitions from the antecedent behavior to behaviors that occurred two positions removed in the sequence.

Analyses of transitions at lags other than 1 may not be as substantively interesting as they first might appear. To detect an interactive pattern at lag 2, the pattern must occur consistently at lag 2. For example, if the wife's response to the husband is delayed (i.e., does not occur at lag 1), but occurs at indefinite lags (i.e., sometimes at lag 2, sometimes at lag 3, etc.), then it will not be detected with a lag 2 analysis. For that reason, those studies that have examined several lags typically have found that the patterns are strongest at lag 1, followed by lag 2, and so forth (e.g., Margolin & Wampold, 1981).

Autodependence in Sequential Data

The analyses illustrated in this chapter have focused on transitions from one member of the system to another (e.g., from husband to wife). However, a person's behavior may also be related to their own behavior. For example, a

---

[7]Actually, the formulas for lags greater than 1 are slightly different from those presented here because there are $N - L$ transitions, where L is the lag, rather than $N - 1$ transitions.

baby's crying may increase the probability that the next baby response will also be crying (i.e., self-stimulating behavior). In the context of sequential analysis, the dependencies between one's own behaviors has been called autocorrelation or serial dependence (Faraone & Dorfman, 1987; Gardner & Hartmann, 1984; Gardner, Hartmann, & Mitchell, 1982), although the term autodependency is more compatible with the method of analyzing sequential categorical data. In the model presented in this chapter, autodependence presents no particular problems. At lag 1, autodependence is just one nonrandom pattern in the data that could be tested along with dependencies among behaviors of different members of the system.

It is possible, however, that one's behavior could be due to his or her own behavior at lag 2 and not to the other's behavior behavior at lag 1; for example,

$$\ldots \; H(+) \; W(0) \; H(+) \; W(-) \; H(+) \; W(0) \; (H(+) \ldots$$

Such a conceptualization requires that the sequence alternate between the two members of the system. However, constraining the sequence to alternate between members of the system violates the assumptions of the methods discussed in this chapter (alternating sequences will be mentioned later). Autodependence becomes a difficult problem when the sequential data are not restricted to a single sequence, as will be seen in the following section.

Simultaneous Sequences

One of the requirements to this point has been that the social interaction yields a single sequence of behaviors. This is a reasonable format for many types of behaviors, especially verbal behavior where there are few overlaps. However, the single sequence of behaviors assumes that while one member of the system is exhibiting behavior, other members are not exhibiting behavior. Clearly, this limits the richness of the interaction that might be captured with a coding system. For instance, while the husband is emitting a negative verbal behavior, the wife may be attending, not tracking, withdrawing, and so forth. If it is desirable to code all members of the system simultaneously, then multiple sequences result. An example of a double sequence for the marital example follows:

Position	1	2	3	4	5	6	7	8	9
Husband	+	o	+	+	+	−	−	−	+
Wife	+	+	+	+	+	+	−	−	−

An intuitively appealing way to handle this double sequence with the methods presented in this chapter is to consider it a single sequence of dyadic behavioral units (DBU; Weiss & Summers, 1983), yielding (with the husband's behavior as first in the DBU):

Position	1	2	3	4	5	6	7	8	9
DBU	(+, +)	(o, +)	(+, +)	(+, +)	(+, +)	(−, +)	(−, −)	(−, −)	(+, −)

Because there were three behaviors in the original system (viz., +, 0, −), then there are nine dyadic behavioral units.

One of the complications of multiple sequences of behaviors is autodependence. In the given sequence it is not clear at position 4 whether the wife is reciprocating the husband's positive behavior (at position 3) or is continuing her positive behavior (at position 3 and before). In double behavioral sequences, it is necessary to sort out the cross-dependencies from the autodependencies. This is complicated by the fact that some transitions contain both auto- and cross-dependencies. Faraone and Dorfman (1987) have presented some methods for examining auto- and cross-dependencies.

Alternating Sequences

One of the requirements of the sequences discussed in this chapter was that any behavior could follow itself. An interesting format that violates this requirement are sequences in which members alternate positions in the sequence. For example, in the context of marital interactions, a husband behavior would be followed by a wife behavior, which in turn would be followed by a husband behavior. Data of this type would result, for instance, from coding speaker turns rather than behaviors within turns.

Alternating sequences of this type alter the randomization procedure on which the statistics discussed in this chapter are based. Partitioning the behaviors based on the member of the interacting system and permuting within the partitions is a possible solution to this problem (see Hubert, 1987, chap. 6), although the autodependency at lag 2 would need to be considered.

Assumptions

The methods discussed in this chapter assume that the probability of the emission of a behavior is independent of the position of the sequence and under the null hypothesis of randomness independent of the other behaviors in the sequence. The assumption that the probability of emission is independent of the position in the sequence is customarily referred to as stationarity. In effect, stationarity means that the patterns of interaction do not change over the course of the interaction. Clearly, this may be an unreasonable assumption for some interactions. For example, if the Weeks's interview discussed earlier (Holloway, Wampold, & Nelson, 1989) had been analyzed without segmentation, the results would have been misleading because it was clear that the interactional patterns changed after Weeks's intervention. In many interactions, there are social and cultural patterns that characterize greetings and terminations. In cases where stationarity is not present, it is necessary to analyze segments of the sequence; for example, if the greetings and terminations were not of substantive interest, the sequence should be truncated. However, typically the status of the stationarity assumption is unknown. Furthermore, segmenting the sequence reduces the length of the sequence analyzed, which reduces the precision of the statistical tests.

That behaviors are independent of other behaviors in the sequence under the null hypothesis dictates that behaviors must not be constrained structurally in any way. The alternating sequence discussed earlier is an example of a constrained sequence. Another example of a structurally constrained sequence is a sequence where a behavior is not allowed to follow itself. This type of sequence is formed, for example, from coding systems that record behavior only when a change of behavior occurs. In such a system, a baby's cry is recorded once for the duration of the cry and the subsequent behavior is recorded when there is a change in behavior (e.g., thumb sucking); thus baby's crying is not allowed to follow baby's crying. Misleading conclusions will results from ignoring structural constrains (see Wampold, 1986).

Distribution of Statistics

The statistical tests involving z-scores have been conducted by comparing the z-scores to the standard normal distribution. However, convergence to a normal distribution has not been proved, although there is strong evidence to suggest that convergence is not a problem. For the unidirectional case, the skewness parameter was calculated from the formula given by Mielke (1979) and was shown that it approaches zero as n increases (Wampold & Margolin, 1982). However, more valid critical values could be established for the z-scores by using a Pearson Type III distribution, as suggested by Mielke, Berry, and Brier (1981) and Hubert (1987). Tables exist for establishing critical values for z-scores for given levels of skewness (Harter, 1969; Hubert, 1987; Salvosa, 1930), where the skewness parameters could be calculated with Mielke's (1979) formula.

As mentioned previously, the distributions of kappa and transformed kappa are not well understood. As an index of effect size, this poses little problem. However, when used as observations to be subjected to statistical tests, the distributions of kappa and transformed kappa are important. In one sense, the distributions of these indexes are dependent on the particular interactions. Nevertheless, further investigations are needed to understand how these indexes perform in various situations.

Limitations, Extensions, and Other Issues

Throughout this chapter, the case has been made for the merit of the procedures presented. Nevertheless, there exist a number of limitations that need to be considered before the methods are undertaken. First, although not related to the statistical analyses, procuring sequential data consumes time and resources. The social interaction typically is taped and then coded. Each hour of tape takes many times as many hours of coding; informally researchers report ranges from 5 to 50 hours of coding time per hour of tape, depending on the coding system. These estimates do not include training of coders and time spent monitoring observer agreement. Once a reliable sequence of behaviors is obtained, statistical analysis with computer assistance is relatively straightforward. The Sequential Analysis Program (SAP; Wampold, Roll, & East, 1989) has been developed to analyze sequential data. The input to this program is the sequence of behaviors; SAP generates transition frequency matrices and the values of z and kappa (transformed and untransformed) related to unidirectional independence, bidirectional dependence, and dominance.

A second limitation of sequential analysis is that it is aimed at repetitive patterns that occur at close proximities (Wampold, 1986). Important events that occur infrequently or irregularly will not be detected with a sequential analysis. For example, Hill et al. (1983) claimed that the counselor used confrontation in response to description, a pattern that was not revealed by the sequential analysis of these data (Wampold & Kim, 1989). However, the counselor may have used a few strategic and powerful confrontations.

Another potential limitation centers around the validity of the methods. A very rich and complex social interaction is reduced to a sequence of behaviors. To what extent are the sequence and the results from the sequential analysis reflective of the true phenomenon? This probably is an unanswerable epistemological question. Nevertheless, the important substantive results that have been obtained from using these methods attest, in part, to their validity, although it is clear that these methods are sensitive to the regular patterns of proximal behaviors. To a certain degree, all research methods reduce reality (Cook & Campbell, 1979; although some behaviorists might raise some philosophical questions about this). Whether these methods are sensitive to aspects of the interaction that answer given research questions is a determination that will need to be made by individual researchers.

Although the focus of this chapter has been on social interactions, the methods presented are applicable to any sequential data that meet the assumptions discussed in this chapter. For example, one might want to analyze the solitary play of an infant to determine the behavioral antecedents of crying. Or, there might be an interest in recording and analyzing the behavior of a target child and natural reinforcers in the environment. Furthermore, the analyses are not restricted to dyadic interactions and extensions to larger systems are not problematical.

REFERENCES

Abadie, P. D. (1985). *A study of interpersonal communication processes in the supervision of counseling.* Unpublished doctoral dissertation, Kansas State University, Manhattan.

Allison, P. D., & Liker, J. K. (1982). Analyzing sequential categorical data on dyadic interaction: A comment on Gottman. *Psychological Bulletin, 91,* 393–403.

Asher, L. M., & Turner, R. M. (1979). Paradoxical intention and insomnia: An experimental investigation. *Behavioral Research and Therapy, 17,* 408–411.

Bakeman, R., & Gottman, J. M. (1986). *Observing interaction: An introduction to sequential analysis.* Cambridge, England: Cambridge University Press.

Budescu, D. V. (1984). Tests of lagged dominance in sequential dyadic interaction. *Psychological Bulletin, 96,* 402–414.

Cohen, J. (1960). A coefficient of agreement for nominal scales. *Educational and Psychological Measurement, 20,* 37–46.

Cook, T. D., & Campbell, D. T. (1979). *Quasi-experimentation: Design and analysis issues for field settings.* Chicago: Rand McNally.

Cottone, R. R. (1981). Ethical issues related to use of paradoxical techniques in work adjustment. *Vocational and Work Adjustment Bulletin, 14,* 167–170.

Cronbach, L. J., Gleser, G. C., Nanda, N., & Rajaratnam, N. (1972). *The dependability of behavioral measurements: Theory of generalizability for scores and profiles.* New York: Wiley.

Ekman, P. W., & Friesen, W. (1978). *Manual for the facial action coding system.* Palo Alto, CA: Consulting Psychologist Press.

Elliott, R. (1980). *Therapy session report: Short-forms for client and therapist.* Unpublished manuscript, University of Toledo, Ohio.

Faraone, S. V., & Dorfman, D. D. (1987). Lag sequential analysis: Robust statistical methods. *Psychological Bulletin, 101,* 312–323.

Feick, L. F., & Novak, J. A. (1985). Analyzing sequential categorical data on dyadic interaction: Log–linear models exploring order in variables. *Psychological Bulletin, 98,* 600–611.

Frankl, V. E. (1985). Paradoxical intention. In G. Weeks (Ed.), *Promoting change through paradoxical therapy,* Homewood, IL: Dow–Jones Irwin, pp. 99–110.

Friedlander, M. L., & Ward, G. W. (1984). Development and validation of the Supervisory Styles Inventory. *Journal of Counseling Psychology, 31,* 541–557.

Gardner, W., & Hartmann, D. P. (1984). On Markov dependence in the analysis of social interaction. *Behavioral Assessment, 6,* 229–236.

Gardner, W., Hartmann, D. P., & Mitchell, C. (1982). The effects of serial dependence on the use of χ^2 for analyzing sequential data in dyadic interactions. *Behavioral Assessment, 4,* 75–82.

Goodyear, R. K., Abadie, P. D., & Efros, F. (1984). Supervisory theory into practice: Differential perception of supervision by Ekstein, Ellis, Polster, and Rogers. *Journal of Counseling Psychology, 31,* 228–237.

Gottman, J. M. (1979). *Marital interaction: Experimental investigations,* New York: Academic Press.

Gottman, J. M. (1980). Analyzing for sequential connection and assessing interobserver reliability for the sequential analysis of observational data. *Behavioral Assessment, 2,* 361–368.

Gottman, J. M., & Ringland, J. T. (1981). The analysis of dominance and bidirectionality in social development. *Child Development, 52,* 393–412.

Haley, J. (1976). *Problem-solving therapy.* San Francisco: Jossey–Bass.

Harter, H. L. (1969). A new table of percentage points of the Pearson type III distribution. *Technometrics, 11,* 177–187.

Hartmann, D. P. (1977). Considerations in the choice of interobserver reliability estimates. *Journal of applied Behavior Analysis, 10,* 103–116.

Hill, C. E., Carter, J. A., & O'Farrell, M. K. (1983). A case study of the process and outcome of time-limited counseling. *Journal of Counseling Psychology, 30,* 3–18.

Holland, P. W. (1986). Statistics and causal inference. *Journal of the American Statistical Association, 81,* 945–960.

Holloway, E. L., Freund, R. D., Gardner, S. L., Nelson, M. L., & Walker, B. R. (1989). The relation of power and involvement to theoretical orientation in supervision: An analysis of discourse. *Journal of Counseling Psychology, 36,* 88–102.

Holloway, E. L., Wampold, B. E., & Nelson, M. L. (1989). *Gerald Weeks' use of a paradoxical intervention with a couple: A case of dynamic change.* Manuscript submitted for publication.

Hubert, L. J. (1977). Kappa revisited. *Psychological Bulletin, 84,* 289–297.

Hubert, L. J. (1987). *Assignment methods in combinatorial data analysis.* New York: Marcel Dekker.

Hubert, L. J., & Baker, F. B. (1977). The comparison and fitting of given classification schemes. *Journal of Mathematical Psychology, 16,* 233–253.

Hubert, L. J., & Levin, J. R. (1976). Evaluating object set partitions: Free-sort analysis and some generalizations. *Journal of Verbal Learning and Verbal Behavior, 15,* 459–470.

Hubert, L. J., & Schultz, J. V. (1976). Quadratic assignment as a general data analysis strategy. *British Journal of Mathematical and Statistical Psychology, 29,* 190–241.

Iacobucci, D., & Wasserman, S. (1988). A general framework for the statistical analysis of sequential dyadic interaction data. *Psychological Bulletin, 103,* 379–390.

Johnston, S. M., & Bolstad, O. D. (1973). Methodological issues in naturalistic observation: Some problems and solutions to field research. In L. A. Hamerlynck, L. C. Handy, & E. J. Mash (Eds.), *Behavior change: Methodology, concepts, and practice* (pp. 7–67). Champaign, IL: Research Press.

Jöreskog, K. G., & Sörbom, D. (1988). *LISREL VII: A guide to the program and applications.* Chicago: SPSS.

Margolin, G., & Wampold, B. E. (1981). Sequential analysis of conflict and accord in distressed and nondistressed marital partners. *Journal of Consulting and Clinical Psychology, 49,* 554–567.

Mielke, P. W. (1979). On asymptotic non-normality of null distributions of MRPP statistics. *Communication in Statistics—Theory and Methods, A8,* 1541–1550.

Mielke, P. W., Berry, K. J., & Brier, G. W. (1981). Application of multi-response permutation procedures for examining seasonal changes in monthly mean sea-level pressure patterns. *Monthly Weather Review, 109,* 120–126.

Orlinsky, D. E., & Howard, K. I. (1975). *Varieties of psychotherapeutic experience.* New York: Teachers College Press.

Patterson, G. R. (1976). The aggressive child: A victim and architect of a coercive system. In E. J. Mash, L. A. Hamerlynck, & L. C. Handy (Eds.), *Behavior modification and families: Theory and research* (Vol. 1). New York: Brunner/Mazel.

Penman, R. (1980). *Communication processes and relationships.* London: Academic Press.

Pett, M. A., Vaughan–Cole, B., Egger, M., & Dorsey, P. (1988). Wrestling meaning from interactional data: An empirically-based strategy for deriving multiple molar constructs in parent–child interaction. *Behavioral Assessment, 10,* 299–318.

Pett, M. A., Vaughan-Cole, B., Wampold, B. E., Egger, M., & East, T. (1987, November). *Reciprocity and dominance in young divorced families.* Paper presented at the meeting of the National Council on Family Relations, Atlanta, GA.

Rohrbaugh, M., Tennen, H., Press, S., & White, L. (1981). Compliance, defiance, and therapeutic paradox: Guidelines for strategic use of paradoxical interventions. *American Journal of Orthopsychiatry, 51,* 454–467.

Salvosa, L. R. (1930). Tables of Pearson's type III function. *Annals of Mathematical Statistics, 1,* 191–198.

Sulzer–Azaroff, B., & Mayer, G. R. (1986). *Achieving educational excellence using behavioral strategies.* New York: Holt, Rinehart, & Winston.

Suppes, P. C. (1970). *A probabilistic theory of causation.* Amsterdam: North–Holland.

Tracey, T. J. (1985). Dominance and outcome: A sequential examination. *Journal of Counseling Psychology, 32,* 119–122.

Wampold, B. E. (1984). Tests of dominance in sequential categorical data. *Psychological Bulletin, 96,* 424–429.

Wampold, B. E. (1986). State of the art in sequential analysis: Comment on Lichtenberg and Heck. *Journal of Counseling Psychology, 33,* 182–185.

Wampold, B. E. (1989). Kappa as a measure of pattern in sequential data. *Quality and Quantity, 23,* 171–187.

Wampold, B. E., Davis, B., & Good, R. H., III (1990). The hypothesis validity of clinical research. *Journal of Consulting and Clinical Psychology.*

Wampold, B. E., & Holloway, E. L. (1983). A note on interobserver reliability for sequential data. *Journal of Behavioral Assessment, 5,* 217–225.

Wampold, B. E., & Kim, K. (1989). Sequential analysis applied to counseling process and outcome: A case study revisited. *Journal of Counseling Psychology, 36,* 357–364.

Wampold, B. E., & Margolin, G. (1982). Nonparametric strategies to test the independence of behavioral states in sequential data. *Psychological Bulletin, 92,* 755–765.

Wampold, B. E., Roll, R., & East, T. (1989). *Sequential analysis program (SAP)* [Computer program]. Salt Lake City: University of Utah.

Watzlawick, P., Beavin, J., & Jackson, D. (1967). *Pragmatics of human communication.* New York. Norton.

Weeks, G. R. & L'Abate, L. (1982). *Paradoxical psychotherapy: Theory and practice with individuals, couples, and families.* New York: Brunner/Mazel.

Weiss, R. L., & Summers, K. J. (1983). Marital Interaction Coding System–III. In E. E. Filsinger (Ed.), *Marriage and family assessment: A sourcebook for family therapy* (pp. 65–84). Beverly Hills, CA: Sage.

5 Nonparametric Tests for Single-Case Experiments

Eugene S. Edgington
University of Calgary, Alberta, Canada

RANDOMIZATION

This chapter describes statistical tests that can be employed to draw valid statistical inferences about treatment effects in single-subject experiments. As the validity of these tests depends on randomization (random assignment), randomization will be discussed briefly before considering specific statistical tests.

In fields of research in which statistical tests are used, it has long been recognized that randomization is necessary in order to draw causal inferences from experimental data. The manner in which randomization is employed is a basic component of experimental design. Although commonly ignored in statistics books, randomization is a standard topic in books on experimental design. Campbell and Stanley (1963) considered randomization important enough to serve as a criterion for distinguishing between experiments and quasi-experiments. This distinction, which is now widely accepted in the behavioral sciences, is made on the basis of the presence or absence of random assignment of "the when and to whom of exposures [to treatments]" (p. 204). Absence of randomness in the assignment of subjects to treatments in a between-subjects experiment makes it impossible to perform an internally valid statistical test of treatment effects, and nonrandom sequencing of "the when" of treatments in a within-subjects experiment also invalidates a statistical test of treatment effects. Like multisubject repeated-measures experiments, single-subject experiments also are within-subjects experiments and as such require random assignment of treatment times to treatments. (Although it is customary to refer to random ordering of treatments within subjects as the randomization that is required for within-subjects designs, it is, in fact, necessary also to ensure that the set of

133

treatment times that is divided among treatment conditions is independent of the ordering of treatments, so treatment times should be randomly assigned to treatments.)

In the field of behavior therapy, the necessity of randomization in single-subject experimentation has not generally been recognized. After pointing out that conventional experimental designs are preplanned with respect to assignment of treatments, Kazdin (1982, p. 263) stressed that this is not so for single-subject behavior therapy designs:

> In single-subject designs, many crucial decisions about the design can be made only as the data are collected. Decisions such as how long baseline data should be collected and when to present or withdraw experimental conditions are made during the investigation itself.

This approach has been called response-guided experimentation (Edgington, 1983) because, contrary to conventional experimental practice, the experimental conditions are adjusted on the basis of responses the subject makes during the experiment. Honig (1966, p. 21) gives a quotation from Skinner that shows Skinner's advocacy of response-guided experimentation:

> A prior design in which variables are distributed, for example, in a Latin square, may be a severe handicap. When effects on behavior can be immediately observed, it is most efficient to explore relevant variables by manipulating them in an improvised and rapidly changing design.

Skinner's second sentence seems plausible enough, but it should be noted that it begins with "When," not "Because." Randomized designs and statistical tests are employed in experimental research precisely because "effects on behavior" of a manipulated treatment usually cannot be "immediately observed;" differences or changes in the dependent variable may not be treatment effects at all.

In behavior therapy response-guided experimentation seems to be a common practice in single-subject experimentation. Since this methodology has not been advocated for multiple-subject research, evidently it is regarded as being especially suited to single-subject behavior therapy research.

There are problems with the application of statistical tests to data from response-guided experiments. Response-guided experimentation is incompatible with randomization and thus provides no basis for statistical tests. Randomizing controls for unknown as well as known sources of confounding, whereas arguments that a research procedure involving nonrandom manipulation is not biased can concern only known sources.

Because they lack randomization, the typical research designs in behavior therapy are not conducive to statistical testing. Unlike *nonexperimental* research, where time-series analysis and other complex procedures have been used in adjusting for trends, research that involves experimental manipulation of variables to determine their effect must utilize randomization because no statistical adjustments can compensate for lack of randomization.

TESTS THAT DO NOT ASSUME RANDOM SAMPLING

Having considered the necessity of experimental randomization, we will now turn to consideration of statistical tests that can be based on randomization alone, in the absence of random sampling. These are randomization tests and other nonparametric tests. First, we will consider the value of these tests for experiments in general, then their value for single-subject experiments in particular.

Randomization Tests

Randomization tests are nonparametric, as they require no assumptions about populations, not even the assumption of random sampling from a population. The physical act of randomization is the random process providing a basis for the tests. The freedom of these tests from the assumption of random sampling is extremely important in behavioral experimentation because very few samples employed in such experimentation are random samples. Cotton (1967, pp. 64–65) indicated that because randomization tests are not based on the random sampling assumption, they, not parametric tests, are the appropriate tests to be applied in behavioral research. In the absence of random sampling, parametric tests are valid only to the extent that their P-values approximate those that would be provided by a randomization test.

Randomization tests are appropriate for single-subject experimentation because random sampling is as rare in single-subject as in multiple-subject experimentation, and randomization tests are the only statistical tests that are valid in the absence of random sampling. Random selection of a subject from a population frequently is inappropriate for a single-subject experiment because of interest in a particular subject, not just any subject that might be selected from a population. Even if an inference about a population of subjects were of interest, random selection of a subject from the population would provide no basis for a parametric statistical test because measurements from a single subject provide no basis for estimating the between-subject variability within the population. An apparent alternative to random sampling of a population of subjects would be to select treatment times randomly from a large population of treatment times, but having a sample of treatment times scattered over a span of time long enough to approximate the "infinite population" assumed by parametric tests would be unpalatable to most experimenters. Furthermore, it is difficult to conceive of an experimenter having a special interest in statistical inferences concerning a particular span of time from which treatment times are to be drawn. Since random sampling is not associated with single-subject experiments, freedom from the random sampling assumption makes randomization tests of considerable importance for analysis of single-subject data.

To understand the rationale for a randomization test it should be kept in mind that the randomization test null hypothesis is the hypothesis of no differential effect of the treatments for any of the experimental units (e.g., subjects or treatment times) that were assigned to the treatments. Random assignment of experimental units to treatments, under the null hypothesis, randomly assigns the unit measurements to the treatments. A distribution of test statistic values derived by permuting (dividing or rearranging) the data therefore consists of values which, under the null hypothesis, would have been obtained under alternative assignments. The steps in performing a randomization test thus are as follows. With the aid of a computer a conventional test statistic, such as t or F, or an unconventional test statistic, such as $\bar{X}_A - \bar{X}_B$ or $|\bar{X}_A - \bar{X}_B|$, is computed for the experimental results, and for repeated permutations (divisions or rearrangements) of the data. The test statistic is computed for each data permutation, and the proportion of the test statistics that are as large as the obtained value is the significance or probability value (P-value). (Occasionally, it is the *smallness* of a test statistic that is indicative of a treatment effect, and in such cases the P-value is the proportion of data permutations with a test statistic value as *small* as the value for the experimental results.) For example, if the obtained t for a t- test was 2.30 and only 4% of the data divisions for which ts were computed yielded ts as large as 2.30, the P-value would be .04; thus, the results would be significant at the .05 level. The objective of a randomization test is to determine how rarely a test statistic value as extreme as the experimental value would result from random assignment alone, in the absence of a treatment effect.

When the data are permuted in a way that provides a data permutation for each possible assignment, the randomization test procedure is called a *systematic* procedure. When the number of possible assignments is so large that it would be impractical to use a systematic procedure, a randomization test may be conducted on the basis of a random sample of all possible data permutations; such a procedure is called a *random* procedure.

Other Nonparametric Tests

Nonparametric tests for ranks and dichotomous data are randomization tests and thus do not require random sampling. To avoid confusion, we will refer to those tests by their familiar names, like "Mann–Whitney U test" or "sign test," and will reserve the term "randomization test" for applications to raw data. The P-values that are given in conventional nonparametric tables are those that a randomization test applied to ranks or dichotomous data would provide.

In examples that will be discussed in this chapter, the application of randomization tests to raw data will be described and, in addition, the application of rank tests to ranks and other nonparametric tests to dichotomous data will be described. It must be stressed, however, that one should not reduce the precision of data by transforming to ranks or categories in order to achieve a nonparametric test; that is unnecessary because a randomization test can be applied directly to the data without such transformations. If, however, the data appear in the form of ranks or categories, the use of conventional nonparametric tests may be useful because reference to tables may be faster than performing a randomization test on the ranks or categories.

TESTS FOR VARIOUS SINGLE-CASE DESIGNS

We will next consider randomization tests and other nonparametric tests for randomized versions of these common single-subject experimental designs: AB . . . AB, alternating treatments, AB, and multiple-baseline designs. Following discussion of tests for those designs, we will describe a testing procedure for a single-subject factorial design. These are only some of the nonparametric tests for randomized single-subject designs that have been published. Some of these are from chapters (Edgington, 1984, 1987; Levin, Marascuilo, & Hubert, 1978), that discuss several additional tests (see also Busk & Marascuilo, this volume).

AB . . . AB Experiments: 2 Treatments

An example of a statistical test for a completely randomized AB . . . AB experiment follows. Quantitative dependent variables are more characteristic of behavior modification experiments than are qualitative dependent variables, so we will first show how to apply a randomization test to quantitative data. The test will be described in detail, and additional nonparametric tests will be discussed.

Consider a randomized single-subject experiment conducted over 12 days, with 6 days for treatment A and 6 for treatment B. We predict that the measurements under treatment A will be larger than those under treatment B. Six days are randomly selected for treatment A, and the other 6 days are assigned to treatment B. Thus, there are $12!/6!6! = 924$ possible randomizations. The null hypothesis is that the subject's response on any particular day is the same as it would have been on that day to the alternative treatment. Results are shown in Table 5.1.

Randomization Tests

If the randomization test null hypothesis is true, then any difference between the measurements under the two treatments is due solely to a difference in the times the two treatments were administered. As the treatment times were randomized, the null hypothesis attributes differences between treatments to the chance assignment of certain treatment times rather than others to a treatment.

TABLE 5.1
Quantitative Data for Two Methods of Reinforcement

	Days											
	1	2	3	4	5	6	7	8	9	10	11	12
Treatments	A	B	B	A	B	A	A	B	A	B	A	B
Responses	17	14	15	17	14	19	21	16	20	16	20	18
Ranks	6.5	1.5	3	6.5	1.5	9	12	4.5	10.5	4.5	10.5	8

For a one-tailed test where A is predicted to provide the larger measurements, $\bar{X}_A - \bar{X}_B$ is an appropriate test statistic. The value of $\bar{X}_A - \bar{X}_B$ for the obtained results is 3.5. For determining significance by the randomization test procedure, the 12 measurements are divided between ("assigned to") A and B (with 6 for each treatment category) in all 924 ways, and the test statistic is computed for each of the data permutations (divisions). The proportion of those data permutations with a test statistic as large as 3.5, the obtained value, is the P-value associated with the results. Performance of the one-tailed test by computer shows that only 5 of the 924 data permutations have a test statistic value as large as 3.5, and so the P-value for the one-tailed test is 5/924, or about .005. For a two-tailed test, the P-value is the proportion of the data permutations with as large an absolute difference between means as 3.5, and this proportion is found to be 10/924, or about .011.

Program 4.4 or Program 4.5 in Edgington (1987) can be used to carry out this test. Program 4.4 systematically permutes the data to derive all data permutations, whereas Program 4.5 randomly permutes the data as many times as the user desires.

Mann–Whitney U Test

Suppose that instead of using frequencies within sessions as the dependent variable the researcher chose to have the 12 sessions ranked with respect to the degree of social adjustment exhibited. (In such a case, the judge doing the ranking could attend to the behavior in general rather than focusing upon a single indicator of social adjustment.) The subject's behavior is videotaped for each session and an independent judge who is blind to the treatment conditions ranks the behavior shown on the videotapes. One could divide the ranks repeatedly to derive a distribution of test statistics, using the same program as was described for raw data, to perform a randomization test. However, one could find the significance more simply by performing the Mann–Whitney U test, which is based on ranks. The last row in Table 5.1 shows the ranks of the measurements, with the smaller ranks assigned to the smaller measurements. Tied measurements each are given the average rank they would have had if they were not tied. The Mann–Whitney U test (Siegel, 1956, pp. 116–127) can be applied validly to the ranks because it is a randomization test for ranks. The value of the test statistic U for the obtained results is 2. The significance table (Siegel, 1956, p. 271) for the Mann–Whitney U test shows a P-value of .004 for a one-tailed test and a P-value of .008 for a two-tailed test.

Fisher's Exact Test

Even if the data were qualitative instead of quantitative, valid nonparametric tests could be conducted. For instance, suppose that for each of the 12 days it was recorded that the subject did or did not show aggression. Assume that an aggressive act occurred on 5 of the 7 days for treatment A and on none of the 7 days for treatment B. By assigning a 0 to days without aggression and a 1 to days with aggression, the researcher can obtain 12 "measurements" to which the randomization test program can be applied. (The test statistics computed by the program are $\bar{X}_A - \bar{X}_B$ for a one-tailed test and $|\bar{X}_A - \bar{X}_B|$ for a two-tailed test. The P-value that a one-tailed randomization test would provide for dichotomous data can be determined directly by computation for Fisher's exact test (Siegel, 1956, p. 98) or tables (pp. 256–270). The significance table for Fisher's exact test shows the results for the present example to be significant at the .01 level, for a one-tailed randomization test.

Siegel (1956, p. 100) doubles the significance value given in the table for Fisher's exact test to get a two-tailed significance value, but it must be stressed that such a procedure will not necessarily give the two-tailed significance value that a two-tailed randomization test would give.

2 Published Examples

McLeod's Experiment.   A single-subject randomized experiment was conducted on a patient who had been taking the drug metronidazole for 3 years following an operation for ulcerative colitis (McLeod, Taylor, Cohen, & Cullen, 1986). The physician, McLeod, and her patient agreed on the desirability of performing an experiment to determine whether the medication was relieving unpleasant symptoms, such as nausea and abdominal pain, because if metronidazole was not effective, both the cost of the drug and the risk of cancer associated with its long-term use dictated discontinuing it.

The experiment lasted 20 weeks. The 20 weeks were divided into 10 blocks of 2-week intervals. Five of the intervals were randomly selected as the times when the patient received metronidazole daily, and the remaining five 2-week intervals were assigned to "an identical placebo capsule." The principal source of data was a diary in which the patient was asked to report the presence or absence, or the magnitude, of each of seven symptoms, which included nausea, abdominal pain, abdominal gas, and watery stool. Because of the possibility that the effects of metronidazole would carry over to days after it was withdrawn, only data from the second week of each 2-week session were subjected to a statistical test. A single weekly measurement for each different symptom was obtained by combining daily observations. There were, therefore, 10 measurements for each dependent variable (symptom). Since there were only $10!/5!5! = 252$ data permutations, the experimenters carried out a systematic randomization test, using the data permuting procedure in Program 4.4 in *Randomization Tests* (Edgington, 1980, 1987).

Reductions in six of the seven symptoms under metronidazole were significant at the .05 level: two P-values were .024 and four were .004. These results confirmed the effectiveness of the drug, so the patient was advised to continue taking it.

Let us briefly consider carry-over effects, a consideration that is important in many single-subject experiments. The use of the first week of each block to "wash out" possible effects of metronidazole was unnecessary for ensuring the *validity* of the test, but allowing sufficient time between sessions for carry-over of effects to be diminished increases the *power* of the study. If metronidazole had an effect that carried over into a control week immediately following its administration and the study did not allow for such carry-over, a statistical test of treatment effect would be based on comparisons of metronidazole effect weeks with other metronidazole effect weeks and would be quite insensitive. A related consideration to carry-over in planning a single-subject experiment is the delay or lag in a treatment showing its effect. If it had been expected that metronidazole would probably not show any effect for about a day, then in McLeod's study the measurements used should be only for the last 6 days of the second week in each block.

Weiss's Experiment.   Weiss and 9 colleagues (Weiss et al., 1980) carried out a study to determine the effect of artificial food colors on aversive (undesirable) behavior in children, such as whining, running away, or breaking and throwing things. The children in the study had not been diagnosed as hyperactive, but the experimenters expected artificial food additives to have a similar effect on their behavior to that which those additives have on hyperactive children.

The study consisted of 22 single-subject experiments, carried out on children between 2.5 and 7 years of age. On each of 77 days a child consumed a bottle of soft drink containing either natural or artificial food coloring. The authors stated that "the two drinks were indistinguishable by sight, smell, taste or stain color," and that neither the children nor their parents, whose record of the child's behavior was the principal source of data, knew which drink was given on any particular day. Eight of the 77 days were randomly selected for giving the artificially colored drink, and the other soft drink was given on the other 69 days.

Ten different measures served as dependent variables. Many of them consisted of the frequency of occurrence of a certain type of aversive behavior. The number of data permutations was too great for a systematic test to be practical, so random data permutation involving 10,000 randomly selected data permutations from the systematic reference set of all data permutations was used to determine significance for a randomization test. (Program 4.5, in *Randomization Tests* was used, as it is the random data permuting counterpart of Program 4.4.) Significance was determined for each child on each dependent variable. "Twenty of the children displayed no convincing evidence of sensitivity to the color challenge" (p. 1488). A 3-year-old boy had P-values of .01 and .02 for two types of aversive behavior, but such P-values are not small, considering the multiplicity of testing: 10 dependent variables for each of 22 children. A 34-month-old girl, however, provided very strong evidence of treatment effects even when the number of children tested and number of variables are taken into account. The P-value for 3 of the 10 dependent variables for that child was .0001, and P-values for 5 others were .0003, .0004, .0006, .001, and .03. As a consequence of the statistical test results from this girl and because the food additive used in the experiment was "about 50 times less than the maximum allowable intakes (ADIs) recommended by the Food and Drug Administration" (p. 1488), the authors stressed the need for more stringent testing of additives. The single-subject experimental results of a single exceptionally sensitive child showed an effect of a small dose of food coloring that might have been missed in other experimental designs.

This study, like that of McLeod and her associates, has some interesting aspects that concern many single-subject experiments. One aspect of the study that is interesting from the standpoint of experimental design is the use of a large number of single-subject experiments. Unlike the study by McLeod, there was no interest in a particular subject; rather, a replicated single-subject design was used as a procedure for determining whether any of the 22 children was sensitive to food coloring. Nowadays, with regard to health issues, identification of even a few apparently healthy persons who are adversely affected by an artificial food additive can be of great importance, especially when the amount of the additive was much lower than is currently allowed.

Despite the difference in objectives of this study and unreplicated single-subject studies, both replicated and unreplicated single-subject studies require a number of measurements from a subject in order to have a sensitive test of treatment effect, and Weiss and associates managed this in a way that has implications for other single-subject experiments in which it is undesirable to have a large number of measurements under one of the treatment conditions. For each subject they assigned 69 days to the control drink but only 8 days to artificial food coloring. Even with only 8 days for artificial food coloring, the large number of control days allowed for the possibility of a P-value as small as $1/(77!/8!69!)$, which is about 1 in 20 billion. (Since the researchers used only 10,000 randomly selected data permutations, however, the smallest P-value they could attain was .0001.)

The use by Weiss and associates of a large number of single-subject experiments in a single study raises special problems in determining the statistical significance of the results, as does their recording of several dependent variable measures for each subject. The researchers certainly got very small P-values on several dependent variables for one of the 22 children, but since they were not looking for effects in that child alone but in any of the 22 children, and since the dependent variables might have been highly correlated, the multiplicity of testing should be taken into consideration in assessing the significance of the results. The multiplicity of measures for each subject can be accommodated by using one of the multivariate randomization tests described in Edgington (1987, chap. 7), which would provide a single P-value for each subject. How that set of 22 P-values then would be used to determine whether there was a significant effect depends on the prediction (and associated statistical decision rule) established prior to the study. For example, if it was expected that the 22 subjects would all be affected similarly by the food additive, it would be appropriate to determine whether the study as a whole showed significance by using probability combining (Edgington, 1987, pp. 170–176). On the other hand, suppose that the experimenters had expected the sensitivity to food additives to vary over the 22 subjects with one or perhaps a few subjects being very sensitive. In that case a different approach would be better than probability combining. If the preset level of significance was .01, the results for any subject would be significant if the individual P-value for that subject multiplied by 22 was no greater than .01. In other words, one could control for Type 1 error rate by multiplying each P-value by the number of P-values computed in the study (see Edgington, 1987, pp. 85–87). Other types of expectations would lead to other ways of determining significance based on the set of 22 P-values. The point to keep in mind is that in a replicated single-subject design, the many ways in which one might determine the overall significance make it essential that the rule for determining a significant effect be specified prior to data collection.

AB . . . AB Experiments: 3 or More Treatments

When there are more than two treatment conditions, a randomization test for a completely randomized single-subject experiment can, of course, also be conducted. If, for instance, there was a control condition and two different experimental conditions, F for one-way analysis of variance could be used as the test statistic to be computed over all data permutations. F could be computed in the same way as if each measurement was from a different subject in a multiple-subject experiment. The degrees of freedom for the numerator of F would be 2, and the degrees of freedom for the denominator of F would be the total number of measurements minus 3. Instead of determining significance by referring F to F tables, the researcher determines the significance as the proportion of data permutations with Fs as large as the obtained F. Program 4.2 or 4.3 in Edgington (1987) can be used to determine the significance of a computed F for this design.

Kruskal–Wallis analysis of variance (Siegel, 1956, pp. 184–193) is a rank test that could be employed. For dichotomous data, a 2×3 contingency chi-square test would provide a close approximation to the P-value that would be given by a randomization test with F as the test statistic, where categorical membership is represented by a 0 or a 1.

Alternating Treatments Experiments: 2 Treatments

Alternating treatments single-subject experiments are related to randomized block experiments in multisubject experimentation. In multisubject experimentation a randomized block design is a design in which subjects are "blocked" or grouped according to some variable that is not experimentally manipulated, such as sex, age, or education. There is random assignment to the experimental treatments within each block. A repeated-measures experiment is a special type of randomized block design, one in which each block consists of treatment times for a particular subject. The following randomized block design for a single-subject experiment, which has sometimes been called an alternating treatments design, is analogous to a repeated-measures design: Within each block there is just one treatment time for each treatment.

One method of blocking for an alternating treatments single-subject design is to group the treatment times into successive pairs, within each of which we randomly determine which member of the pair will be subjected to a particular treatment. For example, a block could consist of the morning and afternoon of each day, as in the study by McCullough, Cornell, McDaniel, and Mueller (1974) of cooperative behavior in a 6-year-old boy. This type of design is what Barlow and Hayes (1979) call an alternating treatments design because the treatments are repeatedly introduced and withdrawn. Kratochwill and Levin (1980) discussed various statistical procedures that might be applied to data from the McCullough et al. study and other studies with similar designs. One of the procedures was a randomization test. Another type of randomization test for alternating treatments designs will be described here.

Randomization Test

Consider a single-subject experiment involving random assignment within blocks. On each of 4 days one treatment is given in the morning and another in the afternoon to determine the relative effectiveness of the two treatments on sociability. Which treatment to give in the morning and which to give in the afternoon is randomly determined for each day. There are $2^4 = 16$ possible assignments of treatments A and B to morning (M) and afternoon (A) of the four days. Table 5.2 shows an assignment of times of day to treatments and the resulting measurements, where larger measurements indicate greater sociability. The null hypothesis is that on each day the measurement associated with the time of day is the same as it would have been if the alternative treatment had been

TABLE 5.2
Data From an Alternating Treatments Experiment

			Treatment Times (Mornings and Afternoons)					
	M	*A*	*M*	*A*	*M*	*A*	*M*	*A*
Treatments	B	A	B	A	A	B	A	B
Measurements	11	9	9	6	8	7	8	10

given at that time of day. The 16 data permutations to determine the significance consist of all possible ways the letters A and B in Table 5.2 can be associated with the eight measurements, with one measurement in each successive pair for A and the other for B. For a one-tailed test $\bar{X}_B - \bar{X}_A$ would be an appropriate test statistic for a randomization test. The obtained value of the test statistic is 1.5. Suppose B was predicted to provide the larger measurements. Two of the 16 data permutations have a test statistic value as large as 1.5, and so the P-value for the one-tailed test is $\frac{2}{16}$, or .125. The results would not have been significant at the .05 level even if the most significant results possible for the randomization test had been achieved. While designing the experiment the experimenter should bear in mind that the number of possible assignments is 2^n, so that the smallest possible P-value is $\frac{1}{2^n}$. Then it would be recognized that with only 16 possible assignments for a 4-day experimental session, the experimenter could not possibly get significance at the .05 or .01 level.

Program 5.1 or Program 5.2 in Edgington (1987) can be used to perform this randomization test.

Wilcoxon's Matched-pairs, Signed-ranks Test.   Instead of a randomization test, Wilcoxon's matched-pairs, signed-ranks test (Siegel, 1956, pp. 75–83) could be applied to the data. For this test the data would be arranged in pairs as shown in Table 5.3. The Wilcoxon test uses T as a test statistic, where T is defined as the smaller of two sums: the sum of ranks for $|B - A|$ where $B - A$ is

TABLE 5.3
Ranking of Differences for Wilcoxon's Test

	Days			
	1	*2*	*3*	*4*
Treatment A	9	6	8	8
Treatment B	11	9	7	10
B - A	+2	+3	-1	+2
|B - A| Ranks	2.5	4	1	2.5

positive or the sum of ranks for |B − A| where B − A is negative. The smaller sum of ranks for the obtained results is the sum of ranks for the negative difference scores, which is 1. The significance table in Siegel's (1956, p. 254) book does not show significance for situations with fewer than six pairs of measurements. (The significance table is to be used for either one-tailed or two-tailed tests, and at least six pairs of measurements are required to permit significance for a two-tailed test at the .05 level.) However, Wilcoxon's test is a randomization test, so the P-value could be determined directly by switching the paired measurements in all $2^4 = 16$ ways and computing test statistic T for each data permutation. Two data permutations give such a small T as 1, and so the P-value is $\frac{2}{16}$, or .125, the same as for the randomization test using $\bar{X}_B - \bar{X}_A$ as the test statistic. (This is an occasion when the *smallness* of the test statistic is indicative of a treatment effect, and so the P-value is the proportion of data permutations with such a *small* test statistic as the obtained value.)

As pointed out earlier, the precision of the data should not be reduced by transforming to ranks or dichotomies for the sake of conducting a nonparametric test; a randomization test can always be employed on the data in the form in which the measurements are made. In earlier examples we assumed that ranks were sometimes reasonable because only relative magnitude was observable or that the presence or absence of some characteristic, such as aggression, in a session, may be more important than the amount of a characteristic. In those cases, use of ranks or dichotomies for the statistical tests would not involve degrading precision of measurement. On the other hand, in the present instance, a rank test was described for application where the ranking was unnecessary. The differences that were ranked for the Wilcoxon test were quantitative differences, which were then diminished in precision by ranking. If there were no nonparametric test that could use the differences between raw data without ranking them, one might justify the Wilcoxon matched-pairs, signed-ranks test as being useful as a nonparametric test. That is, however, not the case; randomization tests can be employed on the raw data without ranking. To summarize, Wilcoxon's matched-pairs, signed-ranks test necessarily loses some of the precision of the original measurements in computing the test statistic value and thus cannot utilize the precision of the measurements to the extent that a randomization test can.

Sign Test

If, instead of quantitative measurements, the time of day (morning or afternoon) when the behavior seemed more sociable was recorded, a sign test could be applied to the data. (The judgment of the relative sociability of morning and afternoon behavior should be made without knowledge of the treatment condition associated with times of day.) Suppose mornings were judged more sociable for days 1, 2, and 3, and afternoon more sociable for day 4. Table 5.3 shows that on

3 of the days (days 1, 2, and 4) the behavior for the time of day associated with B was judged to be more sociable, and on only 1 day was the behavior associated with the time of day for A judged to be more sociable. Application of a sign test (Siegel, 1956, pp. 36–42), where B is predicted to result in more sociable behavior than A, provides a one-tailed P-value of $\frac{5}{16}$, or about .31. (With so few days, a sign test cannot be very sensitive.)

Alternating Treatments Experiments: 3 Treatments

Published Example

An investigation by Smith (1963) of the effect of certain drugs on narcolepsy was one of the early single-subject experiments employing random assignment. As Smith stated, narcolepsy is so rare that it is important to learn as much as possible from the individual case. Consequently, he performed a rigorous investigation of the single case that was available. He used a randomized block design with a single narcoleptic subject to compare the effectiveness of three drugs. Although Smith computed a repeated-measures F and determined significance by reference to F tables, it will be instructive to consider how he could have determined the exact significance by use of a randomization test, considering the way in which randomization was carried out. He investigated the relative effects of three drugs—methamphetamine, dextroamphetamine, and adrenaline methyl ether—on narcolepsy. To provide control over systematic variation in narcolepsy over the time span of the experiment, Smith used a randomized block design in which he divided 15 days into five 3-day blocks. He gave all three treatments in each 3-day block, randomly determining for each block, separately, how the drugs would be distributed over the 3 days. The dependent variable was a score on a rating scale on which the subject indicated the strength of various symptoms of narcolepsy each day. Smith did not provide the raw data for the 15 days, so we will use hypothetical data, shown in Table 5.4, to illustrate application of a randomization test.

TABLE 5.4
Comparison of Three Drugs

	3-Day Blocks				
	1	2	3	4	5
Methamphetamine	4	8	7	8	4
Dextroamphetamine	2	2	3	6	1
Adrenaline methyl ether	3	6	8	7	3

Randomization Test

A randomization test can be performed by using repeated-measures analysis of variance F as a test statistic, where blocks correspond to "subjects" and drugs is the repeated measure. Repeated-measures F for the data is 12.99. F is computed for $(3!)^5 = 7,776$ data permutations to determine significance. If the null hypothesis were true, random assignment of the treatment times to the treatments within each block randomly assigned the measurements for that block to the treatments. Thus, data permutations are produced by switching the measurements between treatments within blocks in every possible way. Thirty of the data permutations, including the one for the obtained results, provide as large a value of F as 12.99, the value for the obtained results; thus, the P-value is $^{30}/_{7776}$, or about .0039.

The significance of F can be determined for this randomization test by using Program 5.1 or 5.2 in Edgington (1987).

Friedman's Analysis of Variance

Smith had the subject rank the 3 days within each block with respect to freedom from narcolepsy. He did not say whether a statistical analysis was performed on those ranks, but Friedman's analysis of variance (Siegel, 1956, pp. 166–172) would be suitable because the tables for that test are based on the randomization test procedure with ranks, using Friedman's special test statistic.

Dichotomous Data

For some symptoms of narcolepsy it might make sense simply to record for each day whether that symptom was present or absent. In that case, the "data" for the randomization test described here could be 1 or 0 for each day, depending on whether the symptom was present or absent.

AB Experimental Designs

In some single-subject studies withdrawal of a treatment that has been introduced is regarded as undesirable; therefore, in those studies there may be introduction of a treatment with no subsequent withdrawal. An assessment of a treatment effect involves a comparison of measurements before and after intervention. (In behavior therapy research such experimental designs are commonly called AB designs.) Sometimes graphical comparisons are used for the assessment. A consistent upward or downward trend in measurements over the course of the experiment would tend to make the treatment measurements systematically lower or higher than the control measurements even if there was no treatment effect. A single-treatment intervention without withdrawal, therefore, is not generally regarded as an acceptable single-subject research design. A valid randomization test, however, can be carried out, provided the point of intervention is randomly determined.

Randomization Test

One-tailed Test.   Suppose an experimenter decides to test the effectiveness of a method for reinforcing a certain type of behavior and uses the frequency of the behavior as the dependent variable. The experimenter chooses to introduce the reinforcement once and not withdraw it. Twenty 5-minute treatment blocks (blocks of time or "treatment sessions") are specified, and the frequency of the behavior within each of the 20 blocks of time constitute the data. The experimental treatment is expected to increase the frequency of the desired behavior, and so a one-tailed test is desired. As the treatment that is introduced is not withdrawn at a later time, the point of introduction divides the 20 treatment blocks into two classes: control blocks, which are the blocks prior to treatment intervention, and experimental blocks, which are those after intervention. The experimenter decides to select the intervention block randomly somewhere within the interval block 6 to block 16. This constraint ensures that there will be at least 5 control and at least 5 experimental blocks, no matter how early or late the intervention might occur. One of the 11 blocks is randomly selected, and the treatment is introduced at the beginning of that block of time. Suppose that the block that was randomly selected for intervention was block 7. The experimental results are shown here, where the underlined numbers indicate the experimental treatment blocks and the measurements (frequencies of response) for those blocks:

Block 1 2 3 4 5 6 7 8 9 10 11 12 13 14 15 16 17 18 19 20
Data   3 4 5 4 3 4 7 8 7 8 9 7 8 8 7 9 8 8

To carry out a one-tailed test where the experimental treatment blocks are expected to provide the larger measurements, the experimenter uses $\bar{X}_E - \bar{X}_C$, the mean of the experimental measurements minus the mean of the control measurements, as the test statistic. The data permutations for which $\bar{X}_E - \bar{X}_C$ is computed are the data permutations for the 11 possible blocks that could be selected for intervention of the experimental treatment: blocks 6 to 16. The test statistic value for the first data permutation is the mean of the last 15 measurements minus the mean of the first 5 measurements, which is 3.87. The test statistic value for the second data permutation (the data permutation associated with the experimental results) is the mean of the last 14 measurements minus the mean of the first 6 measurements, which is 5.02. When the test statistic is computed for the remaining nine data permutations, it is found that only the obtained data permutation provides a test statistic value as large as 5.02, and so the P-value for the obtained results is $\frac{1}{11}$, or about .09.

2-tailed Test

The absolute difference between means, $|\bar{X}_E - \bar{X}_C|$, would be an appropriate test statistic for a two-tailed test if there were no general upward or downward trend in measurements over time that would exist without treatment intervention, but an example will show the inappropriateness of that test statistic when such a trend exists. Suppose we collect data from 12 treatment blocks, where a treatment block for intervention is randomly selected from 1 of the middle 8 blocks and the following results were obtained:

Block 1 2 3 4 5 6 <u>7 8 9 10 11 12</u>
Data   8 7 6 5 4 3 <u>8 7 6 5 4 3</u>

As the treatment was introduced at the beginning of block 7, the first six measurements are control measurements, and the last six are experimental measurements. The results suggest an effect of treatment intervention because the measurements were consistently dropping until treatment intervention, then showed an immediate rise to a higher level before again declining. It is as though fatigue, boredom, or some other factor caused the measurements to decrease in size over time, and that the treatment intervention raised the magnitude of the measurements even though the decline resumed. Notice that despite the appearance of a treatment effect, the two-tailed test statistic $|\bar{X}_E - \bar{X}_C|$ would give a P-value of 1, because the test statistic value for the experimental results is 0, the smallest possible value for all data permutations. The superposition of a treatment effect on an existing opposite trend will not necessarily provide an absolute difference between means equal to 0, as in this example, but the absolute difference between means will in general be insensitive to a treatment effect when there are such trends. Since such trends may exist in some degree or other, it is worthwhile to consider a test statistic to use as an alternative to the absolute difference between control and treatment means.

One test statistic that would not be adversely affected by such trends is F for analysis of covariance. Use of the block number (i.e., 1 for the first block, 2 for the second, and so on) as a covariate provides statistical control over temporal trends within treatment conditions. For each data permutation, F for analysis of covariance would be computed to provide a distribution of Fs with which to compare the obtained F. For the preceding data, use of the absolute difference between means as a two-tailed test statistic would provide a P-value of 1, whereas F for analysis of covariance, with the block number as the covariate, would provide $\frac{1}{8}$, or .125, the smallest P-value possible, since F would have the largest value for the experimental results.

Other Nonparametric Tests.   If the initial observations were in the form of ranks or dichotomies, the randomization test for the AB design could, of course, be applied to those rank values or, for dichotomous data, to 0s and 1s. Tables do not exist to provide the P-values, however, and, in fact, would be so extensive as to be impractical. For example, consider a table of values of differences between mean experimental and mean control ranks for a short series of observations, namely observations for 10 sessions, where the intervention block can be any one of the middle eight blocks. A complete nonparametric table for AB designs with 10 sessions would contain 10! = 3,628,800 different subtables, one for each of the ways ranks 1 to 10 can be arranged in a sequence. Such a table would enable a researcher to select the subtable showing the experimentally obtained sequence of ranks and the significance value for the experimentally obtained difference between mean ranks. For dichotomous data, distinctive sequences of 0s and 1s would not be as numerous as distinctive sequences of ranks, but the number would have to be very large to enable any researcher to pick out the subtable for the experimentally obtained sequence, such as 0,0,1,1,1,1,0,1,1,1. Thus, nonparametric tables for ranked or dichotomous data would be impractical for most AB designs.

Multiple-baseline Experiments

The traditional, nonrandomized, multiple-baseline experiment is a replicated AB (single-intervention) experiment. The separate baselines may be data sequences for different subjects or all of the baselines may refer to a single subject where, for example, each different baseline consists of measurements on a different type of behavior. Treatments are introduced at different times for the different baselines in order to reveal associations between intervention and baseline changes.

As shown in the previous section, it is unnecessary to have more than one AB baseline to ensure *validity* when intervention for that baseline is randomized. A randomized multiple-baseline design, however, may be useful for increasing the *power* (sensitivity) of AB designs when it is impractical to have long baselines. When a baseline does not contain enough data points to be sensitive to treatment effects, it may be helpful to use several baselines. There are many ways the AB experiment can be replicated to provide multiple baselines and randomization tests for those multiple baselines. Two procedures which have been proposed for replicating over subjects will be described. Following the descriptions will be a discussion of their relevance to single-subject multiple-baseline designs where the replications are over behaviors within a single subject.

Wampold–Worsham Test

Wampold and Worsham (1986) developed a randomization test for a randomized multiple-baseline experimental design that is very similar to a traditional, nonrandomized, multiple-baseline design. In their design each baseline is for a separate subject and k different points in time for interventions for the k

subjects are spaced according to the demands of the researcher. After setting the different points of intervention for the different subjects it is randomly determined which subject takes the earliest intervention, which the next, and so on. Wampold and Worsham pointed out that opponents of randomized single-subject designs would not be likely to object to the design because a researcher seldom would have a reason for a particular ordering of the intervention points over subjects. Wampold and Worsham's one-tailed test statistic is determined in this manner: subtract the mean of the control (pre-experimental or "baseline") measurements from the mean of the experimental measurements for each baseline and then add those differences between means over all baselines. To illustrate his procedure, let us consider three subjects providing data over 12 sessions, where the underlined measurements are for the treatment condition:

Sessions:	1	2	3	4	5	6	7	8	9	10	11	12
Subject A:	5	7	4	5	3	7	5	8	10	_8_	_15_	_10_
Subject B:	8	9	7	_7_	_10_	_11_	_10_	_13_	_14_	_10_	_13_	_11_
Subject C:	6	6	7	5	4	8	_7_	_9_	_10_	_11_	_13_	_10_

It was decided that the treatments would be introduced at the beginning of the 4th, 7th, and 10th sessions. Random assignment determined that subject B received the earliest intervention, subject C the next intervention, and subject A the latest intervention. The one-tailed test statistic computed for these results is $(11 - 6) + (11 - 8) + (10 - 6) = 12$. For the randomization test, the value of the test statistic is computed for each of the $3! = 6$ different ways the interventions could be introduced on the 4th, 7th, and 10th sessions, simulating the results that, under the null hypothesis, would have been obtained under other assignments of the interventions to the three subjects. For a one-tailed test where the experimental measurements are expected to be larger than the control measurements, the proportion of those test statistic values that are as large as the value for the experimental results is the P-value. With only three subjects, the smallest possible P-value in only ⅙, but as the number of subjects increases the number of possible assignments increases and consequently the size of the smallest possible P-value decreases; for example, it would be possible to get significance at the .05 level with four subjects.

Marascuilo–Busk Test

Marascuilo and Busk (1988) developed a number of randomization tests for replications of single-subject designs over subjects. One of them was a test for an AB multiple-baseline design. They employed independent application of the assignment procedure given in the previous section for the AB design, wherein any of a set of potential intervention points could be randomly selected for subject X, then any one of those members of the same set could be selected for the next subject, and so on. For all i^k possible interventions, where i is the number of possible intervention points for a subject and k is the number of subjects, the test statistic computed was that of Wampold and Worsham: The difference between the experimental and control means was computed for each subject, and those differences were summed over all subjects.

Single-subject Applications

The two randomization tests just described were published as tests of multiple baselines, replicated over subjects. The randomization tests of Wampold and Worsham (1986) and Marascuilo and Busk (1988) were the central topics of their papers, and in both papers there was mention of the relevance of their procedures to single-subject, multiple baseline designs. Wampold and Worsham regarded their procedure to be applicable not only to multiple subject multiple-baseline designs but also to single-subject designs in which the multiple baselines are for different behaviors. That is shown by their reference to "randomly selecting the order in which the *subjects, behaviors, or situations* [italics added] are subjected to the treatment" (p. 136) in relation to the experimental design for their randomization test. Marascuilo and Busk, on the other hand, believed that correlations between behaviors within a subject usually would make the Marascuilo–Busk procedure inappropriate for single-subject designs:

> One might be tempted to use the proposed methods with multiple-baseline designs across behaviors. In most cases, the application cannot be justified because of the correlations that exist between the measures of different behaviors made at the same time (p. 23).

The multiple-baseline randomization test of Marascuilo and Busk discussed in the preceding paragraph was one of the "proposed methods" whose applicability to multiple baselines for a single subject was so strongly questioned by them.

Two ways in which behaviors in single-subject multiple baselines are likely to be correlated are these: (1) Behaviors covary in the absence of treatment interventions, and (2) A treatment intervention affects more than one behavior. No matter which of these types of correlation was that to which Marascuilo and Busk referred in the foregoing quotation, they were correct in noting that such a correlation is very likely to arise in single-subject baseline designs with different behaviors. The correlation between behaviors causes difficulty in interpreting significant results for both tests that have been discussed, but the *validity* of those tests is unaffected. Both procedures are valid for application to multiple-baseline data from correlated behaviors within a subject. This can be appreciated by considering the null hypothesis, which in conjunction with the random assignment procedure determines the way the data are divided up to generate the theoretical distribution of test statistic values for determining statistical significance. The null hypothesis for each procedure is that the data for all baselines are the same as they would have been under any possible alternative treatment intervention. Therefore, if the null hypothesis is rejected, the alternative hypothesis that is accepted is that treatment intervention had an effect on one or more of the baselines. The two procedures, however, do not permit one to infer which baseline or baselines were affected. Furthermore, rejection of the null hypothesis is not necessarily indicative of the effect of a treatment manipulation on behavior that the treatment was intended to modify; rejection would be appropriate if a treatment manipulation for one type of behavior did not affect that behavior but affected a behavior for a different baseline.

In other words, the two multiple-baseline procedures can validly be applied to single-subject designs with correlated behaviors, but the statistical inference that can be drawn from significant results is not very specific. A statistically significant finding simply implies that somewhere within the configuration of baselines, at least one of the treatment interventions affected at least one of the behaviors. Nevertheless, such an implication can be quite useful to a knowledgeable researcher. Although the correlation between behaviors might frequently make it difficult to conclude that a treatment intervention would not affect more than one behavior, the conclusion that at least one of the behaviors affected would be the target behavior might be very tenable. Given that a researcher is justified in regarding significant results as evidence that at least one of the interventions affected the target behavior, how useful would such an inference be if one could not identify which baseline or baselines were affected? Depending on the nature of the interventions and behaviors, that inference could be very useful. Suppose that the intervention for each baseline was praise given to a very young child for correct performance of the task associated with that baseline. Then, even if one could not infer which task or tasks were performed better as a consequence of praise, having evidence that praise was effective on performance of tasks in the experiment might be very useful, if that child had not previously been known to be responsive to praise.

We have considered two types of correlation between behaviors in single-subject multiple baselines: (1) covariation of behaviors in the absence of treatment intervention, and (2) the effect of treatment intervention on more than one behavior. For either of these two types of correlation, a high correlation between different behaviors makes the two randomization tests less powerful (less likely to detect treatment effects that exist). When behaviors covary to a great extent when no treatments are administered, it is difficult to detect treatment effects that may be small relative to other variation. And when there are correlated responses to a single intervention, a related problem makes it difficult to detect multiple-baseline treatment effects: If an intervention on one baseline tends to affect other baselines as well, causing data shifts before interventions on those baselines, or after interventions on those baselines, there may be difficulty in detecting intervention effects. These problems of reduced sensitivity to treatment effects may be dealt with by selecting interventions likely to have large effects relative to variation in the baseline and by selecting interventions and behaviors to ensure that the intervention for a baseline will primarily affect the behavior for that baseline rather than the behavior for other baselines. Both of the randomization tests just cited should therefore be employed with designs that minimize the effects of correlated behaviors and correlated effects on behaviors of a baseline intervention in order to make the tests sensitive, despite the fact that they are valid even when those effects are not minimized.

Factorial Experiments

Randomization tests can be applied to data from rather complex single-subject experimental designs. An example of this is a factorial design (Edgington, 1987, pp. 261–263). Instead of conducting a number of experiments with a subject, each for the purpose of investigating a certain variable, it is possible to use the same data to test hypotheses about different variables. Note that this is not like comparing several different treatment conditions, where the data for a certain set of days is for a single treatment condition. Instead, with a factorial design, the same data for a given day can be used in the comparison of days with and without condition X and also in the comparison of days with and without condition Y. For some reason, the factorial design does not seem to have received much attention in single-subject research. The following example will illustrate a randomization test for a factorial single-subject experiment.

Two factors, illumination and sound, each with two levels, are investigated to determine their effects on physical strength in a weight lifter. The interest is in the particular weight lifter, as people in general may not be affected in the same way. Although the trainer is limited in his control over illumination and sound conditions during competition, he expects to be able to utilize such information in training and possibly in imagery for the weight lifter during lifting. Ten treatment times are randomly drawn from 20 treatment times and assigned to the "light" condition and the remaining 10 times are allocated to the "dark" condition. Then the 10 treatment times for each of those treatments are randomly divided into 5 for a "quiet" and 5 for a "noise" condition. There are thus four combinations of sound and illumination conditions: quiet and light, quiet and dark, noise and light, and noise and dark, with five measurements for each treatment combination. Table 5.5 shows the outcome of a hypothetical experiment where measures of strength are expressed in arbitrary units.

Randomization Test

First, consider a randomization test for determining whether the sound variable had any effect on strength within the light condition. This involves a com-

TABLE 5.5
Factorial Experimental Data

	Quiet		Noise	
Light	11 12 15	14 14	16 18 20	22 24
Dark	15 8 14	8 6	12 4 5	3 12

parison of the two upper cells. The null hypothesis is that the measurements for the light condition are independent of level of noise. In other words, H_0 is that the presence or absence of noise had no effect on physical strength in the light condition. We divide the 10 measurements in the upper row in every possible way into 5 for the upper left cell and 5 for the upper right cell and compute the difference between means for each division. Program 4.4 (Edgington, 1987) can be used to determine significance by systematic data permutation. A test is unnecessary for these particular results because visual inspection indicates that the two cells differ maximally, so the P-value for the obtained results would be $1/252$ for a one-tailed test with the direction of difference correctly predicted or $2/252$ for a two-tailed test, since there are $10!/5!5! = 252$ permutations of the measurements to be considered.

Similar comparisons could be made, of course, to determine the effect of sound within the dark condition, the effect of illumination within the quiet condition, or the effect of illumination within the noise condition. Program 4.4 could be used for each comparison to determine the significance.

In addition to evaluating the effects of the illumination and sound factors within particular levels of the other factor, one also can test the main effect of illumination or noise over both levels of the other factor combined. Consider how a test would be conducted to test the illumination effect over both quiet and noise conditions. Within each sound condition, the measurements are divided between the light and dark conditions to test the H_0 of no differential effect of the illumination conditions on strength. The number of permutations of data within the two levels of sound between the two illumination conditions will be $10!/5!5! \times 10!/5!5! = 63,504$, since each division of the 10 measurements for the quiet condition can be paired with each of the 252 divisions of the 10 measurements for the noise condition. Program 6.1 (Edgington, 1987) can be used to test the overall main effect of illumination. Analogous permuting of the data by Program 6.1 could test the overall main effect of sound.

Other Nonparametric Tests

Although the randomization test for factorial designs can deal with ranked or dichotomous data, there are no nonparametric tables for test statistics for such data.

OTHER RANDOMIZATION TESTS
FOR SINGLE-SUBJECT EXPERIMENTS

Several single-subject experimental designs, reflecting different procedures of random assignment of treatment times to treatments, have been discussed from the standpoint of the application of nonparametric tests of the null hypothesis of no treatment effect. The designs that were discussed represent some of the more common designs, but, as was pointed out earlier, the tests described are not the only nonparametric tests for single-subject experiments that have been published. It should be noted that randomization tests can be devised for any single-subject experimental design in which there is some form of random assignment of treatment times to treatments. For example, with only six treatment times one could have a potentially sensitive test of treatment effect by randomly assigning six dosages of a drug to the treatment times, where a correlation between drug dosage and strength of response is sought. This test has been described by Edgington (1987, p. 261). Another example would be an ABA design, in which there is treatment intervention and a subsequent withdrawal of the treatment. All possible combinations of time of intervention and time of withdrawal are listed, and one is randomly selected. The randomization test for this design is described by Edgington (1987, pp. 272–274).

In addition to developing new randomization tests to fit other designs involving different forms of randomization, existing randomization tests may be slightly modified for the same experimental design by changing the test statistic to make it sensitive to some alternative type of effect the treatment is expected to have. In McLeod's study of the effect of metronidazole, for example, if metronidazole was expected only to manifest its effect after at least a day's delay, the difference between treatment and control means might be computed on the basis of measures for the last 6 days of each of the sessions, instead of all 7 days of the week. In general, one should consider how to take lag in effect into consideration in choosing a test statistic. If, in an AB design, treatment intervention is expected to produce an immediate sharp change in level, followed very quickly by a return to pre-intervention level, it would be better to use as a test statistic the difference between the measurements for the two treatment blocks that enclose the point of intervention than to use the difference between postintervention and preintervention means. An additional point to consider in devising a test statistic is that there may be several measures of the dependent variable that are relevant, making a multivariate test statistic useful. Edgington (1987, pp. 184–189) described a procedure for producing a multivariate test statistic that can be employed with any single-subject experimental design. It consists in transforming the measurements for each of the dependent variables into z-scores and using the sum of the z-scores for a particular measurement situation as a composite score.

REFERENCES

Barlow, D. H., & Hayes, S. C. (1979). Alternating treatments design: One strategy for comparing the effects of two treatments in a single subject. *Journal of Applied Behavior Analysis, 12,* 199–210.

Campbell, D. T., & Stanley, J. C. (1963). Experimental and quasi-experimental designs for research on teaching. In N. L. Gage (Ed.), *Handbook of research on teaching.* Chicago: Rand McNally.

Cotton, J. W. (1967). *Elementary statistical theory for behavior scientists.* Reading, MA: Addison–Wesley.

Edgington, E. S. (1980). *Randomization tests.* New York: Marcel Dekker.

Edgington, E. S. (1983). Response-guided experimentation. *Contemporary Psychology, 28,* 64–65.

Edgington, E. S. (1984). Statistics and single case analysis. In M. Hersen, R. M. Eisler, & P. M. Miller (Eds.), *Progress in behavior modification* (Vol. 16). New York: Academic Press

Edgington, E. S. (1987). *Randomization tests* (2nd ed). New York: Marcel Dekker.

Honig, W. K. (Ed.). (1966). *Operant behavior: Areas of research and application.* New York: Appleton–Century–Crofts.

Kazdin, A. E. (1982). *Single-case research designs: Methods for clinical and applied settings.* New York: Oxford University Press.

Kratochwill, T. R., & Levin, J. R. (1980). On the applicability of various data analysis procedures to the simultaneous and alternating treatment designs in behavior therapy research. *Behavioral Assessment, 2,* 353–360.

Levin, J. R., Marascuilo, L. A., & Hubert, L. J. (1978). N − nonparametric randomization tests. In T. R. Kratochwill (Ed.), Single subject research: Strategies for evaluating change. New York: Academic Press.

Marascuilo, L. A., & Busk, P. L. (1988). Combining statistics for multiple-baseline AB and replicated ABAB designs across subjects. *Behavioral Assessment, 10,* 1–28.

McCullough, J. P., Cornell, J. E., McDaniel, M. H., & Mueller, R. K. (1974). Utilization of the simultaneous treatment design to improve student behavior in a first-grade classroom. *Journal of Consulting and Clinical Psychology, 42,* 288–292.

McLeod, R. S., Taylor, D. W., Cohen, A., & Cullen, J. B. (1986). Single patient randomized clinical trial: Its use in determining optimal treatment for patient with inflammation of a Kock continent ileostomy reservoir. *Lancet, 1*(March 29), 726–728.

Siegel, S. (1956). *Nonparametric statistics for the behavioral sciences.* New York: McGraw–Hill.

Smith, C. M. (1963). Controlled observations on the single subject. *Canadian Medical Association Journal, 88,* 410–412.

Wampold, B. E., & Worsham, N. L. (1986). Randomization tests for multiple-baseline designs. *Behavioral Assessment, 8,* 135–143.

Weiss, B., Williams, J. H., Margen, S., Abrams, B., Caan, B., Citron, L. J., Cox, C., McKibben, J., Ogar, D., & Schultz, S. (1980). Behavioral responses to artificial food colors. *Science, 297,* 1487–1489.

Statistical Analysis in Single-Case Research: Issues, Procedures, and Recommendations, with Applications to Multiple Behaviors

6

Patricia L. Busk
University of San Francisco

Leonard A. Marascuilo
University of California, Berkeley

Misconceptions and misunderstandings regarding the use of statistical procedures for analyzing data from single-subject designs can be found in the research literature (cf. Barlow & Hersen, 1984). Authors have contended that statistical procedures are not appropriate for single-subject designs because the purposes of such methods are at odds with the identification of reliable intervention effects associated with individuals. The objections to the use of statistical procedures are based on the unique "clinical" significance of individual differences in single-case research, where visual inspection is the preferred method of analysis versus the between-group and within-group differences in experimental research wherein researchers use statistical procedures as the method of analysis to provide generalizations to human populations. Arguments have been presented that each individual's uniqueness contradicts the use of statistics. The very fact of variation is the chief argument for the use of statistics. If individuals responded equally to treatment, then there would be no need for statistics. "The argument that statistics cannot be used because of such variability or uniqueness is no more than a special application of an argument that one cannot learn from experience" (Chassan, 1979, p. 102).

There are statistical procedures known as *randomization tests* that focus on individual differences. Such methods have been proposed for single-case ($N = 1$) and small-sample ($N > 1$) studies by Edgington (1967, 1969, 1975a, 1975b, 1980b, 1980c, this volume), Krathocwill and Levin (1980), and by Levin, Marascuilo, and Hubert (1978). In particular, the randomization methods have been recommended as a supplement to the visual inspection method (Edgington, 1967; Gorsuch, 1983; Jones, Vaught, & Weinrott, 1977; Kazdin, 1976; Wolery & Billingsley, 1982). More recently, randomization tests have been extended by

Wampold and Worsham (1986) and Marascuilo and Busk (1988) to combine data from replicated designs in a manner that still preserves the individual differences of the single-case design used to focus on clinical practice. The purpose of combining data from replicated designs is to gain statistical power for rejecting the null hypothesis of no treatment effects that allows extending clinical decisions on individuals to populations of similar subjects.

Visual inspection, however, has long been recommended as the only method for evaluating single-case data (Baer, 1977, 1988; Baer & Parsonson, 1981; Michael, 1974; Parsonson & Baer, 1978; Sidman, 1960) and is the most commonly used method to determine single-case intervention effects. The fact that visual inspection is the predominant method of analyzing single-case research studies is supported by a review of the articles published in the *Journal of Applied Behavioral Analysis* during 1988. All of the articles involving single-case research designs used visual inspection as the method for analyzing the data. Statistical procedures were used, however, in the analysis of data from between-group designs reported in the same journal. Kratochwill and Brody (1978) conducted a survey of four behavior modification journals regarding the connection between research practices and the use of statistical inference. The four empirical research journals examined for their statistical practices were *Behavior Therapy, Behaviour Research and Therapy, Journal of Applied Behavior Analysis,* and *Journal of Behavior Therapy and Experimental Psychiatry.* The percentage of all experimental research studies using statistical inference ranged from 18% to 69%. Designs classified as single-case studies that used statistical inference ranged from a low of 4% to a high of 9%. Results from both investigations support the contention that visual inspection has been and continues to be the predominant mode for analyzing single-case data.

The reliability of visual inspection has been shown to be biased (Furlong & Wampold, 1982; Wampold & Furlong, 1981b). Results of both studies indicated that subjects trained in visual inference ignore small intervention effects that can be detected by examining the relative individual-subject variation in the data that is the object of randomization tests.

Other misconceptions and misunderstandings involve the appropriateness of parametric procedures such as the t and F tests, time-case analyses, and split-middle techniques. Serial dependency and autocorrelation in single-case studies invalidate parametric procedures such as the t and F tests and the use of split-middle techniques (Barlow & Hersen, 1984). Erroneous recommendations to use parametric procedures under the assumption of no autocorrelation in single-case research have been made by Kazdin (1984, pp. 290, 294) and Huitema (1985). These recommendations have been questioned recently and in the past by several methodologists (Busk & Marascuilo, 1988; Jones, Weinrott, & Vaught, 1978; Sharpley & Alavosius, 1988; Suen & Ary, 1987; Toothaker, Banz, Noble, Camp, & Davis, 1983). Kazdin proposed that t and F tests should be preceded by a test of serial dependency. If the tests are not significant, then parametric procedures are justified. Showing that an autocorrelation is not statistically significant is not proof that an autocorrelation does not exist (Busk & Marascuilo, 1988). In many cases, the number of observations is too small to determine whether there is an autocorrelation different from zero between errors (Suen & Ary, 1987). Such tests usually are based on too few data points, which means that most tests lack statistical power to detect a nonsignificant autocorrelation. In addition, such tests are based on data that may not reflect the autocorrelated nature of the behavior because of the duration of the interval between observations of the behavior (Busk & Marascuilo, 1988). Details regarding the violations of assumptions for parametric tests due to serial dependency are found in Busk and Marascuilo, Jones et al., Toothaker et al., and Kazdin (1984, pp. 287–290).

In this chapter, these issues are re-examined in light of recent discussions and proposed methods of analysis. In addition, procedures are described for analyzing data from multiple-baseline designs across behaviors.

VISUAL INSPECTION AS A METHOD OF ANALYZING SINGLE-CASE DATA

In visual inspection, single-case researchers are instructed to look for pronounced changes in levels of behavior and changes in trend in behavior across a phase (Barlow & Hersen, 1984). The difficulty with this recommendation is that in practice one is not always able to detect such pronounced changes reliably (DeProspero & Cohen, 1979; Furlong & Wampold, 1981, 1982; Jones et al., 1978; Wampold & Furlong, 1981b). Experimental evidence collected by Wampold and Furlong (1981b) has shown that visual inspection is unreliable in that different evaluators come to different conclusions. In a study in which visual inspection was evaluated, a group of 14 graduate students who were counselors in training and who had completed a seminar in single-case research were compared with a group of 10 graduate students who had completed two or three quarters of a multivariate statistical analysis course. The former group, trained in identifying pronounced changes, "appeared to use a scaling heuristic in which they attended to large changes in a time series regardless of the relative variation" (p. 79) and ignored small intervention effects that subjects trained in statistics identified with greater skill and ease. A follow-up study by Furlong and Wampold (1982) further confirmed the findings of the original study. One would think that the results of these studies would lead researchers performing single-case investigation away from a methodology that has been shown to have serious deficiencies in replicability.

Knapp (1983) and Bailey (1984) have proposed the use of judgmental aids or alternate charting techniques as methods to improve ratings based on visual analysis. Based on the results of experimental evidence, they found that even with additional aids visual inspection is unreliable. In particular, Knapp's conclusions supported the results of previous studies that inconsistency among subjects is present in visually appraising data. His conclusions resulted from an investigation of judgments made by behavior analysts of whether or not change had occurred from baseline to intervention. Three graphing techniques and three types of intervention were used as interpretative aids. The findings of De-Prospero and Clark (1979) and Jones et al. (1978) were documented by Bailey in his study of interrater agreement and ratings of significance on both changes in level and trend using lines of progress and semilogarithmic charts.

What is needed are procedures that can consistently detect the changes in levels of behavior and changes in trends of behavior if they are real. One solution is to supplement visual inspection with the application of randomization tests to measures of central tendency for changes in levels of behavior and to measures of slopes for changes in trends of behavior.

AUTOCORRELATED ERRORS IN SINGLE-CASE RESEARCH

There are two issues involving autocorrelated errors in single-case research. The first is the effects of the presence of autocorrelations on statistical procedures requiring independence. These effects have been recognized. The second involves the existence of autocorrelation or serial dependency in single-case data. This latter issue has been the controversial one. In social science research, the presence of a correlation between repeated observations on individuals is unquestioned, and the data analysis procedures take into consideration the correlated nature of the data (Hays, 1981, p. 402; Kerlinger, 1973, p. 247). For example, dichotomous responses to two survey questions would be analyzed using the McNemar (1947) test or dichotomous responses to the same question before or after treatment would be analyzed with the same statistical technique. For continuous variables, a repeated measures analysis of variance would be used. In single-case research, however, the existence of correlated observations is debated. On the one side, there is the position that empirical analyses of single-case data have found that there is little or no autocorrelation in typical behavioral data (Huitema, 1985). On the other side, there is the position that repeated observations on the same individual through time usually consist of measures that are not independent. "While the degree of this dependency can usually be reduced by lengthening the time interval between successive observations, it is difficult to eliminate entirely" (Holtzman, 1963, p. 200). There are two aspects of the measurement in single-case research that affect the serial dependency—one is the behavior itself and the second is the way that the behavior is assessed. Measurements made by the same observer will induce structure into the data and hence serial dependency.

Two factors must be considered when attempting to assess the magnitude of serial dependency in behavioral data. The first is the precision of the estimate of the coefficient, and the second is the power of the statistical test to determine whether the coefficient is significantly different from zero. The precision of the estimate of serial dependency is directly related to the size of the sample of behavior. This same relationship holds for power. If the sample size is small, the sample correlation will be quite variable. Because the researcher takes a sample of the behavior and does not measure the behavior to assess its continuous nature, it is not possible to assess accurately the magnitude of the serial dependency in the behavioral data.

As an illustration of this situation, consider the data reported by Holtzman (1963) on three functions over 245 successive days on a single schizophrenic patient who had been studied intensively by Mefferd and his colleagues. The Series A measurements consisted of 100 daily observations of creatinine in the urine, Perceptual Speed, and Word Association Relatedness Score. The latter two scores were from a simple mental abilities test with a large number of parallel forms that could be used for daily testing. The 100 observations on the three functions can be considered as an adequate measurement of the behavior so that any serial dependency in the three functions would be estimated with precision. The time series plotted for creatinine showed a rapid fluctuation together with an undulating trend. The correlogram indicated that the serial correlation dropped off sharply in four lags to a trivial value. Hence the amount of serial correlation is small as it disappears after four lags. The correlogram for Perceptual Speed drops off very gradually and continues in a downward trend in the negative direction, indicative of serial correlation in Perceptual Speed. The correlogram for Word Association Relatedness Score shows essentially no association. The serial correlation or lag on autocorrelation for creatinine was .60, for Perceptual Speed was .75, and for Word Association Relatedness Scores was .25. The first two are statistically significant, and the latter is nonsignificant. Estimates of the lag one autocorrelation based on the first 6, 10, 15, 30, and 50 observations were made for each of the three functions with the following results. For creatinine, the values were .22, .30, .38, .36, and .69, respectively. For Perceptual Speed, the values were $-.17$, .04, .54, .57, and .69, respectively. For Word Association Relatedness Scores, the values were $-.19$, $-.19$, .12, .31, and .38, respectively. These estimates of the lag one autocorrelation for each of the time series based on 100 observations vary widely from those obtained for each sample size considered. Confidence intervals constructed for each of the functions and each of the estimates covered the autocorrelations based on the 100 observation series, indicating that these estimates were not out of range of the original time series. For this illustration, decisions regarding the magnitude of the autocorrelated nature of the measured behavior vary, depending on the sample size, which indicates that trying to infer the "true" or underlying magnitude of serial dependency of the behavior being measured is questionable with sample sizes that are less than 50.

If the autocorrelation is tested for statistical significance, the power to detect a nonzero autocorrelation is dependent on the size of the time series as well. For the function with the nonzero autocorrelation estimate of .25, all but the estimate based on 50 observations were nonsignificant. These tests are consistent with the 100 time-series nonsignificant result. For the other two functions with statistically significant autocorrelations, those estimates based on samples of sizes 6 and 10 failed to reject the null hypothesis, which is indicative of lack of power. For the Perceptual Speed function, the autocorrelation based on the sample size of 15 also failed to reject the null hypothesis. The magnitude of the serial dependency for these two functions are indicative of strong dependency.

This illustration provides the basis for a warning that serial dependency does exist in behavioral data and that trying to detect serial dependency using small samples will not be precise and may lead to erroneous conclusions.

The selection of sample sizes of 6, 10, 15, 30, and 50 to represent typical size of behavior samples were based on the findings of Busk and Marascuilo (1988). Their data were obtained from graphed data for 44 studies published in the *Journal of Applied Behavior Analysis* from 1975 to 1985. In their study of 101 baseline phases, 47% were from samples of size 6 to 15, 38% were from samples of size 15 to 30, and only 15% were from samples of 30 or more. Generally, phases contain less than 30 observations. Sample sizes for the intervention phase were grouped into the same categories as for baseline data, and the following percentages were found: 43, for 6 to 15; 30 for 15 to 30; and 27 for 30 and more.

Busk and Marascuilo (1988) computed lag one autocorrelations for the graphed data from 44 research studies. A total of 248 independent data sets were available from the 44 studies. Of these sets, 101 were for baseline phases, 125 were for intervention phases, and 22 were for phases beyond the intervention. The major finding was that many single-case studies are based on data in which the autocorrelations tend to be larger than zero. In particular, they found that 80% of the autocorrelations were in the range of .10 to .49 for phases of size 5 to 18 observations. More importantly, 40% of the baseline sets of data produced autocorrelations greater than .25 (see p. 239 of Busk & Marascuilo), and, during the intervention phases, the percentage increased to 59. Statistical tests requiring the assumption of independence performed on data from these studies would have an inflated Type I error.

Jones et al. (1977) initially sounded a warning about the presence of autocorrelation in single-case research. They investigated serial dependency in 24 graphs of experimental data from research studies sampled from the *Journal of Applied Behavior Analysis* and found evidence of 20 significant autocorrelations. Huitema (1985) reanalyzed the Jones et al. data, claiming that baseline and intervention data were erroneously combined. Additionally he analyzed graphs from 441 other published single-case research studies, concluding that behavioral data are not autocorrelated or are lowly autocorrelated. His findings were challenged (Busk & Marascuilo, 1988; Suen, 1987; Suen & Ary, 1987). In particular, Huitema tested autocorrelations for statistical significance. These autocorrelations were based on samples of size 6 to 53 with a median of 10. As has been shown, such estimates are not precise indicators of the actual autocorrelated nature of the behavior under observation. A conclusion that behavioral data are not correlated or are correlated to a low degree cannot be justified based on data from a small sample that are not indicative of the underlying trend in the behavior. With such small sample sizes, the statistical tests of no autocorrelation have low power, and the serial dependency estimates are not precise indicators of the underlying autocorrelated nature of the behavior.

Single-case research studies are based on samples of behavior for which the test for identifying a nonzero autocorrelation as statistically significant has very low power. In addition to the inability to test for a statistically significant autocorrelation with adequate power, there is the problem with the points at which observations are made. Busk and Marascuilo (1988) and Holtzman (1963) have pointed out that data observations may be too far apart in time of measurement to detect the autocorrelated nature of the behavior. Or as has been demonstrated, the behavior may have serial dependency but based on few observations, the true dependency is unable to be estimated with precision. Many single-case research studies rely on observers to provide measurements of the behavior. Observers interject their own unique structure on the data thus adding to the serial dependency in the data. Lastly,

> The process of testing to determine if the level of autocorrelation present in a data series is significant, and then deciding on the basis of the presence or not of a significant autocorrelation whether traditional statistical procedures can be used to test for effects, is unwise, as well as not in keeping with the methodological rigour which requires that data analysis procedures are stipulated prior to data collection. (Sharpley, 1988, p. 583)

When the behavior is viewed over an extended period of time as in the example given, the dependency in the data is seen readily. If, however, only a small segment of that behavior is assessed for a research study, then it is difficult to detect empirically the serial dependency. Because of this difficulty in empirically validating the serial dependency in behavioral data, single-case researchers should analyze their data not assuming independence of observations. Parametric procedures are designed for independent, static data and have been proposed as an alternative to visual inspection of single-case data (Gentile, Roden, & Klein, 1972; Huitema, 1985; Shine & Bower, 1971). Parametric tests can be invalidated by using original observations at each time period as the unit of analysis because of significant autocorrelation (Phillips, 1983; Scheffé, 1959;

Toothaker et al., 1983). Autocorrelation poses two problems for these traditional tests: (a) Because the errors are not independent, the statistical test overestimates the number of independent sources of information (Kazdin, 1976) and (b) Positive autocorrelation can spuriously decrease the error variance and thereby creates a liberal bias, whereas negative autocorrelation can spuriously increase error variance and thereby creates a conservative bias (Hartmann et al., 1980; Kenny & Judd, 1986; Phillips, 1983; Sharpley, 1988). In particular, Gardner, Hartmann, and Mitchell (1982) demonstrated that, when there is an autocorrelation of .25, the probability of a Type I error can be misrepresented by 25% to 40% for an $\propto$ = .05 for a chi-square analysis. Phillips (1983) showed that serially correlated errors affect the analysis of variance results of systematic designs used by single-case researchers. Toothaker et al. (1983) have shown that even traditional analysis of variance F tests modified to account for autocorrelation have inflated Type I errors in the presence of autocorrelated errors. A t-test can be inflated by 110% when the autocorrelation is only .10 and as much as 435% when the autocorrelation is .90 (Sharpley, 1988, p. 583).

Scheffé (1959), in examining departures from the assumptions for the analysis of variance, concluded that lack of independence departures are the most formidable with which to cope. In addition, Scheffé (1959) has shown that, in the presence of autocorrelation of .30, the risk of a Type I error is increased from .05 to .12 and, even if the autocorrelation is as small as .20, the risk of a Type I error of .05 is doubled to .10. As the autocorrelation increases, the risk of a Type I error increases rapidly (see p. 339 of Scheffé, 1959). Crosbie (1987) provided an illustration of the effects of autocorrelation on the use of a t-test to analyze data from a two-phase, single-case study.

Single-case data should be analyzed using time-series methods or randomization tests. Time-series analysis (cf. Box & Jenkins, 1970) is a statistical procedure that can accommodate serial dependency or autocorrelated errors because the data are transformed to remove autocorrelation before a statistical test is performed. Glass, Willson, and Gottman (1975) discussed in detail time-series analysis methods for describing and for testing statistical effects of intervention in studies with repeated measurements over time. The combining of least squares regression and time-series methods in analyzing data from single-case studies is suggested by Horne, Yang, and Ware (1982).

Crosbie (1987) correctly warned that "considerable statistical expertise is required for its proper use (Glass et al., 1975; Hartmann et al., 1980), and reliable model fitting (particularly producing stationarity by differencing) requires a considerable number of data points" (p. 142). His warning has been echoed by other researchers (Kratochwill & Levin, 1980). At least 35 to 40 observations are needed for each phase in order to justify the time-series model (Box & Jenkins, 1970; Glass et al., 1975; Gottman & Glass, 1978; Horne et al., 1982).

Interested researchers should consult these references and the chapter by Richard McCleary in this volume for details on time-series methods.

UNIT-OF-ANALYSIS PROBLEM

Levin et al. (1978) discussed the problem of using original observations as the unit of analysis for autocorrelated single-case data. Their method for treating this problem is to define a *phase* as the unit of analysis and use a summary measure on each phase, provided that the summary measure is based on a sufficiently large sample size that produces autocorrelations between the summary measures that are close to zero. According to their guidelines, if the autocorrelation between adjacent observations is .50 or smaller, then nonparametric procedures based on the summary measures is justified if there are 15 or more observations per phase. If the autocorrelations are smaller than .50, then the number of observations per phase can be considerably smaller than 15. For additional information on the sample-size topic, see Table 3.1 of Levin et al. (1978, p. 179) and Marascuilo and Busk (1988, pp. 23–24).

An analogy to a study done in several classrooms at the same grade level within one school should help to illustrate the concept of "unit of analysis." Suppose that in a research study the treatments were randomly assigned to the classrooms within the school. If the students are treated individually or the treatment is tailored to each individual and students performed independently of all other students in the *same* and in *different* classrooms, then students could be the appropriate unit of analysis and the scores of each of the students would be used as the dependent variable for the analysis. If in each classroom, however, the treatment is directed to the class as a whole rather than to the individual student, then the students' performances are related to one another, and the classroom must be treated as the unit of analysis. Instead of using the scores of each student, one must use the mean or the median as a measure of performance in the classroom. In this way, the analysis of the data of the intact classroom preserves the classroom as a unit receiving the treatment. In terms of the analog, phases correspond to classrooms. If there is autocorrelation between the observations within a phase, then the analysis must be carried out at the phase level. If there should be multiple observations within a phase that are known to be statistically independent, then these writers would recommend that individual time periods be treated as the unit of analysis. In this case, the t and F statistics would be valid.

APPROPRIATE SUMMARY MEASURES FOR ANALYZING SINGLE-CASE DATA

Another issue raised by Levin et al. (1978) and Marascuilo and Busk (1988) was the appropriate summary measure for the unit of analysis. The selection of the summary measure should be based on knowledge of the behavior under investigation and the magnitude of the autocorrelation. If the autocorrelations were equal to zero, then parametric procedures such as t and F tests would be valid.

Unfortunately, autocorrelations are not zero. That is why Levin et al. argued for the phase as the unit of analysis. There is a misconception regarding the definition of the meaning of *unit of analysis*. For Levin et al., unit of analysis for most single-case studies is synonymous with the phases.

Recently, Haring and Kennedy (1988) used the term in an idiosyncratic way in that they called the summary measure or dependent variable the unit of analysis. For example, the percentage correct over a phase, percentage of opportunities meeting criterion over a phase, the number of trials to criterion that ends a phase, percentage correct with competent performance coded across a phase, and percentage correct with competent performance coded and task analysis grid are called incorrectly by Haring and Kennedy "unit of analyses" when in reality they are dependent measures made across each phase.

Selection of the appropriate summary measure for phase behavior is based upon whether the researcher is investigating changes in levels of behavior or changes in trends of the behavior. If the behavior shows only level differences, then the appropriate summary measure to be observed on each unit of analysis is a measure of central tendency, such as the mean or median of the phase. When the distributions of the phase observations are skewed, then medians may be preferred to means as they are not affected by extreme observations. If outliers are encountered, trimmed or Winsorized means may be substituted (Marascuilo & McSweeney, 1977, pp. 420–421).

Sometimes the behavior may be subject to carry-over effects from one phase to another. If it is known that the behavior is affected in this manner, then the observations affected by the carry-over would not be used in determining the summary measure. For example, if the first few observations in the B phase of an ABAB design have a carry-over component, then these first few observations should be removed before the determination of the measure of central tendency used as the dependent variable. With behavior that shows trend differences, the appropriate dependent variable would be the slope of the best-fitting straight line to the observations within a phase. When there are carry-over effects operating in a study where effects are exhibited in changes in trend, the effects would be observed by an A phase slope continued over to the initial B phase observations. If such a trend is noted, then these initial observations should be eliminated from the computation of the slope for the B phase. Observations that are based on success or failure for each trial can be summarized as the proportion of successes or the proportion of failures.

In the case of delayed effects, the first few observations of the intervention phase could be removed from the computation of the mean values. Determining the number of values to eliminate from the computations must be done a priori to the data collection. Using this method to eliminate delayed effects would require additional observations within a phase. Another way to reduce the impact of carry-over effects on the proposed statistical test is to space observations far apart in time (Edgington, 1980a).

Another problem that may exist in a time series is that a researcher finds that stability in the A phase takes more trails for one subject than another. One way to handle this problem is to eliminate from the computation of the A phase mean the initial trials. Again, however, it would be important to specify the cutoff point before data collection.

The use of summary measures may be questioned in terms of loss of information. This is not the case, however, as summary measures are more precise in conveying information regarding intervention effects than individual observations. The precision of the summary measure is based on the squared standard error of the measure. For an autocorrelation of size ρ, the squared standard error of the mean is given by

$$\sigma_{\bar{x}}^2 = \sigma_x^2[(1/N) + \rho(N - 1)/N]$$

and for large sample sizes $\sigma_{\bar{x}}^2$ is approximately equal to

$$\sigma_x^2[1/N + \rho],$$

which is considerably smaller than σ_x^2, the squared standard deviation for the original observations.

RANDOMIZATION TESTS FOR SINGLE-CASE AB AND ABAB DESIGNS

As a supplement to visual inspection, randomization tests that utilize individual data have been proposed by Edgington (1967, 1969, 1975a, 1975b, 1980b, 1980c, 1987), by Kratochwill and Levin (1980), and by Levin et al. (1978). More recently Wampold and Worsham (1986) and Marascuilo and Busk (1988) have extended these randomization tests to multiple-baseline and reversal single-case designs across subjects. Limited use has been made, however, of randomization tests (Ewart, Burnett, & Taylor, 1983; Hunt, 1988/1989; Ischi, 1980; Kratochwill, 1978; Kratochwill & Brody, 1978; Sacks, 1988). The validity of randomization tests has been discussed by Edgington (1980c) and Levin et al. (1978).

Randomization procedures can be used with original data or with ranks. With summary measures derived from the original observations, more detailed computational work is involved, whereas using rank procedures reduces the amount of computation. Test statistics, decision rules, and significance probabilities are easy to generate for both original and rank data. For single-case studies, these methods have been illustrated by Wampold and Furlong (1981a). For replicated single-case studies, Marascuilo and Busk (1988) and Wampold and Worsham (1986) provided step-by-step illustrations of the combined randomization tests across subjects. One of the advantages of replication is that a researcher can develop tests with acceptable Type I error rates. In many cases, with two or more subjects, risks of Type I error rates less than .05 can be generated and normal approximations to the exact probability distributions can be utilized.

The use of ranks in the randomization procedures has an added benefit in that ranks can be employed with subjects do not provide comparable data on the same scale of measurement. For example, the measurements may differ across subjects, because the targeted behaviors may be different for each subject. In any case, the same underlying characteristic or behavior must be observed.

One might think that the use of ranks results in a loss of information. The same theory that holds for the comparison of the rank tests to normal curve tests applies here. For example, if tests based on the normal distribution are replaced by ranked data and the normal distribution assumptions are valid, the loss in power is less than 5%. The power efficiency of the rank tests relative to normal curve tests is equal to $3/\pi = .955$. Further details on this topic may be found in Lehmann (1975, pp. 76–81).

If the underlying variables are compact about the mean, a more powerful test can be obtained by using normal scores in place of ranks (Marascuilo & McSweeney, 1977, p. 278).

The combined randomization methods are used whenever a single-case design has been replicated with independent subjects. If the data from the two or more subjects are related in any way, these procedures cannot be used to analyze information pooled across the subjects. For example, husbands and wives observed over time in a counseling situation could not have their data treated collectively if the information were correlated. Information across husbands could be pooled as could the information across wives, which provides data for two separate analyses.

Random assignment of intervention is required for the AB design. The random intervention point is not necessary for the ABAB design. What would be needed is a stable estimate of the summary measure. As has been discussed, the number of observations per phase that would be required to generate a stable estimate depends on the magnitude of the autocorrelation. Because the value of the autocorrelation is unknown and not able to be estimated (Busk & Marascuilo, 1988), at least 10 to 15 observations per phase should yield a stable estimate.

If a researcher used a random intervention point for each B phase in the replicated ABAB design, then the treatment would be delivered in a time-lagged fashion across the subjects. Such a design would be called a multiple-baseline ABAB design across subjects.

To combine data across multiple subjects, one must be certain that the treatment effects are in the same direction. In other words, there must not be a disordinal (crossover) subject by treatment interaction, otherwise the combining procedure is invalid.

Additional information regarding the summary measures for the combined randomization tests can be found in Marascuilo and Busk (1988).

The use of randomization tests and combined randomization tests are not restricted to AB and ABAB designs. These methods can be extended to accommodate any number of designs that researchers use. For example, an AB design with a follow-up can be treated as a planned analysis where three randomization tests are performed: a randomization test for the A and B phases, a randomization test for the A and follow-up phases, and a randomization test for the B and follow-up phases. The Type I error can be controlled using Dunn's (1961) procedure (see Marascuilo & Serlin, 1988, for details regarding the use of Dunn's method and Sacks, 1988, for an application of the randomization procedure for this design). Designs where two treatments (B and C) are applied in a replicated design and then reversed (C and B) for half of the subjects can be handled in a planned manner. The randomization tests for those subjects with the same treatment pattern can be combined using the procedures referred by Marascuilo and Busk (1988). Again, the error rate should be controlled for each of the three individual randomization tests: A with B, A with C, and B with C or A with C, A with B, and C with B for the reversed interventions.

Hypotheses regarding trends in the data have been tested with randomization procedures (see Levin et al., 1978; Marascuilo & Busk, 1988). Such tests are usually more powerful than the ABAB randomization tests.

In addition to randomization tests for analyzing single-case data, Edgington (1982) has described how nonparametric tests can be used for multiple schedule designs (or "alternating treatments designs," as referred to by Barlow & Hersen, 1984, pp. 254–256). Application of Wilcoxon matched-pairs, signed-ranks test, the Mann–Whitney U test, the Sign test, and the Fisher's exact test are illustrated for research studies where there is more than one possible source of a treatment or reinforcement that alternates during the course of the experiment.

Randomization procedures have been criticized by Kazdin (1980, 1984) as not being of utility to single-case researchers in the analyses of results. In particular, he specified that

> [w]ithout consistently rapid reversals in performance, differences between A and B conditions may not be detected. In situations where performance does not reverse, where there is a carryover effect from one condition to the next, or where attempting to reverse behavior is undesirable for clinical or ethical reasons, use of the randomization test may be limited. (Kazdin, 1984, p. 307)

Whereas this conclusion may hold in some studies, it cannot be construed to mean that it holds for all studies. In fact, it is shown through an example that these criticisms are not valid for a specific set of data where differences across phases are small.

RANK PROCEDURES FOR SINGLE-CASE, MULTIPLE-BASELINE DESIGNS ACROSS BEHAVIORS

For replicated designs, Marascuilo and Busk (1988) have illustrated combined randomization tests for original and ranked data. Often in single-case research, data are collected on more than one behavior to assess treatment effectiveness across behaviors. If a researcher is interested in a test of the null hypothesis that the treatment was effective across the measured behaviors, then an extension of the Marascuilo and Busk (1988) procedure could be used. In this section, we present a step-by-step illustration of the extension of their procedure to multiple behaviors. The extension is valid only for data converted to ranks.

The restriction to ranks is based on the fact that, if the scales for the summary measures vary across behaviors, differences across phases between summary measures are not commensurate across behaviors. In addition, the use of ranks simplifies the statistical theory.

To test for treatment effectiveness across behaviors, the behaviors must all be measuring the same underlying construct, as required in meta-analysis (Hedges & Olkin, 1985, p. xv; Marascuilo, Busk, & Serlin, 1988, p. 69). Behaviors measuring different constructs must not be combined either within or between subjects.

Typically in single-case research, the case are not selected randomly. They are selected, observed, and the treatment is applied to each subject after a search for appropriate subjects. Internal validity can be satisfied for the study, but external validity involving the generalization to a larger population is probably always questionable. In single-subject research, great detail is provided regarding the characteristics of the subjects. Therefore, the generalizations to a larger population would be to those individuals similar to the subjects in the research study.

Two rank procedures are presented: one for a replicated AB multiple-baseline design across behaviors and one for a replicated ABAB multiple-baseline design across behaviors. These methods for analyzing single-case data can be extended to other replicated designs. The extension follows the methods described in a later section for replicated ABC designs and an AB design with a follow-up.

A. *Rank procedure for the replicated AB multiple-baseline design across behaviors.* Consider the following hypothetical study patterned after the study by Hunt (1988/1989) designed to help determine whether the motivation that is generated when well-established behavior chains are interrupted is related to environmental contingencies or whether a major source of motivation is reinstatement of a predicted sequence of events. A multiple-baseline across 4 subjects with a simultaneous treatment design was used to compare the acquisition of communicative responses during traditional instruction (A phase) and interrupted chain training (B phase). The initiation of the B phase was randomly assigned for each of the 4 subjects and each of the behaviors. The proportion of correct responses during each of the phases was the dependent variable. For each subject, three behaviors specific to each individual were targeted and assessed. Results of the treatment for each of the 4 subjects on the three responses are presented in Table 6.1.

Each of the three responses could be analyzed separately using a combined Edgington randomization test across subjects (Marascuilo & Busk, 1988). If a

TABLE 6.1
Proportion of Correct Responses During Phases 1 and 2 for Four Subjects

Subject	Response	Item Requested	A Phase		B Phase		Ranks
			p_A	p_B	R_A	R_A	d
Hiep	1	basketball	.00	.80	1	2	+1
	2	key to locker	.00	.68	1	2	+1
	3	tape recorder	.00	.36	1	2	+1
Total difference							+3
Yung	1	vending machine	.08	.86	1	2	+1
	2	trash can	.00	.15	1	2	+1
	3	game	.08	.45	1	2	+1
Total difference							+3
Manora	1	cup of tea	.00	.29	1	2	+1
	2	key to locker	.05	.29	1	2	+1
	3	photo album	.10	.11	1	2	+1
Total difference							+3
Teresa	1	snack item	.14	.82	1	2	+1
	2	key to locker	.18	.39	1	2	+1
	3	game	.11	.44	1	2	+1
Total difference							+3

test across behaviors were desired, however, Edgington's method cannot be used. In general, Edgington's randomization method of analysis will be more powerful than the one to be illustrated here. The rationale for using the method of combining behaviors with the AB design is that it can be readily extended to the ABAB design.

Let the summary measure for this study be the proportion of correct responses within a phase. Using a summary statistic avoids the problem of autocorrelated behaviors within a phase, provided the autocorrelations and sample sizes satisfy the recommendations made by Levin et al. (1978).

To test the null hypothesis that there is no treatment effect or no difference between traditional instruction and interrupted behavior chain procedures, the summary measures are ranked for each behavior across phases; then the difference between the phase ranks is obtained. For the first subject Hiep, the difference in the ranks for each of the three responses is $+1$, with a resulting total difference of $+3$. This total difference or the number of positive differences can be used as a criterion for testing the null hypothesis. Under the null hypothesis, the number of positive differences has a binomial distribution with $p = \frac{1}{2}$. Thus, one can use the Sign test within each subject (Marascuilo & Serlin, 1988, pp.

170–173). In addition, information across subjects can be pooled, making use of the combined Sign test (see Marascuilo & McSweeney, 1977, p. 627).

Under the null hypothesis of no intervention effects, the proportion of successes could be larger in either the intervention phase or the baseline phase. In addition, under the null hypothesis the ranks assigned to the summary measures of behaviors are independent so that the correlation coefficients between phases are theoretically equal to zero. This condition would not be expected under the alternative. Under the alternative, the ranks assigned to the summary measures of behaviors should be collected and a large proportion of successes should be present in the intervention phase. Thus, it is sensible to test the null hypothesis that the probability of a positive difference in the two phases is equal to $\frac{1}{2}$ versus the alternative hypothesis that the probability of a positive difference between the two phases is greater than $\frac{1}{2}$.

The Sign test uses as its criterion for deciding whether or not to reject the null hypothesis an index of success or failure, that is, a dichotomous outcome. When the differences in ranks across the two phases is obtained, the resulting measure is addressed in a dichotomous way by referring to the number of positive or negative differences and not to the magnitude of the difference. The number of positive differences can be considered as the number of successes, and the number of negative differences can be considered as the number of failures. For 3 response behaviors, there is only one outcome that is compatible with the alternative hypothesis. It is 3 positive signs. For this outcome, the probability of rejecting the null hypothesis is $(\frac{1}{2})^3$ or .125. With 2 phases and 3 behaviors, statistical power is lacking to reject the null hypothesis. By combining the results for one or more subjects, the probability of rejecting the null hypothesis can be increased, provided that there is no interaction between treatment and behaviors.

For the remaining 3 subjects, each of their responses resulted in a positive difference. Across all 4 subjects and the 3 response behaviors, the number of positive signs is 12. Because of the independence under the null hypothesis, the critical values for the Sign test (see Marascuilo & Serlin, 1988, p. 756) can be used to determine the rejection region. In this case, the rejection region for $\alpha =$ .05 is to reject the null hypothesis if 10, 11, or 12 positive differences are present. Because there were 12 positive differences, the null hypothesis is rejected at the .05 level, and it is concluded that the intervention has been successful across the 12 item requests, that is, the proportion of correct responses under the interrupted behavior chain procedures is greater than under the traditional procedure.

It is important to recognize that the critical region for the Sign test is constructed under the assumption that the null hypothesis is true, that the probability of a positive difference is $\frac{1}{2}$, and that the ranks of the summary measures across behaviors for each subject are independent. Under the alternative hypothesis, the last assumption is clearly in question. If one views this as a problem, one can treat the subject as the unit of analysis and define the success or failure dependent variable strictly in terms of the overall pattern for each subject. The overall pattern of positive and negative differences for an individual subject would be considered positive if the number of positive differences is greater then the number of negative differences. The overall pattern of differences would be considered negative if the number of negative differences were greater than the number of positive differences. For this example using the subject as the unit of analysis, the new criterion would be four positive differences for which the significance probability is $(1/2)^4$ or .0625. The null hypothesis could be rejected if the level of significance was set at .10. If the number of subjects were increased to five, then the chance for statistical significance at the .05 level is possible.

B. *Rank procedure for the ABAB replicated multiple-baseline design across behaviors.* The extension to the ABAB design is straightforward. After an appropriate summary measure is obtained for each phase, the measures are ranked for each behavior and for each subject. The ranks 1, 2, 3, and 4 are assigned to the phases for each behavior. This time the ranks for the two A and the two B phases are summed and the difference between these two sums is used in the test of the null hypothesis, that is,

$$d = (R_{B1} + R_{B2}) - (R_{A1} + R_{A2}).$$

For a given behavior under the null hypothesis, all assignments of the four ranks are equally likely and given by $P! = 4! = 24$, where P is the number of phases. These 24 permutations with the associated d are listed in Table 6.2. The d value for the first permutation is given by

$$d = (2 + 4) - (1 + 3) = 2.$$

Each of the permutations has an associated probability of $1/P! = 1/24 = .0417$. The critical region for rejecting the null hypothesis is determined from this distribution, which is summarized in Table 6.3. There is no acceptable critical region for one subject and one behavior as each of the d values has an associated probability greater than .05. For this method, there would be more than one behavior so that the d values for each behavior would be summed and used as the criterion for deciding whether to reject the null hypothesis.

The randomization distribution for 2 behaviors is found in Table 6.4. Frequencies associated with each D value are presented in Table 6.5. Probabilities corresponding to each D value are found by adding all of the frequencies associated with the D value and dividing by the total possible number of frequencies (576). A value of $D = 4$ could be obtained in three ways: $d_1 = 4$ and $d_2 = 0$, $d_1 = 2$ and $d_2 = 2$, and $d_1 = 0$ and $d_2 = 4$. The corresponding probability for $D = d_1 + d_2 = 4$ is

$$P = (32 + 16 + 32)/576 = 80/576 = .1389.$$

The remaining probabilities are found in Table 6.6. The decision rule for a one-tailed test, based on $\alpha = .05$, is

TABLE 6.2
Permutation Distribution of Ranks for ABAB Design

Permutation						
A_1	B_1	A_2	B_2	$(R_{B1} + R_{B2})$	$(R_{A1} + R_{B2})$	d
1	2	3	4	6	4	2
1	2	4	3	5	5	0
1	3	2	4	7	3	4
1	3	4	2	5	5	0
1	4	2	3	7	3	4
1	4	3	2	6	4	2
2	1	3	4	5	5	0
2	1	4	3	4	6	-2
2	3	1	4	7	3	4
2	3	4	1	4	6	-2
2	4	1	3	7	3	4
2	4	3	1	5	5	0
3	1	2	4	5	5	0
3	1	4	2	3	7	-4
3	2	1	4	6	4	2
3	2	4	1	3	7	-4
3	4	1	2	6	4	2
3	4	2	1	5	5	0
4	1	2	3	4	6	-2
4	1	3	2	3	7	-4
4	2	1	3	5	5	0
4	2	3	1	3	7	-4
4	3	1	2	5	5	0
4	3	2	1	4	6	-2

TABLE 6.3
Probability Distribution for d

d	Frequency	Probability
-4	4	.1667
-2	4	.1667
0	8	.3333
2	4	.1667
4	4	.1667
Total	24	1.0000

TABLE 6.4
The Randomization Distribution for Combining Two Behaviors in an ABAB Design

d_1	-4	-2	0	2	4
d_2					
-4	-8	-6	-4	-2	0
-2	-6	-4	-2	0	2
0	-4	-2	0	2	4
2	-2	0	2	4	6
4	0	2	4	6	8

TABLE 6.5
Frequencies Associates with the Randomization Distribution for Combining Two Behaviors
in an ABAB Design

d_1	-4	-2	0	2	4
f	4	4	8	4	4
d_2 f					
-4 4	16	16	32	16	16
-2 4	16	16	32	16	16
0 8	32	32	64	32	32
2 4	16	16	32	16	16
4 4	16	16	32	16	16

DR: Reject the null hypothesis if $D = 8$.

In this case, the actual risk of a Type I error is $16/576 = .0278$.

Like combining statistics for multiple-baseline replicated designs across sub jects, the randomization distribution for two behaviors can be approximated by a normal distribution, based on the results of the Lilliefors (1967) test. But because the number of outcomes is so small, it is not possible to generate critical values that correspond to nominal α values. Hence the use of the normal approximation for 2 behaviors is not recommended. The distribution for 3 behaviors is found in the same manner as for 2 behaviors (see Table 6.4). The D values and their corresponding probabilities are found in Table 6.7. For 3 behaviors, the one-tailed, $\alpha = .05$, decision rule is given by

DR: Reject the null hypothesis if $D = 10$ or 12.

The actual risk of a Type I error is $\alpha = (64 + 192)/13824 = .0185$. As for 2 behaviors, the Lilliefors test results indicate that the normal approximation could be used, but it is not recommended for the same reason given for two behaviors. For four or more behaviors, the normal approximation is acceptable.

For one behavior over P phases, the expected value for d is

$$E(d) = 0.$$

TABLE 6.6
Probability Distribution for D Based on Combining Data for Two Behaviors

$D = d_1 + d_2$	Frequency	Probability
-8	16	.0278
-6	32	.0556
-4	80	.1389
-2	96	.1667
0	128	.2222
2	96	.1667
4	80	.1389
6	32	.0556
8	16	.0278
Total	576	1.0000

TABLE 6.7
Probability Distribution for Combining Three Behaviors in an ABAB Design

D	Frequency	Probability
-12	64	.0005
-10	192	.0139
-8	576	.0417
-6	1024	.0741
-4	1728	.1250
-2	2112	.1528
0	2432	.1758
2	2112	.1528
4	1728	.1250
6	1024	.0741
8	576	.0417
10	192	.0139
12	64	.0005
Total	13,824	1.0000

Also under the null hypothesis,

$$\sigma_R^2 = (P^2 - 1)/12.$$

In addition, the autocorrelation is

$$\rho = -1/(P - 1)$$

so that the variance of d is given by

$$\text{Var}(d) = P[(P^2 - 1)/12][P/(P - 1)].$$

For four phases,

$$\text{Var}(d) = 4[(4^2 - 1)/12][4/(4 - 1)] = 20/3.$$

As a consequence for B behaviors and P phases, the expected value of $D = d_1 + d_2 + \ldots + d_B$ is given by

$$E(D) = 0$$

and $\text{Var}(D) = BP[(P^2 - 1)/12][P/(P - 1)]$.

To illustrate the test of no effect of treatment across behaviors, consider the data of Table 6.8. The figures in this table come from a hypothetical study based on the dissertation research of Sacks (1988). Sacks examined the effectiveness of implementing a peer-mediated, social-skills training strategy with elementary-aged visually handicapped students who were served in resource room programs. Through a multiple-baseline design across behaviors, changes in duration of gaze measured in seconds, number of positive initiations, and frequency of joining group activities served as the outcome variables that were evaluated for the experimental condition of peer-mediated. The average of a behavior over the

TABLE 6.8
Hypothetical Data for Three Subjects and Three Behaviors Collected Using an ABAB Design

Subject	Behavior	Phase Means				Phase Length				Ranks				
		A_1	B_1	A_2	B_2	A_1	B_1	A_2	B_2	R_{A1}	R_{B1}	R_{A2}	R_{B2}	d
1	Duration of gaze (seconds)	3.2	5.1	3.6	4.9	11	8	6	4	1	4	2	3	4
	No. of positive social initiations	2.4	6.9	4.4	5.2	15	4	5	5	1	4	2	3	4
	Freq. of joining in group activities	2.1	3.0	2.9	3.2	7	12	7	6	1	3	2	4	4
Rank Total D														12
2	Duration of gaze (seconds)	1.5	3.0	3.2	5.9	15	6	4	6	1	2	3	4	2
	No. of positive social initiations	3.1	4.0	4.2	4.9	7	13	6	4	1	2	3	4	2
	Freq. of joining in group activities	2.7	3.8	3.2	3.5	11	10	4	7	1	4	2	3	4
Rank Total D														8
3	Duration of gaze (seconds)	3.5	4.2	2.5	4.0	11	8	6	4	2	4	1	3	4
	No. of positive social initiations	1.3	6.0	4.0	6.1	7	12	5	7	1	3	2	4	4
	Freq. of joining in group activities	1.5	6.3	2.5	5.5	16	3	6	5	1	4	2	3	4
Rank Total D														12
Total of ranks across subjects														32

sessions within a phase provided an appropriate summary measure. Three students were the subjects of this investigation. The introduction of behaviors for training were counterbalanced across participants and were introduced weekly over 12 training sessions. Sacks collected social validation data from nonhandicapped peers. Also, regular classroom teachers were employed to help substantiate the positive outcomes resulting from the social skills training.

Consider the data for Subject one. We begin by ranking the phase means for each behavior separately. For Subject one's duration of gaze, the four means are 3.2, 5.1, 3.6, and 4.9, which are assigned the rank values of 1, 4, 2, and 3, respectively. For this behavior, the value of d is

$$d = (4 + 3) - (1 + 2) = 4.$$

The values for the remaining 2 behaviors for Subject one are reported in Table 6.7. For this subject, D is

$$D = d_1 + d_2 + d_3 = 4 + 4 + 4 = 12.$$

D is compared with the distribution of values presented in Table 6.7. For a one-tailed alternative, which states that the effects of intervention are positive the $\alpha = .05$ decision rule is given by

DR: Reject the null hypothesis of no treatment effects
    across the three behaviors if $D = 10$ or 12.

For Subject one, the null hypothesis is rejected, and it is concluded that the intervention has had a positive effect across the 3 behaviors. For the remaining 2 subjects, $D_2 = 8$ and $D_3 = 12$. The null hypothesis is rejected also for Subject three but not for Subject two. As before, if one views this as a problem, one can treat the subject as the unit of analysis and define the success or failure dependent variable strictly in terms of the overall pattern for each subject.

To combine data across S subjects and across B behaviors in a study, the criterion variable is defined as

$$L = D_1 + D_2 + \ldots + D_S.$$

When the null hypothesis of no effect of treatment is true, the expected value of L is

$$E(L) = 0.$$

and

$$\text{Var}(L) = S\text{Var}(D) = SBP[(P^2 - 1)/12][P/(P - 1)].$$

For the data of Table 6.7,

$$L = D_1 + D_2 + D_3 = 12 + 8 + 12 = 32.$$

and

$$\text{Var}(L) = 3(3) \ (3)[(4^2 - 1)/12][4/(4 - 1)]$$

$$= 60.$$

Here the normal approximation can be justified. In particular, the test statistic that is used to evaluate the null hypothesis is given by

$$Z = [(L \pm 1) - E(L)]/ \ \text{Var}(L),$$

where ± 1 is the correction for continuity because the distance between adjacent values is 2 units (see Table 6.6) and the correction is half of the distance between adjacent values. The value of one is added if $L < E(L)$, and one is subtracted if $L > E(L)$. The value of Z is compared with the critical value from the standard normal distribution, which under the null hypothesis has a mean of zero and a standard deviation of one.

For the data of Table 6.7,

$$Z = [(32 - 1) - 0]/ \ 60$$

$$= 4.13.$$

With $\alpha = .05$, the one-tailed decision rule determined from the standard normal distribution is

DR: Reject the null hypothesis of no treatment effect if $Z > 1.645$.

For 3 behaviors and 3 subjects, the null hypothesis of no treatment effect across subjects and behaviors is rejected. It is concluded that the treatment was effective.

It can be shown that the use of the normal approximation for determining the critical value for rejection of the null hypothesis is valid for four or more behaviors observed on one subject. In addition, the normal approximation provides Type I error control for testing the null hypothesis by a combined test with at least 2 subjects observed on at least 2 behaviors.

SUMMARY

Based on the information presented in this chapter, there is evidence to support the use of statistical procedures for *supplementing* visual inspection in the analysis of single-case data. Statistical methods known as randomization tests deal with the individual nature of single-case data unlike the statistical procedures that deal with group variation. Many single-case methodologists have raised objections to the use of group procedures.

The autocorrelated nature of repeated-measures data is widely accepted in the fields of education and psychology. Researchers in those fields use procedures that take into account the correlation between observations when analyzing data. Single-case data are repeated measures on one individual and hence a special case of the usual repeated-measures design. For this special case, the correlated nature of observations would be recognized by researchers in the fields of education and psychology.

In behavioral research, the concept of serial dependency in the data has been debated. Repeated observations on a single subject generate data that are difficult to analyze from a statistical point of view. The difficulty arises because one cannot assume with any degree of certainty that errors between observations made close in time for a single individual are statistically independent. Statistical proof is difficult to obtain, because the behavior is observed over a small number of time points and does not provide a basis for a precise estimate of the underlying serial dependency. Experience suggests that performance deviations are neither *random* nor due to chance alone. Fluctuations in observed behavior are influenced primarily by characteristics within the individual and not by the treatment applied by the researcher. The use of observers to record the behavior in single-subject studies also induces structure into the data and hence adds to the serial nature of the data.

In light of these arguments, if a single-subject researcher still is tempted to test the data from a single-case research study in order to determine whether the autocorrelation is statistically significant to justify the use of traditional statistical procedures, then all statistical methods must be specified before the study is undertaken. To be in keeping with methodological rigor, the decision to employ any statistical processes must be made before any data are collected (Sharpley, 1988, p. 583).

A variety of procedures can be used, depending on the type of design and on the number of observations collected. If the number of observations per phase is large (35 or more per phase), then time-series analyses are justified. Otherwise, nonparametric and randomization tests are recommended for analyzing data from replicated and nonreplicated single-case studies. These latter procedures are much simpler to understand and to carry out than time-series methods. It is our position that single-case researchers should no longer hesitate to supplement their visual analyses with statistical methods. In this chapter, guidelines for the use of such statistical procedures have been presented, along with references where these methods have been illustrated step by step.

REFERENCES

Baer, D. M. (1977). Perhaps it would be better not to know everything. *Journal of Applied Behavior Analysis, 10,* 167–172.

Baer, D. M. (1988). An autocorrelated commentary on the need for a different debate. *Behavioral Assessment, 10,* 295–297.

Baer, D. M., & Parsonson, B. S. (1981). Applied changes from steady state: Still a problem in the visual analysis of data. In C. M. Bradshaw, E. Szobadi, & C. F. Lowe (Eds.), *Quantification of steady-state operant behavior*. Amsterdam: Elsevier.

Bailey, D. B., Jr. (1984). Effects of lines of progress and semilogarithmic charts on ratings of charted data. *Journal of Applied Behavior Analysis, 17,* 359–365.

Barlow, D. H., & Hersen, M. (Eds.). (1984). *Single case experimental* designs: Strategies for studying behavior change (2nd ed.). New York: Pergamon Press.

Box, G. E. P., & Jenkins, G. M. (1970). *Time-series analysis: Forecasting and control.* New York: Cambridge University Press.

Busk, P. L., & Marascuilo, L. A. (1988). Autocorrelation in single-subject research: A counterargument to the myth of no autocorrelation. *Behavioral Assessment, 10,* 229–242.

Chassan, J. B. (1979). *Research design in clinical psychology and psychiatry* (2nd ed.). New York: Irvington Publications.

Crosbie, J. (1987). The inability of the binomial test to control Type I error with single-subject data. *Behavioral Assessment, 9,* 141–150.

DeProspero, A., & Cohen, S. (1979). Inconsistent visual analysis of intrasubject data. *Journal of Applied Behavior Analysis, 12,* 513–519.

Dunn, O. J. (1961). Multiple comparisons among means. *Journal of the American Statistical Association, 56,* 52–64.

Edgington, E. S. (1967). Statistical inference from N = 1 experiments. *Journal of Psychology, 65,* 195–199.

Edgington, E. S. (1969). Approximate randomization tests. *Journal of Psychology, 72,* 143–179.

Edgington, E. S. (1975a). Randomization tests for one-subject operant experiments. *Journal of Psychology, 90,* 57–68.

Edgington, E. S. (1975b). Randomization test for predicted trends. *Canadian Psychological Review, 16,* 49–53.

Edgington, E. S. (1980a). Overcoming obstacles to single-subject experimentation. *Journal of Educational Statistics, 5,* 261–267.

Edgington, E. S. (1980b). *Randomization tests.* New York: Marcel Dekker.

Edgington, E. S. (1980c). Validity of randomization tests for one-subject experiments. *Journal of Educational Statistics, 5,* 235–251.

Edgington, E. S. (1982). Nonparametric tests for single-subject multiple schedule experiments. *Behavioral Assessment, 4,* 83–91.

Edgington, E. S. (1987). Randomized single-subject experiments and statistical tests. *Journal of Counseling Psychology, 34,* 437–442.

Ewart, C. K., Burnett, K. F., & Taylor, C. B. (1983). Communication behaviors that affect blood pressure: An A–B–A–B analysis of marital interaction. *Behavior Modification, 7,* 331–334.

Furlong, M. J., & Wampold, B. E. (1981). Visual analysis of single-subject studies by school psychologists. *Psychology in the Schools, 18,* 80–86.

Furlong, M. J., & Wampold, B. E. (1982). Intervention effects and relative variation as dimensions in experts' use of visual inspection. *Journal of Applied Behavioral Analysis, 15,* 415–421.

Gardner, W., Hartmann, D. P., & Mitchell, C. (1982). The effects of serial dependency on the use of chi-square for analyzing sequential data in dyadic interactions. *Behavioral Assessment, 4,* 75–82.

Gentile, J. R., Roden, A. H., & Klein, R. D. (1972). An analysis-of-variance model for the intrasubject replication design. *Journal of Applied Behavior Analysis, 5,* 193–198.

Glass, G. V., Willson, V. L., & Gottman, J. M. (1975). *Design and analysis of time-series experiments.* Boulder: Colorado Associated University Press.

Gorsuch, R. L. (1983). Three methods for analyzing limited time-series (N of 1) data. *Behavioral Assessment, 5,* 141–154.

Gottman, J. M., & Glass, G. V. (1978). Analysis of interrupted time-series experiments. In T. R.

Kratochwill (Ed.), *Single-subject research: Strategies for evaluating change*. New York: Academic Press.

Haring, T. G., & Kennedy, C. H. (1988). Units of analysis in task-analytic research. *Journal of Applied Behavior Analysis, 21*, 207–215.

Hartmann, D. P., Gottman, J. M., Jones, R. R., Gardner, W., Kazdin, A. E., & Vaught, R. S. (1980). Interrupted time-series and its application to behavioral data. *Journal of Applied Behavior Analysis, 13*, 543–559.

Hays, W. L. (1981). *Statistics* (2nd ed.). New York: Holt, Rinehart, & Winston.

Hedges, L. V., & Olkin, I. (1985). *Statistical methods for meta-analysis*. Orlando, FL: Academic Press.

Holtzman, W. H. (1963). Statistical methods for the study of change in the single case. In C. W. Harris (Ed.), *Problems in measuring change* (pp. 199–211). Madison: University of Wisconsin Press.

Horne, G. P., Yang, M. C. K., & Ware, W. B. (1982). Time series analysis for single-subject designs. *Psychological Bulletin, 91*, 178–189.

Huitema, B. E. (1985). Autocorrelation in applied behavior analysis: A myth. *Behavioral Analysis, 7*, 107–110.

Hunt, P. C. (1988/1989). Increasing motivation with an interrupted behavior chain strategy (Doctoral dissertation, University of California, Berkeley, with San Francisco State University, 1988). *Dissertation Abstracts International, 50*, 863A.

Ischi, N. (1980). Analyse des fondements technologiques de la modification des contingencies sociales en classe. *Revue Suissage Psychologie, 39*, 113–132.

Jones, R. R., Vaught, R. S., & Weinrott, M. (1977). Time-series analysis and operant research. *Journal of Applied Behavior Analysis, 10*, 151–166.

Jones, R. R., Weinrott, M., & Vaught, R. S. (1978). Effects of serial dependency on the agreement between visual and statistical inference. *Journal of Applied Behavior Analysis, 11*, 277–283.

Kazdin, A. E. (1976). Statistical analyses for single-case experimental designs. In M. Hersen & D. H. Barlow (Eds.), *Single case experimental designs: Strategies for behavioral change*. New York: Pergamon Press.

Kazdin, A. E. (1980). Obstacles in using randomization tests in single-case experimentation. *Journal of Educational Statistics, 5*, 253–260.

Kazdin, A. E. (1984). Statistical analyses for single-case experimental designs. In D. H. Barlow & M. Hersen (Eds.), *Single case experimental designs: Strategies for studying behavior change* (2nd ed., pp. 285–324). New York: Pergamon Press.

Kenny, D. A., & Judd, C. M. (1986). Consequences of violating the independence assumptions in analysis of variance. *Psychological Bulletin, 99*, 422–431.

Kerlinger, F. N. (1973). *Foundations of behavioral research* (2nd ed.). New York: Holt, Rinehart, & Winston.

Knapp, T. J. (1983). Behavior analysts' visual appraisal of behavior change in graphic display. *Behavioral Assessment, 5*, 155–164.

Kratochwill, T. R. (Ed.). (1978). *Single subject research: Strategies for Evaluating change*. New York: Academic Press.

Kratochwill, T. R., & Brody, G. H. (1978). Single subject designs: A perspective on the controversy over employing statistical inference and implications for research and training in behavior modification. *Behavior Modification, 2*, 291–307.

Kratochwill, T. R., & Levin, J. R. (1980). On the applicability of various data analysis procedures to the simultaneous and alternating treatment desings in behavior therapy research. *Behavioral Assessment, 2*, 353–360.

Lehmann, E. I. (1975). *Nonparametrics: Statistical methods based on ranks*. San Francisco: Holden-day.

Levin, J. R., Marascuilo, L. A., & Hubert, L. J. (1978). N = nonparametric randomization tests. In

T. R. Kratochwill (Ed.), *Single subject research: Strategies for evaluating change* (pp. 167–196). New York: Academic Press.

Lilliefors, H. W. (1967). On the Kolmogrov–Smirnov tests for normality with mean and variance unknown. *Journal of the American Statistical Association, 62,* 399–402.

Marascuilo, L. A., & Busk, P. L. (1988). Combining statistics for multiple-baseline AB and replicated ABAB designs across subjects. *Behavioral Assessment, 10,* 1–28.

Marascuilo, L. A., Busk, P. L., & Serlin, R. C. (1988). Large sample multivariate procedures for comparing and combining effect sizes within a single study. *Journal of Experimental Education, 57,* 69–85.

Marascuilo, L. A., & McSweeney, M. A. (1977). *Nonparametric and distribution-free methods for the social sciences.* Monterey, CA: Brooks/Cole.

Marascuilo, L. A., & Serlin, R. C. (1988). *Statistical methods for the social and behavioral sciences.* New York: W. H. Freeman.

McNemar, Q. (1947). Note on sampling error of the difference between correlated proportions or percentages. *Psychometrika, 12,* 153–157.

Michael, J. L. (1974). Statistical inference for individual organism research: Mixed blessing or curse? *Journal of Applied Behavior Analysis, 7,* 647–653.

Parsonson, B. S., & Baer, D. M. (1978). The analysis and presentation of graphic data. In T. R. Kratochwill (Ed.), *Single-subject research: Strategies for evaluating change.* New York: Academic Press.

Phillips, J. P. N. (1983). Serially correlated errors in some single-subject designs. *British Journal of Mathematical and Statistical Psychology, 36,* 269–280.

Sacks, S. Z. (1988). Peer-mediated social skills training: Enhancing the social competence of visually handicapped children in a mainstreamed school setting (Doctoral dissertation, University of California, Berkeley, with San Francisco State University, 1987). *Dissertation Abstracts International, 48,* DA8726430.

Scheffé, H. (1959). *The analysis of variance.* New York: Wiley.

Sharpley, C. F. (1988). Single-subject research. In J. P. Keeves, *Educational research, methodology, and measurement: An international handbook* (pp. 580–586). Oxford, England: Pergamon Press.

Sharpley, C. F., & Alavosius, M. P. (1988). Autocorrelation in behavioral data: An alternative perspective. *Behavioral Assessment, 10,* 243–251.

Shine, L. C., & Bower, S. M. (1971). A one-way analysis of variance for single-subject designs. *Educational and Psychological Measurement, 31,* 105–113.

Sidman, M. (1960). *Tactics for scientific research: Evaluating experimental data in psychology.* New York: Basic Books.

Suen, H. K. (1987). On the epistemology of autocorrelation in applied behavior analysis. *Behavioral Assessment, 9,* 113–124.

Suen, H. K., & Ary, D. (1987). *Application of statistical power in assessing autocorrelation.* A paper presented at the annual meeting of the American Educational Research Association, Washington, DC.

Toothaker, L. E., Banz, M., Noble, C., Camp, J., & Davis, D. (1983). N = 1 designs: The failure of ANOVA-based tests. *Journal of Educational Statistics, 8,* 289–309.

Wampold, B. E., & Furlong, M. J. (1981a). Randomization tests in single-subject designs: Illustrative examples. *Journal of Behavioral Assessment, 3,* 329–341.

Wampold, B. E., & Furlong, M. J. (1981b). The heuristics of visual inspection. *Behavioral Assessment, 3,* 79–92.

Wampold, B. E., & Worsham, N. L. (1986). Randomization tests for multiple-baseline designs. *Behavioral Assessment, 8,* 135–143.

Wolery, M., & Billingsley, F. F. (1982). The application of Revusky's Rn test to slope and level of changes. *Behavioral Assessment, 4,* 93–103.

7

Meta-Analysis for Single-Case Research

Patricia L. Busk
University of San Francisco

Ronald C. Serlin
University of Wisconsin–Madison

In 1976, Glass introduced a general measure of treatment effectiveness. This measure of treatment effectiveness, termed the effect size, is used as an indicator of the practical importance of the treatment or study outcome. Usually the effect size is the ratio of the difference between two sample means—that for the experimental group and that for the control group—to a standard deviation measure. With this ratio, the study's findings are converted to a common metric in terms of standard deviation units. More importantly, the effect-size measure, because it is metric- or scale-free, can be used to summarize and quantify the treatment effects of a body of different studies testing the same hypothesis. By converting the findings of different studies to a common metric, the estimate of average impact of the treatment can be based on a wide range of conceptually related measures and hence a larger sample of studies. Glass used the effect-size measure with a set of other statistical techniques in an empirical review of psychotherapy literature and termed this methodology *meta-analysis*, defining the term as "the statistical analysis of summary findings of many empirical studies" (Glass, McGaw, & Smith, 1981, p. 21). Since Glass's pioneering work, many advances have been made in the original methodology (see Hedges & Olkin, 1985), and meta-analyses have proliferated in the educational and psychological literature.

Focusing on the central role of literature reviews in scientific development, Cook and Leviton pointed out that, traditionally, "psychologists depend on the qualitative literature review to establish 'facts' " (1980, pp. 449–450). Many reviews have been published in such journals as *Review of Educational Research, New England Journal of Medicine, Psychological Bulletin,* and *American Public Health Journal,* or in such annual publications as *Review of Research in Educa-*

tion and *Annual Review of Psychology.* The goal of these reviews is to accumulate empirical research information on a topic. Frequently, research studies are presented in a serial manner. Sometimes the methodological strengths and weaknesses are discussed. Studies can be grouped into three categories: studies that confirm or disconfirm a particular finding or studies that are equivocal. The box in which the highest count falls is voted the winner (Light & Smith, 1971); therefore, a research finding is either confirmed or disconfirmed by the plurality of votes. Such reviews have come under severe criticism (Glass, 1978; Glass & Smith, 1979; Jackson, 1978; Scruggs, Mastropieri, & Casto, 1987b). The main shortcomings of qualitative reviews are that they are subjective, scientifically unsound, and an inefficient way to extract useful information (Light & Pillmer, 1984). In particular, they provide only a crude idea of the outcome of a body of research. There is no way to assess the magnitude of the outcome with a vote-counting approach (see Bangert–Drowns, 1986, pp. 388–389).

Reviews of research studies have been classified into four categories (H. M. Cooper, 1982; Jackson, 1980). Only one of these types of reviews involves an integrative review. It is to this type that meta-analysis belongs. According to Jackson, "the integrative review is primarily interested in inferring generalizations about substantive issues from a set of studies directly bearing on those issues" (p. 438). Meta-analysis involves quantifying the treatment results of research studies and applying statistics to those quantifications. Bangert–Drowns (1986) classified meta-analysis methods into five different approaches and provided suggestions for the use of each. The five approaches are Glassian meta-analysis, study-effect meta-analysis, combined probability method, approximate data pooling with tests of homogeneity, and approximate data pooling with sampling-error corrections. These approaches differ in their purpose, units of analysis, treatment of study variability, and the outcome of the analysis. Interested readers are referred to Bangert–Drowns for details.

Typically single-case researchers have relied on qualitative reviews of the literature to evaluate the generality of treatments. As with other psychological reviews, shortcomings have been identified with reviews of single-case literature. The narrative reviewers may be criticized for not evaluating previous studies critically by failing to examine the research methodology, not examining the relationship of the study quality to study outcomes, and eliminating studies from consideration on an arbitrary basis. If the studies are explored systematically, then the presence or absence of confounding or intervening variables could be investigated. In addition, objective evaluation of study outcomes often is not possible, because most results are based on visual inspection. In spite of these weaknesses, Salzberg, Strain, and Baer (1987) have advocated the narrative review. Such a review may be lengthier and more detailed than a quantitative review. Greater specificity was obtained in the qualitative review by Salzberg et al., but the systematic examination of extraneous variables was lacking (Scruggs et al., 1987b). Given these problems with the qualitative reviews of the literature, single-case researchers may decide to turn to the quantitative approach advocated by Glass (1976), even though this new methodology is not without criticism (cf. Cook & Leviton, 1980; Eysenck, 1978; Slavin, 1984; Strube, Gardner, & Hartmann, 1985; Strube & Hartmann, 1982; Wilson & Rachman, 1983).

Because meta-analysis does not depend on frequency counts and statistical significance as does the vote-counting method, some of the criticisms leveled against the qualitative reviews cannot be directed at a meta-analysis. In addition, the single-case researcher would not find vote counting of utility, because very few studies report statistical significance.

Meta-analysis has been described by Blimling (1988) as having four general purposes: (a) to describe a body of studies, (b) to summarize the overall effect of a particular treatment, (c) to identify variables that influence the magnitude and direction of the study outcomes, and (d) to quantify the magnitude and significance of the treatment's effect. Many of the statistical techniques used in research studies, such as analysis of variance or regression, are used by the meta-analyst to extract and organize the information for the review. The critical evaluation of previous research is carried out in the identification of variables that influence the magnitude and direction of the study outcomes. Such identification is performed consistently for each study in the review, as opposed to the more inconsistent qualitative reviews of the literature. Although there are concerns expressed about how meta-analyses are performed, meta-analysis allows the researcher to investigate systematically the effects of extraneous variables, such as age, duration of the treatment, and varying treatment methods, an advantage typically lacking in the qualitative reviews.

The recommended format for the presentation or publication of the results of the meta-analysis is rigorous—a listing of all the references used in the meta-analysis, criteria on the basis of which inclusion of studies was made, procedures used to achieve the literature review, variables extracted from each study reviewed, methods for computing the effect sizes, and the statistical methods used to investigate the influential variables (cf. Wilson & Putman, 1982, for a review that follows these guidelines).

In spite of several proposed meta-analytic techniques (Center, Skiba, & Casey, 1985–1986; Hartmann & Gardner, 1982; Mastropieri & Scruggs, 1985–1986; Scruggs, Mastropieri, & Casto, 1987a; Scruggs, Mastropieri, & Forness, 1988; Scruggs, Mastropieri & McEwen, 1988; Skiba, Casey, & Center, 1985–1986; Strube, et al., 1985), the wide-scale use of the empirical summary of single-case studies is lacking. On the one hand, single-case researchers may not be inclined to summarize empirically the results of their studies (Salzberg et al., 1987), given their tradition of visual inspection. On the other hand, the techniques proposed may be inappropriate for single-case data or not easy to compute. These issues are discussed in this chapter.

In addition to these two issues, there is the problem of the research methodology of single-case studies. Traditional experimental group designs involve a random sampling from a population of subjects and the random assignment of subjects to one of the experimental groups and the control group. Group differences that occur after intervention are attributed to the intervention, because other plausible explanations are controlled for by random assignment to groups or by various statistical methodological techniques. In applied settings, large numbers of subjects are not used. Single-case researchers have turned to time-series designs, based on the assumption that the behavior of the individual subject is unique (Allport, 1962; Hersen & Barlow, 1976) and because the purpose of the investigation is to describe the intervention to a particular client population. Single-case studies consist of a series of repeated observations separated into at least two distinct phases—baseline and intervention. Usually, single-case designs are replicated across behaviors, settings, or across subjects. Such designs are atypical of the group studies of the originally proposed meta-analytic techniques. In this chapter, an empirical method of summarizing single-case experiments is proposed that addresses the autocorrelated nature of the single-case data and that will be able to take advantage of advances of the Hedges and Olkin (1985) methodology for combining effect sizes across studies.

PREVIOUSLY PROPOSED META-ANALYTIC TECHNIQUES FOR SINGLE-CASE RESEARCH DESIGNS

White, Rusch, Kazdin, and Hartmann (1989) argued that there are obstacles to the application of meta-analysis to single-case studies. One major obstacle is the fact that between-group meta-analyses use summary statistics such as correlation coefficients, effect sizes (the magnitude of the difference between experimental and control group means standardized by a measure of variability), and t-tests to be combined across studies. These measures may not be found in many of the single-case reports. This does not mean, however, that effect-size measures are inappropriate for use in single-case research. If an effect size or summary measure can be defined that accurately assesses the magnitude of the treatment impact across subjects that is metric-free, then the issue whether such a measure is used or reported in such studies is of little consequence. Even in the educational and psychological literature, the effect-size measure is not reported on a consistent basis. Frequently, meta-analysts must approximate the effect size from summary information reported in a research article. Such a problem may not be encountered in single-case research, because all the data for a research study usually are provided in graphic form. Even if these data were not evident from the graphs, they could be obtained from the authors of the research article. Therefore, the meta-analyst could readily generate the effect-size measure from the graphic representation, using a computerized method developed by Smoot and Curlette (1990).

White et al. (1989) have leveled both conceptual and methodological criticisms at meta-analysis, which they claim limit the applicability of this method for single-case studies. We will attempt to address their concerns.

One of the methodological problems involves statistical independence of effect-size measures. As pointed out earlier in this chapter, such an issue is not problematical under the approaches presented here. Methods have been proposed that result in measures that can be combined across studies. The other practical problem concerns the recovery of data from single-case studies. In fact, the determination of effect sizes in single-case research is less problematical than in studies involving between-group designs, because single-case researchers are more open to providing or publishing graphs of their research results. The determination of effect sizes would be more consistent across such studies than across those with group designs, where a variety of summary measures may be reported as correlation coefficients, effect sizes, t-tests, and p values. The challenge for the meta-analyst is to combine these diverse measures to determine treatment effectiveness.

The conceptual criticisms are as follows: (a) The use of an effect size that assesses magnitude on a common metric is merely an attempt to provide statistical control, (b) The determination of generality is made by a statistical process and not by an experimental one, and (c) The growth of scientific knowledge cannot occur because growth can only occur through the process of systematic replication. Each of these concerns will be addressed in turn.

Determining an effect-size measure is not a matter of statistical control, but rather it is a method for quantifying a treatment outcome. The approaches presented in this chapter go beyond obtaining a single value, in that we show how a confidence interval for the effect-size parameter can be constructed and used for comparative purposes. A common metric allows researchers objectively to compare treatments across different subjects within a single study and across different studies. The common metric provides the researcher with the ability to compare the average improvement of the treatment across a wide range of conceptually related measures that otherwise might not be comparable. Presently, results from several subjects within a single-case study are compared by visual inspection, which is a subjective evaluation. Both the visual inspection (the subjective approach) and the effect-size measure (the objective approach) can be used within a given study, as many researchers have argued (Kazdin, 1984; White, 1987).

White, Rusch, Kazdin, and Hartmann (1989) deferred to Salzberg et al. (1987) for the argument that experimental procedures and not statistical procedures should be used to discover the variables that are responsible for a treatment outcome. We would not argue with Salzburg et al. on this matter. Rather we would question the exclusive use of a single experiment to decide whether a variable is responsible for an effect. Meta-analysis allows one to investigate systematically whether a variable is responsible for an effect and to assess under which conditions and with what type of subjects the effect occurs, which we would argue goes beyond the evidence of one or two experiments.

One cannot dispute the claim of White et al. (1989) that "from the standpoint of philosophy of science, direct and systematic replications of studies are superior to either the meta-analytic or narrative review method in assessing generality" (p. 292). The difficulty that a researcher encounters is that there are so many replications that one is unable to review and evaluate the results of these experiments in an objective and a systematic manner.

White et al. (1989) did admit "that the logic of decision making that underlies single-case investigations is compatible with statistical reasoning" (p. 283) but that "the difficulty lies in capturing it in statistical terms" (p. 283). We would argue that the data in single-case research studies indeed can be captured in statistical terms. In fact, Edgington (1980), given certain assumptions, has shown that single-case data can be analyzed for statistical significance by randomization tests. Such tests yield a p value (the probability of a more extreme outcome or outcomes than the observed one given that the hypothesis of no treatment effect is true). Mullen and Rosenthal (1985) have used p values to combine results across studies and derive an effect-size measure from the combined value.

Two study outcomes that are used in traditional meta-analysis are p values, or probability levels that the null hypothesis of no difference is true (Mullen & Rosenthal, 1985), and effect sizes (Hedges & Olkin, 1985). Because the majority of single-case studies are analyzed via visual inspection, p values are not likely to be found but could be determined if a randomization test were used on each subject or a combined test were used across subjects (Marascuilo & Busk, 1988), provided that the assumptions for the randomization test were met. Such tests can be performed relatively easily by the researcher. Therefore, an effect-size measure is the indicator that would be the obvious choice for summarizing study effects. Some of the suggested indicators of treatment effects for single-case studies are (1) Percentage of nonoverlapping data (Scruggs et al., 1987a; (2) Variance accounted for by changes in level, changes in slope, and by the combined effects of level and slope changes using a piece-wise regression approach (Center et al., 1985–1986); (3) Effect size based on the ratio of difference between the average of intervention observations and the average of the baseline observations to the standard deviation of the baseline observations (Andrews, Guitar, & Howie, 1980; Gingerich, 1984); (4) A modification of the latter procedure (Corcoran, 1985); and (5) When norms are available, effect size based on the ratio of the difference between the mean for the treatment and the mean of the normative group to the standard deviation of the normative group (Nietzel & Trull, 1988).

For most single-case studies, normative data are not available. The dependent variable for most studies is a subject's behavior. Given this dependent variable, it is obvious that normative data do not exit. Therefore, Nietzel and Trull's method would not be applicable to most single-case data.

White (1987) has criticized the Scruggs et al. (1987a) method for synthesis (percentage of nonoverlapping data). Although the method is simple to calculate and easy to interpret, the method does not adequately assess meaningful trends in the data, is too sensitive to atypical baseline data, and is not sufficiently powerful to detect important treatment differences. There are benefits, however, from the use of this method, as White et al. (1989) have pointed out. "The meta-analysis revealed that social interaction effects were stronger when target children were directly reinforced for interaction" (p. 282). Whether these conclusions would differ if a more appropriate effect-size measure were used in the meta-analysis remains to be determined.

Center et al. (1985–1986) proposed a variance estimate for an effect-size measure that includes changes in level, changes in slope, and the combined effects in the estimate. Their model had three limitations. First, three effect-size measures that were interdependent were generated. Multiple-effect sizes within a study create problems for combining across studies. Second, as a result of generating three measures, interpretation problems arise as to which measure is the key indicator of the magnitude of the treatment effect. Third, unless there are a substantial number of data points in a single-case research study, the fitting of regression lines to a series of a few points will not provide a reliable estimate. Finally, Center et al.'s regression approach is based on independence of observations (as are the preceding estimates, e.g., Scruggs et al., 1987a) and often is justified by Huitema's (1985) claim that autocorrelation is not a serious problem for single-case data. Such a claim has been questioned by several methodologists (Busk & Marascuilo, 1988; Sharpley & Alavosius, 1988; Suen, 1987; Suen & Ary, 1987). Nonindependence can cause problems when the estimates are to be combined across subjects or behaviors within a study and across studies. Effect-size estimates that are based on a standard deviation composed of either baseline observations or all observations, such as those suggested by Andrews et al. (1980), Corcoran (1985), and Gingerich (1984), could yield a numerator and denominator that are not independent. The lack of independence results in an inability to use existing methods for combining effect-size estimates across studies. What would be ideal is a measure that is both sensitive to changes in level, changes in slope, and the combined effects and that allows the use of existing methodology for combining across subjects, behaviors, and studies.

GUIDELINES FOR DEFINING AN EFFECT-SIZE MEASURE

To provide a rationale for our choice of a single-case effect-size measure, let us reconsider the more traditional two-sample case. Glass's (1976) standardized mean difference, in which the denominator is the control-group standard deviation, indicates the magnitude of the treatment effect by comparing the mean difference with the amount of "natural" variability present in the data, that is, if the difference in group means is large compared with chance variability, then the effect should be considered important. The choice of the control-group standard deviation as the scaling factor is based on a desire to obtain an estimate of variability that is free of possible treatment contamination.

As has been pointed out by many authors (cf. Hedges & Olkin, 1985), if one can assume that the treatment does not affect the variance of the scores, then a more efficient estimate of the common population variance is the mean square within groups (the pooled within-group variance). A researcher must decide if the assumption of variance homogeneity is tenable, for not only does the appropriate denominator depend on this decision but also does the ability to test the effect-size measure directly. Under the assumption of variance homogeneity, the standardized mean difference follows a noncentral t distribution (Hedges & Olkin, 1985, p. 79), whereas if variance homogeneity does not hold, the distribution of the standardized mean difference is unknown. According to Hedges and Olkin (p. 78), the assumption of variance homogeneity is a good one. Nevertheless, in any particular experiment, this decision must once again be made.

Now let us consider what factors may affect the magnitude of the standardized mean difference. Of course, the actual effectiveness of the treatment will do so, as will the variability present in the control (or both) population(s). If the variance is larger than it "naturally" should be, for whatever reason, then the effect size will be underestimated, and conversely for a variance that is smaller than it ought to be. To some extent, the variability in the sample is an issue concerning validity; one wants the population to represent the group to which one wishes to generalize the experimental results. If it contains people whose scores are more or less tightly packed around the mean than desired, then one is sampling the wrong population. The variability in the population is also an issue of reliability. If one improves the reliability of the measure used, then the variability in the scores will be reduced, and the effect size will increase.

In this case, then, a reduction in the unexplained, or error, variability, and the corresponding increase in the magnitude of the effect size, is reasonable, because we are still comparing the mean difference with an estimate of chance variation. But now let us say that we can explain a large amount of the variation in the scores of the subjects with an individual-differences variable, such as motivation. If we do so, then again the unexplained variation is reduced, and again the measure of the treatment effect size is increased. Is this increase problematical in the latter case but not in the former? We think not. Rather, the scientist is rewarded for uncovering another major explanatory variable. Conversely, if the individual-differences variable is not successful in explaining much of the variability in the scores, then the mean squares within can increase, with a subsequent reduction in the estimate of the treatment effect size.

The more that explanatory variables can account for variability in the scores, the smaller the unexplained, chance variation becomes. Let us imagine that *all* of the interindividual variation can be accounted for. Does that mean that the mean square within becomes zero, and the measures of effect size infinite? No, because we are still left with intraindividual variation, which is the province of single-case research. In an experiment in which all of the variability occurs within the subject(s), it only makes sense to assess the magnitude of an effect in terms of the "natural" chance variability present in the within-subject scores.

In parallel with the between-subject experiment, then, the within-subject effect size should be defined as a ratio of the control-treatment mean difference to the baseline standard deviation. And again in parallel with the multiple-group experiment, the researcher must decide if homogeneity of variance is present in the baseline and treatment phases. If it is, then one would again use the pooled standard deviation in the denominator. In the single-case case, however, the problem is slightly more complex, for if one cannot assume a kind of compound symmetry among the measures (called exchangeability by Puri & Sen, 1985), then the numerator and denominator of the standardized mean difference are not independent, and the distribution of the effect-size measure is no longer that of the noncentral t. Compound symmetry is a weaker assumption than that of independence or no correlation between observations. The simplest (although not necessarily the most likely to occur in practice) covariance structure that allows this independence is one in which all of the variances and all of the covariances among the measures are equal, respectively. This same independence is required of the numerator and denominator for the F ratio in an analysis of variance. One design that makes the compound symmetry assumption easier to justify is Edgington's randomization design.

In summary, we suggest that in both between-subjects and within-subjects experiments, given that assumptions of variance homogeneity or compound symmetry are valid, the effect-size measure be defined as the standardized mean difference, where the scale factor is the square root of the mean square error in the design. The advantages that accrue from this definition are three-fold. First, one single definition holds for all experimental designs. Second, because the distribution of the effect-size measure is known, one can test the effect size directly and find a confidence interval for it (see Serlin & Lapsley, 1986). Third, Hedges and Olkin's meta-analytic techniques can be used, because they are based on large-sample, normal approximations to the noncentral t distribution. And fourth, it is straightforward to convert individual ts to effect sizes.

If, in single-case research, the assumptions required to make the numerator and denominator independent cannot be met, then some other technique must be used to test effect sizes. We now describe such a technique, and then we provide examples of analyses of effect sizes in single-case research in which we assume compound symmetry among the measures.

AN EFFECT-SIZE MEASURE FOR SINGLE-CASE RESEARCH

This section focuses on obtaining an effect-size measure for single-case designs, which takes into account *the lack of independence* in the data. Although effect-size measures will be defined in general terms of mean differences and the mean-square residual within subjects, with particular examples provided in the context of within series designs (e.g., ABAB and ABC) and multiple-baseline designs (across subjects, behaviors, and designs), extensions to other designs logically follow one of the designs that have been discussed. We will present three approaches to obtaining an effect-size estimate for single-case research studies. The approaches differ in the assumptions that are made to obtain the estimate. A general discussion of assumptions follows.

The assumptions underlying univariate repeated-measures analysis of variance include normality and "sphericity," where sphericity involves the variances and covariances of the measures (cf. Kirk, 1968, p. 136). If all measures have the same variance and all pairs of measures have the same covariances (i.e., if compound symmetry is present), then sphericity holds and the analysis is valid. In this case, the most efficient estimate of the unexplained intrasubject variability is the mean-square residual within subjects, which is our third approach to defining an effect-size estimate. We suggest the square root of this error estimate as the denominator for all within-subjects effect-size estimates. In all approaches to determining effect sizes, the numerator is the difference between treatment-condition effect and the control-condition effect, which is typically assessed in the single-case design with baseline and treatment observations. In defining the effect-size estimates in this manner, we have a definition that parallels the one that would be used in between-subjects experiments.

If the assumptions underlying repeated-measures analysis of variance cannot be thought to hold, then we need an alternative method of dealing with the autocorrelated data, but we still desire a definition that makes sense in terms of the discussion of the previous section. Levin, Marascuilo, and Hubert (1978) defined a phase unit as the unit of analysis in single-case designs and used a summary measure of each phase to overcome the difficulty posed by the data that do not meet the assumptions of univariate repeated-measures analysis of variance. We will make use of the Levin et al. emphasis on phases, and we will use it for two of our approaches to defining an estimate, where the specific approach depends on the nature of tenable distributional assumptions.

SUGGESTED PROCEDURES FOR META-ANALYSIS IN SINGLE-CASE RESEARCH

Consider the data for the multiple-baseline design across subjects presented by Wampold and Worsham (1986) and found in Table 7.1. We will use the data for the four subjects to illustrate the three approaches that differ in the distributional and variability assumptions made regarding the data. These approaches are presented in order of weakest to strongest assumptions.

TABLE 7.1
Data for Four Subjects Used to Illustrate Effect Sizes for the Multiple-Baseline
Across Subjects Model

Block	1	2	3	4	5	6	7	8	9	10	11	12	13	14	15	16	17	18	19	20
								Subject One (Bob)												
Phase	A	A	A	A	A	B	B	B	B	B	B	B	B	B	B	B	B	B	B	B
Value	8	7	6	7	4	5	6	5	4	4	5	2	4	3	4	5	4	3	2	2
								Subject Two (Candy)												
Phase	A	A	A	A	A	A	A	A	B	B	B	B	B	B	B	B	B	B	B	B
Value	6	7	8	7	5	7	6	8	6	5	4	4	4	3	2	5	3	4	3	6
								Subject Three (Abby)												
Phase	A	A	A	A	A	A	A	A	A	A	A	A	B	B	B	B	B	B	B	B
Value	5	5	4	6	4	5	6	7	4	5	6	5	2	3	2	4	1	0	2	3
								Subject Four (Dave)												
Phase	A	A	A	A	A	A	A	A	A	A	A	A	A	A	A	A	B	B	B	B
Value	8	6	7	7	8	5	7	8	7	6	7	8	5	6	8	8	6	4	4	5

Note. These data are taken from Randomization Tests for Multiple-Baseline Designs by B. E. Wampold and N. L. Worsham (1986). *Behavioral Assessment, 8*, 135-143. Copyright (1986) by Pergamon Press. Reproduced with permission of the author.

Approach One—No Assumptions.   With no assumptions concerning population distributional form and equality of intermeasure variances and covariances, the best one can do is calculate a separate effect size for each subject by dividing the difference in phase means by the baseline standard deviation, which is Glass's original effect-size estimate and the one illustrated by White et al. (1989, p. 288) in their article on meta-analysis for single-case research. For the first subject, Bob, the baseline mean is 7.0, and the intervention mean is 3.88. With a baseline standard deviation of 0.82, the effect size for Bob is given by

$$(7.0 - 3.88)/0.82 = 3.8.$$

The means and standard deviations used to compute the effect sizes are found in Table 7.2. With these summary measures the remaining effect sizes are determined and reported in Table 7.3. Assuming that these sample effect sizes are estimating a common population effect size, then, under the null hypothesis of no treatment effects, we would expect that half of the effect sizes to be positive and half to be negative. In this case, the binomial sign-test model can be used to

TABLE 7.2
Summary Measures for the Multiple-Baseline Design in Table 7.1

Subject	$\overline{X}_A$	$\overline{X}_B$	$\overline{X}$	S_A	S_B	S_P	SS_W	SS_T	SS_R
Bob	7.00	3.88	4.50	0.82	1.20	1.15	55.00	31.15	23.55
Candy	6.75	4.08	5.15	1.03	1.24	1.16	58.55	34.22	24.33
Abby	5.17	2.13	3.95	0.94	1.25	1.07	64.95	44.36	20.59
Dave	6.94	4.75	6.50	1.06	0.96	1.04	35.00	15.35	19.65
Total	6.38	3.68	-	–	–	–	213.50	–	–

obtain a confidence interval. A one-tailed confidence interval is obtained whenever there is a priori reason for specifying a directional outcome to the research investigation (see Marascuilo & Serlin, 1988, pp. 180–182 for a discussion of one-tailed confidence intervals). The binomial sign-test model yields a 93.75% one-tailed confidence interval for the median population effect size (Marascuilo & Serlin, 1987, p. 182) of

$$ES > 2.07,$$

which would be interpreted as a large effect. Of course, no effect size can be interpreted by itself; rather, it must be compared with other effect sizes obtained in similar studies, with competing treatments, or in light of practical and clinical considerations. Note that because only four subjects were in the research study, a 95% confidence interval is not obtainable. The best we can do is a 93.75% confidence interval. With five subjects, however, a 95% confidence interval is possible.

Approach Two: Assumption of Equality of Variances Across Baseline and Treatment Phases.   With the slightly more stringent assumptions that the variances in the baseline and treatment phases are the same and that, whatever the intermeasure correlational patterns, they are the same in the two phases, we can pool the within-phase variances to obtain better estimates for the denominators. For example, for Bob, the within-phase standard deviations are 0.82 and 1.2.

TABLE 7.3
Effect-Size Estimates Using Three Approaches for the Four Subjects of the
Multiple-Baseline Design of Table 7.1

Subject	Approach One	Approach Two	Approach Three	ES>
Bob	3.80	2.71	2.71	1.58
Candy	2.57	2.30	2.30	1.30
Abby	3.23	2.84	2.84	1.67
Dave	2.07	2.11	2.11	1.00

These are pooled by squaring them (to obtain variances), multiplying by the within-phase degrees of freedom (3 and 15, respectively), adding the products, and dividing by the overall degrees of freedom (3 + 15 = 18). Numerically, the estimate is

$$[3(0.82)^2 + 15(1.2)^2]/18$$

yielding a pooled variance of 1.32, a standard deviation of 1.15, and an effect size for Bob given by

$$ES = (7.0 - 3.88)/1.15 = 2.71.$$

This is the estimate that White et al. (1989, p. 284) used to define their meta-analysis procedure for single-case research. Proceeding in this fashion, leads one to obtain the other effect-size estimates of 2.3, 2.84, and 2.11 (see Table 7.2 for summary measures and Table 7.3 for effect sizes). Because the variances and covariances in both phases are assumed to be the same, an additional assumption that the population distributions in the two phases are the same implies that the distribution of the effect-size measures is symmetrical. This assumption allows us to use the Wilcoxon model to obtain the 93.75% one-tailed confidence interval for the median population effect size as

$$ES > 2.11.$$

The pooling procedure will not always yield a higher lower limit to the confidence interval, as it did in this example (compare 2.11 with 2.7 under Approach one).

It has been demonstrated (see Tiku, 1986) that for symmetrical distributions the t-test is fairly robust in terms to both Type I and Type II error rates. Applying the one-sample t-test to the effect-size estimates generated under this approach, we obtain a 93.75% (equivalent to the sign and Wilcoxon intervals given earlier, although it typically would be calculated and reported as a 95% confidence interval) one-tailed confidence interval for the mean population effect size as

$$ES > 2.49 + (.34/\sqrt{4})\,(-2.353) = 2.09.$$

(see Marascuilo & Serlin, 1988, p. 415, for details on this method).

Approach Three: Assumptions of a Normal Distribution and Equality of Variances and Intercorrelations Across Baseline and Treatment Phases. Adding the assumption of population normality will not change the methods applied to these data, because without some assumptions concerning pattern of inter-measure correlations, the corresponding numerators and denominators are not independent, and, therefore, the distribution of effect-size estimates still is unknown. If we do assume that the phase scores are normally distributed, that the within-phase variances are the same, and that the within-phase intermeasure correlations are equal, then the effect-size estimates that have been calculated for each subject based on a pooled within-phase error term follow the noncentral t-distribution. For the data of table 7.1, each effect size would have 18 degrees of freedom. If desired, confidence intervals for each can be calculated, using either the methods described in Serlin and Lapsley (1986), which are based on percentiles of the noncentral t-distribution, or the methods described in Hedges and Olkin (1985), which depend on the large-sample normal approximation for the noncentral t-distribution. The advantage of the Serlin and Lapsley method is that for small degrees of freedom, the normal approximation to the noncentral t-distribution is not very precise. The advantage of the normal approximation, however, is that it allows one to use the Hedges and Olkin methodology to test whether the effect sizes appear to be constant across individuals.

Two points should be made at this time. First, the estimate of the within-phase variability differs from that obtained in a standard repeated-measures analysis of variance (Marascuilo & Serlin, 1988, p. 572). The reason for this difference is that the effect sizes have been allowed to differ among the subjects, which is equivalent to the presence of a subject-by-treatment interaction. Only after the case is made, on the basis of theory or prior research, for equal effects across subjects can this interaction be eliminated. Second, even though the assumptions at this point would allow the pooling across subjects of the error terms, this has not been done. If the error terms are pooled, the four effect-size estimates would not be independent, being based on a single common denominator, and the Hedges and Olkin (1985) method for testing their equality could not be used.

Finally, then, let us assume that the effects are equal across subjects. This assumption allows the removal of the subject-by-treatment interaction from the model, and the variances can now be pooled over all subjects by first subtracting the common treatment sum of squares from the combined within-subject sum of squares and then dividing the difference by the combined degrees of freedom. This definition of effect size corresponds to the desired method for estimating the effect size described earlier in the chapter.

In the example, the within-subject sums of squares are found by summing the square of the deviation of each score from the subject mean. This computation yields sums of squares within each subject of 55.0, 58.55, 64.95, and 35.0; overall, the sum of squares within subjects is given by

$$55.0 + 58.55 + 64.95 + 35.0 = 213.5.$$

The treatment sum of squares is obtained in the usual way using the overall baseline and intervention averages of 6.38 and 3.68, respectively. These values yield a treatment sum of squares of 145.8, so that the residual sum of squares found by subtracting the treatment sum of squares from the sum of squares within subjects is given by

$$213.5 - 145.8 = 67.7.$$

With 75 degrees of freedom, the mean square residual becomes $(67.7/75) = 0.9$, and the standard deviation is the given by

$$\sqrt{0.9} = 0.95.$$

Using this value with the baseline and intervention means produces an effect size

$$ES = (6.38 - 3.68)/0.95 = 2.84.$$

Given all of the assumptions, this effect-size estimate follows a noncentral t-distribution with 75 degrees of freedom. Using the methods described in Serlin and Lapsley (1985, 1986), the 93.3% one-tailed confidence interval for the population effect size is

$$ES > 2.34,$$

whereas using the Hedges and Olkin (1985) normal approximation, the 93.3% one-tailed confidence interval for the unbiased estimate of the effect size is

$$ES > 2.31.$$

Effect sizes for each individual based upon this approach are provided in Table 7.3. These estimates are based on the sum of squares within, the between-phase sum of squares, and the residual sum of squares for each individual (see Table 7.2). For subject one,

$$ES = (7.0 - 3.88)/\sqrt{23.55/18} = 2.71.$$

Notice that the effect sizes for Approaches two and three are the same. The advantage to the additional assumptions of Approach three, however, is that one now is able to obtain a confidence interval for individual effect-size estimates. Using the methods of Serlin and Lapsley (1986), a 95% confidence interval for Subject one is given by

$$ES > 1.58.$$

The confidence interval for a single individual is wider than the overall confidence interval, as the individual ones are based on intervention sum of squares and fewer degrees of freedom. The remaining individual effect sizes are reported in Table 7.3.

ILLUSTRATION OF EFFECT-SIZE ESTIMATES
FOR ABAB DESIGN

To illustrate the three approaches for determination of effect sizes for the ABAB design, consider the study by Miller (1973), where a procedure called "retention control training" (RCT) was given to two subjects for the treatment of nocturnal enuresis. Two adolescent "subjects were exposed to the sequential conditions of attention-placebo baseline, RCT, return to baseline, and RCT" (p. 288). Bedwetting episodes were reported weekly. For Subject one, phases consisted of the following number of weeks: Three for attention-placebo baseline, three for RCT,

TABLE 7.4
Summary Measures for the ABAB Design

Subject	$\bar{X}_{A1}$	$\bar{X}_{B1}$	$\bar{X}_{A2}$	$\bar{X}_{B2}$	S_{A1}	S_{B1}	S_{A2}	S_{B2}	$\bar{X}_A$	$\bar{X}_B$	$\bar{X}$	S_P
One	4.67	1.67	4.00	0.40	0.58	1.15	0.00	0.89	4.33	0.88	2.36	0.6997
Two	5.67	2.67	4.33	0.71	0.58	1.15	1.15	1.11	5.00	1.30	2.69	1.0500

Subject	SS_W	SS_T	SS_R
One	51.21	40.93	10.28
Two	75.44	51.34	24.10

three for return to baseline, and seven for RCT. The second subject had the same number of weeks for the first three phases. There were 10 weeks in the last phase. Phase means and standard deviations are reported in Table 7.4 for these subjects.

Approach One: No Assumptions.   Separate effect-size estimates are calculated for each subject under this approach. The effect-size measure would be the difference in average phase means divided by a baseline standard deviation measure. If the two baseline standard deviations are equal, then a pooled standard deviation based on the two baselines would be used in estimating the effect size. In this case for both subjects, it is not possible to pool the standard deviations across the two baseline phases. Therefore, the initial baseline is used in calculating the effect size. For the first subject, the average baseline mean is 4.33 and the average intervention mean is 0.88. With the initial baseline standard deviation of 0.58, the effect size is given by

$$(4.33 - 0.88)/0.58 = 5.98.$$

This effect size and that for Subject 2 are reported in Table 7.5. Because only two subjects were used in the study, it is not possible to obtain a confidence interval.

Approach Two: Assumption of Equality of Variances Across Baseline and Treatment Phases.   Under this approach, the assumption of equality of vari-

TABLE 7.5
Effect-Size Estimates Using Three Approaches for the Two Subjects of the
ABAB Design of Table 7.4

Subject	Approach One	Approach Two	Approach Three	ES>
One	5.98	4.94	3.56	2.04
Two	6.41	3.52	2.72	1.49

ances across the four phases of the study would be made. An inspection of the standard deviations in Table 7.4 would lead one to question whether this assumption would be met. At this point, the researcher would not go beyond Approach one, as an inspection of the standard deviations in Table 7.4 reveals that the four variances are anything but homogeneous, with standard deviations of 0.57, 1.15, 0.0, and 0.89 for Subject one. For illustrative purposes only, however, we will compute the effect sizes under this approach that uses the pooled within-phase variance to obtain a better estimate for the denominator of the effect size. For Subject one, each of the four standard deviations would be squared and weighted by the within-phase degrees of freedom, the weighted variances would be added, and the resulting sum divided by the overall degree of freedom of $2 + 2 + 2 + 6 = 12$. The pooled standard deviation is .6997, and the effect size is estimated by

$$ES = (4.33 - 0.88)/.6997 = 4.94.$$

The effect-size estimate for Subject two is found in the same manner and is listed in Table 7.5.

Because there are only two estimated effect sizes, the Wilcoxon model would not be used to obtain a confidence interval. If the one-sample t-test were used to obtain a 95% confidence interval for the mean population effect size, it would be given by

$$ES > 4.23 + (1.0/\sqrt{2}) (-6.314) = -0.1,$$

which would mean that the population effect size could be zero, that is, that there is no treatment effect. Obviously, caution must be used here as there are only two subjects, and, with so few subjects, the confidence interval will be very broad.

Approach Three: Assumptions of a Normal Distribution and Equality of Variances and Intercorrelations Across Baselines and Treatment Phases. If we failed to meet the assumptions of Approach two, which are weaker ones, then we certainly would fail to meet the assumptions of Approach three, which are even stronger. Again for illustrative purposes, we will continue to determine effect sizes. Under this approach and with more stringent assumptions, it is possible to obtain confidence intervals for individual effect sizes as well as for a pooled effect size.

For this example, the within-subject sum of squares is found by summing the square of the deviation of each score from the subject mean (for Subject one, the mean is 2.54). This computation yields sums of squares within subjects of 51.21 and 75.44; the overall sum of squares within subjects is given by

$$51.21 + 75.44 = 126.65,$$

which has degrees of freedom of 28 (i.e., $(14 - 1) + (16 - 1) = 28$). The treatment sum of squares is obtained using the baseline mean of 4.67 and a treatment mean of 1.11. The squared deviations of each of these values from the overall mean of 2.54 are weighted by 12 (the combined number of baseline observations) for the baseline squared deviations and 18 (the combined number of treatment observations) for the treatment squared deviations. These calculations yield a treatment sum of squares of 91.25. The residual sum of squares is found by subtracting the sum of squares treatment from the sum of squares within subjects and is given by

$$126.65 - 91.25 = 35.4.$$

This sum of squares has $28 - 1$ or 27 degrees of freedom, so that the mean square residual becomes (35.4/27) or 1.31, and the standard deviation is given by

$$\sqrt{1.31} = 1.14.$$

Using this value for the standard deviation of the effect size with the baseline and intervention means of 4.67 and 1.11, respectively, produces

$$ES = (4.67 - 1.11)/1.14 = 3.12.$$

Given the assumptions of this approach, this effect-size estimate follows a noncentral t-distribution with 27 degrees of freedom. Following Serlin and Lapsley (1986), a 95% confidence interval is obtained by finding the confidence interval for the noncentrality parameter and dividing the limit by $\sqrt{n_A n_B/N}$, where n_A is the number of baseline observations in the study and n_B is the number of treatment observations in the study. For this example, $n_A = 12$ and $n_B = 18$. The confidence interval for the noncentrality parameter, and finally for the effect size, can be found using a computer program devised by B. H. Cooper (1968) and corrected by Chou (1985). For this example,

$$ES > 5.82/\sqrt{(12)(18)/30} = 2.17.$$

Effect sizes for each individual under Approach three are provided in Table 7.5. These estimates are based on the sum of squares within, the between sum of squares, and the residual sum of squares for each individual (see Table 7.4). For Subject one,

$$ES = (4.33 - 0.88)/\sqrt{10.28/11} = 3.56.$$

Notice that these effect-size estimates are not the same as under either of the previous approaches. This difference results from the type of design that we are illustrating. The 95% confidence interval for Subject one is determined by obtaining the confidence interval for the noncentrality parameter for the t-distribution with 11 degrees of freedom and dividing it by the square root of the product of the number of baseline and treatment observations divided by the total number of observations. For Subject one,

$$ES > 3.77/\sqrt{(6)(8)/14} = 2.04.$$

The confidence interval for Subject two is obtained by following the same procedure and is found in Table 7.5.

EFFECT-SIZE ESTIMATES FOR OTHER SINGLE-CASE DESIGNS

To determine a single effect size for studies involving other single-case designs, the same procedures as those that have been specified could be used and would be based on the level assumptions made. Studies with ABC designs also can yield effect-size measures. In fact, there are two possible separate measures that could result from this design—a measure of the effect of treatment B the effect of C. Each effect size is determined separately.

If there were two sets of subjects for the study, where one set received the treatments in BC order and a second set received the treatments in CB order, then the researcher would have effect sizes for each treatment order. The effect sizes for the treatment orders could be compared using the two-sample Wilcoxon test. The results of this test would indicate whether the order was a factor in the treatment results.

In determining an effect size for a multiple-baseline study with a follow-up, the measure would be computed in a manner similar to a multiple-baseline study. The effect-size measures would be obtained separately for treatment and then for follow-up. If the researcher so desired, an effect-size measure could be computed between the treatment phase and the follow-up phase. The measure would be an indication of the sustained effectiveness of treatment. For this effect size, and under Approach one, the standard deviation would be the one computed from the treatment observations. Under Approach two, both treatment and follow-up observations would be used in the pooled estimate. Similarly, Approach three calculations would involve the sum of squares within the treatment and follow-up phases.

Effect-size measures for studies with multiple behavior pose an additional problem. Behaviors for the same subject are not independent, and this dependency must be considered before the data can be combined across subjects. Ignoring the dependency can result in erroneous assumptions about the standard errors for the estimates of effect sizes. What this complication means to the researcher is that the methods for testing for homogeneity of effect sizes and for obtaining confidence intervals for the combined effect size would be in error. Glass et al. (1981) used a data set of 14 studies regarding class size and achievement effects to illustrate the effects of interdependence in effect-size measures. The 14 studies yielded 108 different effect sizes. Glass et al. assessed the effect of the interdependency on the confidence interval for the regression coefficient using Tukey's jackknife method. They found that the confidence interval was more than 350% wider when interdependencies were considered. Glass et al. concluded that when regression techniques are used to assess the effect-size differences the best method to use is generalized least squares, which allows correlated errors—interdependencies of the effect sizes. As many single-case researchers may not be utilizing regression techniques for comparing effect sizes and assessing the relevancy of extraneous measures, other ways need to be developed to handle interdependencies that arise from multiple behaviors. Such methods have been developed by Marascuilo, Busk, and Serlin (1988).

If the identical behaviors are observed across subjects, then the methods of Marascuilo et al. (1988) can be used to combine effect sizes for individual behaviors, which were determined across subjects. These methods involve pooling effect sizes across behaviors and then across subjects. In order to pool effect sizes across behaviors, the correlations between behaviors must be known or able to be estimated. If the strength of the relationships are not known or cannot be estimated, then McLaughlin and Marascuilo (1990, p. 341) recommended using .5 as the estimate for the average correlation between behaviors. When combining differences across subjects and combining effect sizes across studies, the measured behavior under investigation must be of the same underlying construct (see Marascuilo & Busk, 1988, for a discussion of this issue).

As we have pointed out, the summary measure is based on the knowledge of the behavior under investigation. Selection of the appropriate summary measure for phase behavior is based on whether the researcher is investigating changes in levels of behavior or changes in trends of the behavior. If the behavior shows only level differences, then the appropriate summary measure to be observed on each unit of analysis is a measure of central tendency, such as the mean of the phase. When the distributions of the phase observations are skewed, then medians may be preferred to means, as they are not affected by extreme observations. If outliers are encountered, trimmed or Winsorized means may be substituted (Marascuilo & McSweeney, 1977, pp. 420–421). If the behavior is based on changes in trends in the behavior, then the slope of the phase would be the appropriate summary measure.

Occasionally, the behavior may involve carry-over effects from one phase to another. If it is known that the behavior is affected in this manner, then the observations affected by the carry-over would not be used in determining the summary measure. For example, if the first few observations in the B phase of an ABAB-reversal design have a carry-over component, then these first few observations should be removed before the determination of the measure of central tendency used as the dependent variable. With behavior that shows trend differences, the appropriate dependent variable would be the slope of the best-fitting straight line to the observations within a phase. When there are carry-over effects operating in a study in which the effects are exhibited in trend changes, the effects would be estimated by an A phase slope continued over to the initial B phase observations. If such a trend is noted, then these initial observations should be eliminated from the computation of the slope for the B phase. Observations that are based on success or failure for each trial can be summarized as the proportion of successes or the proportion of failures.

In the case of delayed effects, the first few observations of the intervention phase could be removed from the computation of the mean values. Determining the number of values to eliminate from the computations must be done prior to the data collection. Using this method to eliminate delayed effects would require additional observations within a phase. Another way to reduce the impact of carry-over effects on the proposed statistical test is to space observations far apart in time (Edgington, 1980).

SUGGESTED PROCEDURES FOR META-ANALYSIS IN SINGLE-CASE RESEARCH

When undertaking a meta-analysis, one of the first decisions that the reviewer must make concerns the purpose of the review. According to Bangert–Drowns (1986), there are two possible alternatives for the meta-analysis. The first is a purely descriptive review following the methods taken by Glass et al. (1981) and Kulik, Kulik, and Cohen (1979), which is the usual intent when one is reviewing the literature. A meta-analyst with this purpose would use Approaches one and two as described in this chapter. If the purpose is to test specific hypotheses and determine a generalizable estimate of the treatment outcome following the procedures taken by Hedges and Olkin (1985), Hunter, Schmidt, and Jackson (1983), Hunter and Schmidt (1990), and Rosenthal and Rubin (1982), then the meta-analyst would use effect-size estimates based on Approach three. This second purpose is akin to a secondary analysis of the literature. Bangert–Drowns likens the latter alternative to a cluster analysis or data pooling. The more recent developments in this area include model building.

> The difference between these alternatives is not a trivial one. A meta-analyst's choice will determine how outcome variation is treated and how the findings are interpreted and generalized. Indeed, it will determine how the meta-analyst conceives of the whole meta-analytic enterprise. (Bangert–Drowns, 1986, p. 396)

Most single-case researchers would identify with the first alternative, because their intent is to discover what the available research says about the effect of a particular behavioral intervention and to summarize accurately the research on this treatment that is reported in the literature. Utilizing such an approach allows the single-case researcher to examine systematically the covariation of study outcomes with factors such as (a) the length of treatment, (b) the timing of the intervention relative to the onset of problems, (c) the experience of the intervening agent, and (d) the level of disability of the subject under treatment. Such a systematic investigation usually is not carried out in the qualitative or traditional literature review. Additionally, the reader of such a review may find it difficult to determine what support there is for the conclusions of the reviewer, because conclusions of a review should be stated explicitly and supported empirically. Such empirical support is difficult to obtain in a traditional review. In particular, Salzberg et al. (1987) provided a traditional narrative review as an alternative to a proposed meta-analysis procedure of Scruggs et al. (1987a). The traditional review covered just six single-case studies and took more than three pages to synthesize. In spite of the details provided in the review, Scruggs et al. argued that it does not examine the study factors in a systematic manner and "provides no information whatsoever regarding their criteria for evaluating study outcomes" (p. 50).

Reviews of single-case literature should be as objective, as systematic, as straightforward, and as replicable as are the individual studies being reviewed. To accomplish this, we recommend procedures that reflect the objective criteria described by Jackson (1980), and detailed by Scruggs et al. (1987b), which include the following:

> (a) define and delimit the topic, (b) cite and review previous reviews, (c) cite procedures for obtaining research articles, (d) describe common, independent, and dependent variables, (e) examine covariation of study outcome with study characteristics, (f) support conclusions with empirical data from the original research, and (g) state criteria by which study outcomes are evaluated. (p. 49)

Many reviewers commonly fail to meet most or even many of these criteria. Rarely are we told exactly what aspects of a topic will be included in a review, what procedures were used to locate relevant articles, or what previous reviewers have concluded on a particular topic. Scruggs et al. (1987b) pointed to a review by McCuller and Salzberg (1982) that failed "to adequately address *any* of these criteria" (p. 50).

SUMMARY

The benefit of using effect-size measures in single-case research in a study is that the researcher is able to go beyond the "controversial" technique of visual inspection to demonstrate empirically the magnitude of the outcome effect. Additional benefits and advantages of meta-analysis have been detailed by Strube and Hartmann (1983), and White et al. (1989) have spelled out the advantages of meta-analysis for the single-case researcher. The interested reader is referred to these sources for specific advantages.

Benefits of an effect-size measure for single-case research apply to the larger research community as well. Using the approaches described in this chapter that yield effect sizes that can be combined with those from other research, meta-analysts who previously may have excluded single-case studies now can include these applied behavior studies in their reviews. When meta-analysts do not include single-case studies in their reviews, the results of those reviews would not be representative of all types of behavioral interventions (White et al., 1989; Wilson & Rachman, 1983). Such reviewers must be willing to use Glass's regression techniques (Glass et al., 1981) with multiple-effect sizes that result from Approaches one and two for each study or Hedges and Olkin's (1985) methods on a single effect size from Approach three for each study. The choice of methods depends on the variance and covariance assumptions that one is willing to make. The researcher must pay particular attention to which assumptions are tenable before deciding on an appropriate analysis. Only the most stringent assumptions will allow for meta-analysis in which the intention is to determine a generalizable estimate of the treatment effect.

In this chapter, procedures have been proposed, based on varying assumptions for determining effect-size estimates from a single-case investigation. The approaches are simple to use. For Approaches one and two, if the number of subjects in the study are greater than three, then a single confidence interval can be obtained for the quantitative measure of the treatment outcome. For Approach three, a confidence interval can be obtained for individual effect sizes as well as a combined effect size.

REFERENCES

Allport, G. W. (1962). The general and unique in psychological science. *Journal of Personality, 30,* 405–422.

Andrews, G., Guitar, B., & Howie, P. (1980). Meta-analysis of the effects of stuttering treatment. *Journal of Speech and Hearing Disorder, 45,* 287–307.

Bangert–Drowns, R. L. (1986). Review of developments in meta-analytic method. *Psychological Bulletin, 99,* 388–399.

Blimling, G. S. (1988). Meta-analysis: A statistical method for integrating the results of empirical studies. *Journal of College Student Development, 29,* 543–549.

Busk, P. L., & Marascuilo, L. A. (1988). Autocorrelation in single-subject research: A counterargument to the myth of no autocorrelation. *Behavioral Assessment, 10,* 229–242.

Center, B. A., Skiba, R. J., & Casey, A. (1985–1986). A methodology for the quantitative synthesis of intra-subject design research. *Journal of Special Education, 19,* 387–400.

Chou, Y. (1985). A remark on algorithm AS5: The integral of the noncentral *t* distribution. *Applied Statistics, 34,* 102.

Cook, T. D., & Leviton, L. C. (1980). Reviewing the literature: A comparison of traditional methods with meta-analysis. *Journal of Personality, 48,* 449–472.

Cooper, B. H. (1968). Algorithm AS5: The integral of the noncentral *t* distribution. *Applied Statistics, 17,* 193–194.

Cooper, H. M. (1982). Scientific guidelines for conducting integrative reviews. *Review of Educational Research, 52,* 291–302.

Corcoran, K. J. (1985). Aggregating the idiographic data of single-subject research. *Social Work Research and Abstracts,* 9–12.

Edgington, E. S. (1980). Overcoming obstacles to single-subject experimentation. *Journal of Educational Statistics, 5,* 261–267.

Eysenck, H. J. (1978). An exercise in mega-silliness. *American Psychologist, 33,* 517.

Gingerich, W. J. (1984). Meta-analysis of applied time-series data. *Journal of Applied Behavioral Science, 20,* 71–79.

Glass, G. V. (1976). Primary, secondary, and meta-analysis of research. *Educational Researcher, 5,* 3–8.

Glass, G. V. (1978). Integrating findings: The meta-analysis of research. *Review of Research in Education, 5,* 351–379.

Glass, G. V., McGaw, B., & Smith, M. L. (1981). *Meta-analysis in social research.* Beverly Hills, CA: Sage.

Glass, G. V., & Smith, M. L. (1979). Meta-analysis of research on class size and achievement. *Educational Evaluation and Policy Analysis, 1,* 2–16.

Hartmann, D. P., & Gardner, W. (1982, November). *Some thoughts on the application of meta-analytic procedures to single subject studies.* Paper presented at the annual meeting of the Association of Advancement of Behavior Therapy, Los Angeles.

Hedges, L. V., & Olkin, I. (1985). *Statistical methods for meta-analysis.* Orlando, FL: Academic Press.

Hersen, M., & Barlow, D. H. (1976). *Single case experimental designs: Strategies for studying behavior change.* New York: Pergamon Press.

Huitema, B. E. (1985). Autocorrelation in applied behavior analysis: A myth. *Behavioral Assessment, 7,* 107–118.

Hunter, J. E., & Schmidt, F. L. (1990). *Methods of meta-analysis: Correcting error and bias in research findings.* Newbury Park, CA: Sage.

Hunter, J. E., Schmidt, F. L., & Jackson, G. B. (1983). *Meta-analysis: Cumulating research findings across studies.* Beverly Hills, CA: Sage.

Jackson, G. B. (1978). *Methods for reviewing and integrating research in the social sciences.* Final Report to the National Science Foundation for Grant No. D1576–20309. Social Science Research Group, George Washington University, Washington, DC.

Jackson, G. B. (1980). Methods for integrative reviews. *Review of Educational Research, 50,* 438–460.

Kazdin, A. (1984). Statistical analysis for single-case experimental designs. In D. H. Barlow & M. Hersen (Eds.), *Single case experimental designs* (2nd ed., pp. 285–324). New York: Pergamon Press.

Kirk, R. E. (1968). *Experimental design: Procedures for the behavioral sciences.* Belmont, CA: Brooks/Cole.

Kulik, J. A., Kulik, C. L. C., & Cohen, P. A. (1979). A meta-analysis of outcome studies of Keller's personalized system of instruction. *American Psychologist, 37,* 307–318.

Levin, J. R., Marascuilo, L. A., & Hubert, L. J. (1978). N = nonparametric randomization tests. In T. R. Kratochwill (Ed.), *Single subject research: Strategies for evaluating change* (pp. 167–196). New York: Academic Press.

Light, R. J., & Pillmer, D. B. (1984). *Summing up: The science of reviewing research.* Cambridge, MA: Harvard University Press.

Light, R. J., & Smith, P. V. (1971). Accumulating evidence: Procedures for resolving contradictions among different research studies. *Harvard Educational Review, 41,* 429–471.

Marascuilo, L. A., & Busk, P. L. (1988). Combining statistics for multiple-baseline AB and replicated ABAB designs across subjects. *Behavioral Assessment, 10,* 1–28.

Marascuilo, L. A., Busk, P. L., & Serlin, R. C. (1988). Large sample multivariate procedures for comparing and combining effect sizes within a single study. *Journal of Experimental Education, 57,* 69–85.

Marascuilo, L. A., & McSweeney, M. A. (1977). *Nonparametric and distribution-free methods for the social sciences.* Monterey, CA: Brooks/Cole.

Marascuilo, L. A., & Serlin, R. C. (1988). *Statistics methods for the social and behavioral sciences.* New York: Freeman.

Mastropieri, M. A., & Scruggs, T. E. (1985–1986). Early intervention for socially withdrawn children. *Journal of Special Education, 19,* 429–441.

McCuller, B., & Salzberg, C. I. (1982). The functional analysis of imitation. In N. R. Ellis (Ed.), *International review of research in mental retardation* (Vol. 11, pp. 285–320). New York: Academic Press.

McLaughlin, F. E., & Marascuilo, L. A. (1990). *Advanced nursing and health care research: Quantification approaches.* Philadelphia: W. B. Saunders.

Miller, P. M. (1973). An experimental analysis of retention control training in the treatment of nocturnal enuresis in two institutionalized adolescents. *Behavior Therapy, 4,* 288–294.

Mullen, B., & Rosenthal, R. (1985). *Basic meta-analysis: Procedures and programs.* Hillsdale, NJ: Lawrence Erlbaum Associates.

Nietzel, M. T., & Trull, T. J. (1988). Metal-analytic approaches to social comparisons: A method for measuring clinical significance. *Behavioral Assessment, 10,* 159–169.

Puri, M. L., & Sen, P. K. (1985). *Nonparametric methods in general linear models.* New York: Wiley.

Rosenthal, R., & Rubin, D. B. (1982). Comparing effect sizes of independent studies. *Psychological Bulletin, 92,* 500–504.

Salzberg, C. L., Strain, P. S., & Baer, D. M. (1987). Meta-analysis for single-subject research: When does it clarify, when does it obscure? *Remedial and Special Education, 8,* 43–48.

Scruggs, T. E., Mastropieri, M. A., & Casto, G. (1987a). The quantitative synthesis of single-subject research: Methodology and validation. *Remedial and Special Education, 8,* 24–33.

Scruggs, T. E., Mastropieri, M. A., & Casto, G. (1987b). Reply to Owen White. *Remedial and Special Education, 8,* 40–42.

Scruggs, T. E., Mastropieri, M. A., Cook, S. B., & Escobar, C. (1986). Early interventions for developmental functioning: A quantitative synthesis of single-subject research. *Behavioral Disorders, 11,* 260–271.

Scruggs, T. E., Mastropieri, M. A., & Forness, S. R. (1988). Early language interventions: A quantitative synthesis of single-subject research. *Journal of Special Education, 22,* 259–283.

Scruggs, T. E., Mastropieri, M. A., & McEwen, T. (1988). Early intervention for children with conduct disorders: The quantitative synthesis. *Journal for the Division of Early Childhood, 12,* 359–367.

Serlin, R. C., & Lapsley, D. K. (1985). Rationality in psychological research: The good-enough principle. *American Psychologist, 40,* 73–83.

Serlin, R. C., & Lapsley, D. K. (1986, April). *Exact tests and confidence intervals for effect sizes and measures of association.* Paper presented at the annual meeting of the American Educational Research Association, San Francisco.

Sharpley, C. F., & Alavosius, M. P. (1988). Autocorrelation in behavioral data: An alternative perspective. *Behavioral Assessment, 10,* 243–251.

Skiba, R. J., Casey, A., & Center, B. A. (1985–1986). Nonaversive procedures in the treatment of classroom behavior. *Journal of Special Education, 19,* 459–481.

Slavin, R. E. (1984). Meta-analysis in education: How has it been used? *Educational Researcher, 13,* 6–15.

Smoot, S., & Curlette, W. (1990, April). *Meta-analysis of single-subject research in education: A common metric and a computerized method.* Paper presented at the annual meeting of the American Educational Research Association, Boston.

Strube, M. J., Gardner, W., & Hartmann, D. P. (1985). Limitations, liabilities, and obstacles in reviews of the literature: The current status of meta-analysis. *Clinical Psychology Review, 5,* 63–78.

Strube, M. J., & Hartmann, D. P. (1982). A critical appraisal of meta-analysis. *British Journal of Clinical Psychology, 21,* 129–139.

Strube, M. J., & Hartmann, D. P. (1983). Meta-analysis: Techniques, applications, and functions. *Journal of Consulting and Clinical Psychology, 51,* 14–27.

Suen, H. K. (1987). On the epistemology of autocorrelation in applied behavioral analysis. *Behavioral Assessment, 9,* 113–124.

Suen, H. S., & Ary, D. (1987). Application of statistical power in assessing autocorrelation. *Behavioral Assessment, 9,* 125–130.

Tiku, M. L. (1986). *Robust inference.* New York: Marcel Dekker.

Wampold, B. E., & Worsham, N. L. (1986). Randomization tests for multiple-baseline designs. *Behavioral Assessment, 8,* 135–143.

White, D. M., Rusch, F. R., Kazdin, A. E., & Hartmann, D. P. (1989). Applications of meta analysis in individual-subject research. *Behavioral Assessment, 11,* 281–296.

White, O. R. (1987). Some comments concerning "The quantitative synthesis of single-subject research." *Remedial and Special Education, 8,* 34–39.

Wilson, G. T., & Rachman, S. J. (1983). Meta-analysis and the evaluation of psychotherapy outcome: Limitations and liabilities. *Journal of Consulting and Clinical Psychology, 51,* 54–64.

Wilson, V. L., & Putman, R. R. (1982). A meta-analysis of pretest sensitization effects in experimental design. *American Educational Research Journal, 19,* 249–258.

8 Single-Case Research Design and Analysis: Comments and Concerns

Joel R. Levin
University of Wisconsin–Madison

In the 13 years since the publication of Tom Kratochwill's first edited volume on the topic of single-subject methodology and methods of data analysis, we have witnessed a number (if not an explosion) of exciting new developments.

Single-Case Terminology

First, and as an interesting historical aside, the term "single subject" (Kratochwill, 1978) appears to have flown the way of the pterosaur. As we enter the 1990s, N of 1 designs are more commonly and uniformly referred to as "single case" (see also Hersen & Barlow, 1976). This is more than likely in keeping with the humanitarian spirit of the American Psychological Association's cherished *Publication Manual* (1983), which within the last generation has seen references to the data providers of an experiment transformed from "Ss" to "subjects" to, currently, "students," "children," or "participants."

Visual Analysis

Second, Parsonson and Baer's chapter in the present volume furnishes adversaries on both sides of the controversy over statistical versus nonstatistical treatment of single-case data with more fuel for their respective fires (e.g., Baer, 1988; DeProspero & Cohen, 1979; Furlong & Wampold, 1982; Knapp, 1983; Maytas & Greenwood, 1990; Ottenbacher, 1990; Sharpley, 1986; Wampold & Furlong, 1981). With so much ado about statistical assumptions—including both their necessity and their reality vis-à-vis the nature of *actual* (as opposed to *presumed*) human behavior—the Parsonson–Baer chapter should leave the non-

213

statistical, graphical proponents with increased confidence in the appropriateness and conciseness of their visual tools.

The graphical opponents (statistical proponents), however, will likely be left with quite a different message: Newer and cleverer ways of presenting data to the eyeball simply represent newer and cleverer ways of reaching unwarranted scientific conclusions and generalizations on the basis of those data. That is, there are surely tradeoffs in: (a) what *initial impressions* a researcher or reader can readily grasp from a graphical plot; and (b) what *reliable, generalizable conclusions* one can reach on that basis alone (i.e., without confirming statistical analyses). More on this later.

Statistical Assumptions

A related third point is that in the half-score and four years since Kratochwill (1978), a massive amount of additional evidence has emerged concerning the validity of the statistical assumptions (notably, the independence/autocorrelation assumption) required to analyze single-case data "properly" (see, for example, Busk & Marascuilo, this volume; Crosbie, 1987, 1989; Gardner, Hartmann, & Mitchell, 1982; Phillips, 1983; Sharpley & Alavosius, 1988; Toothaker, Banz, Noble, Camp, & Davis, 1983). Statisticians remind researchers of the assumptions that are required to maintain interpretable Type I error probabilities in their *t*-tests, ANOVAs, χ^2 analyses, binomial tests, and other nonparametric procedures. Researchers remind statisticians that "the proof is in the pudding" of real-live participants responding operantly, thereby putting the "monkey" squarely back on the back of the statistician. Indeed, sometimes statisticians remind everybody of the perils of assuming too much about statistical assumptions—to wit, independence—as applied to real people in the behavior change literature (e.g., Huitema, 1985); and sometimes statisticians even remind other statisticians of the flaws in their remindings (e.g., Busk & Marascuilo, 1988; Suen & Ary, 1987).

Data Analysis Versatility

Fourth and fortunately, the field is now flooded with an increased variety and sophistication of statistical weaponry to analyze single-case data. The modern-day research analyst's arsenal typically includes (1) *hardware,* in the form of powerful (fast, friendly, and filled with memory) personal computers; (2) *software,* in the form of data analysis techniques that heretofore were inaccessible or impossible to access—notably time-series analyses (e.g., Crosbie & Sharpley, 1989), nonparametric analyses based on complete permutation distributions (e.g., Edgington, 1989), and even publication-quality graphical plots (e.g., Wilkinson, 1987); and (3) *thoughtware,* in the form of the now-voluminous literature on single-case data analysis possibilities, which can be readily be deduced from both my previous points and the previous chapters in the present volume. Not so fortunately, however, along with the thrill of new appropriate data analysis tools comes the agony of new, inappropriate ones, some of which will be alluded to shortly.

Topics and Controversies

Fifth and finally, the past generation of single-case research methodology has given birth to new topics and associated controversies, including controversies in the making. For a flavor of some new topics, see Busk and Serlin's (this volume) discussion of meta-analysis "do's" and "don'ts" for single-case data. Even though the infant meta-analysis was screaming and kicking by 1978 (Glass, 1976), translations to single-case methodology were still in search of a translator. With the appearance of the present Busk–Serlin chapter, what started out rather crudely for would-be single-case meta-analysts (e.g., Scruggs, Mastropieri, & Casto, 1987) has now achieved some measure of sophistication. In particular, Scruggs et al. conceptualized a single-case effect size as the percentage of non-overlapping data in two phases (A and B). As was pointed out by White (1987, pp. 36–37), however, such a measure is extemely wasteful of information—in a manner analogous to the efficiency difference between, say, performing a two-sample Irwin–Fisher median test instead of a two-sample t-test of means when the assumptions for the latter are met. The Busk–Serlin analogs to traditional effect-size measures, on the other hand, represent "powerful" new contributions to the single-case meta-analysis literature.

As a couple nominees for "up and-coming controversies," may I submit: (1) continued misapplication of statistical tests, as a result of the user's faulty or incomplete understanding of their underlying logic and assumptions (e.g., randomization and other nonparametric tests; see Edgington, this volume); (2) the proper number of cases and autoregressive parameters required to produce both valid and powerful time-series analyses (Busk & Marascuilo, this volume; McCleary & Welsh, this volume); and (3) the statistical consequences of scaling kappa "pattern" measures in sequential analyses, as well as the interpretations that result from such scaling (Wampold, this volume). In short, we now have new fields to plow—and axes to grind.

SELECTED ISSUES

The focus of the discussion that follows is on a few selected issues in the design and analysis of single-case research, issues that emanate from the previous chapters in this book.

Discriminant Validity and Transfer-appropriate Processing

I begin by considering Kratochwill's (this volume) Table 1.3, which offers useful guidelines for enhancing the credibility of an intervention's impact (namely, that an observed effect can be unambiguously and uniquely traced to a particular intervention or intervention component). In that sense, most of the research characteristics listed in Kratochwill's table address case-study and single-case-design aspects of the firmly entrenched conventional-design construct of *internal validity* (Campbell & Stanley, 1966).

There is something that I believe needs to be added in relation to enhancing an intervention's credibility, however. That is the advisability of incorporating de-signs and design variations that are capable of producing *differential* or *selective* intervention effects. Yes, it seem reasonable to assume that a particular interven-tion becomes a more plausible proximate cause when it generalizes across par-ticipants (heterogeneity or subjects), dependent measures (impact of treatment), and contexts or settings (generalization and follow-up assessment). It should also be pointed out, however, that in certain situations just such generalization can serve to diminish an intervention's plausibility.

In short, if a given intervention is all things to all people in all contexts, then the intervention may in fact be no thing at all (other than a global attentional, motivational, or placebo effect). Consider, for example, a study in which assert-ive discipline training is used to improve a disruptive student's deportment in a history class. It would certainly be nice to see an improvement in that student's history-class behavior following one or more discipline-training experiences. Maybe it would be nice to see the student's improved behavior generalize to science and English classes as well. But would it also be nice if it generalized to a physical education class, to the lunchroom, or to out-of-school play activities? Or if it led to higher grades in all courses, to less tardiness and truancy, to greater popularity among peers, to less stress and a lower level of blood cholesterol? And what if the same discipline training led to similar improvements when it was noncontingently administered to students who were not at all disruptive? Or if discipline training were found to diminish some other maladaptive behavior, such as a phobia or enuresis? Would such generalizations strengthen one's con-clusions about the credibility of the intervention per se, or would there be some "plausible rival hypotheses" (Campbell & Stanley, 1963) that one might wish to consider?

As I have argued elsewhere (Levin, 1989), the credibility of treatments or interventions is considerably enhanced through research designs that capitalize on the constructs of *discriminant validity* (Campbell & Fiske, 1959) and *transfer-appropriate processing* (Morris, Bransford, & Franks, 1977). Interventions that exhibit discriminant validity are ones that are successful only when applied to those behaviors or situations to which they are conceptually tied. In the preceding example, if one wished to attribute success to a discipline intervention (rather than to an intervention in general, or to the proverbial Hawthorne effect), then a study with high discriminant validity would have discipline training being effective for reducing the student's disruptive behavior (in history class), but not for curing the same student's fear of snakes, not for increasing the student's popularity, and perhaps not even for reducing the student's disruptive behavior on the playground (i.e., transfer to a situation far beyond that which can rightfully be expected).

Transfer-appropriate processing (TAP), as a logical extension of discriminant validity, requires, for example, that Intervention A is more successful than Intervention B for one targeted behavior, setting, or outcome measure (Behavior X, Setting X, or Measure X), but not for another (Behavior Y, Setting Y, or Measure Y). In fact, exactly the opposite pattern might obtain in the Y cases (i.e., Intervention B is more successful than Invervention A). Thus, a study with high TAP validity might demonstrate that assertive discipline training is superior to imagery desensitization therapy when it comes to reducing a student's disruptions of a history class, whereas imagery therapy is superior to assertive discipline training when it comes to reducing a student's fear of snakes.

For single-case research, the multiple-baseline design is exemplary for establishing generalizable effects, on the one hand, and selective effects, on the other. Yet, for as much "press" as that design may receive for its intervention *generalization* (e.g., Kratochwill, this volume), its underlying rationale is clearly founded on the notion of intervention *discrimination*. Consider, for example, the multiple-baseline design implemented across settings. Within each phase of the design, an intervention's credibility rests on the assumption that the desired outcome will occur only in the setting(s) in which the intervention is administered. That is, at each phase of the design, all nonintervened settings serve as "controls" for the setting(s) to which the intervention was administered. The same logic applies to the multiple-baseline design implemented across behaviors. Indeed, if generalization (in the form of spontaneous transfer to nonintervened settings or behaviors) is observed, then one's ability to attribute an outcome to the intervention per se is undermined, both conceptually and in terms of inferential-statistical support for an intervention-based effect (e.g., Revusky, 1967; Wampold & Worsham, 1986).

Single-case designs that are well suited to capitalize on TAP logic are those that provide for a comparison of two or more interventions (e.g., simultaneous- and alternating-treatments designs) or of two more components of an intervention (e.g., reversal designs; see for example, Kratochwill & Levin, 1978). With greater intentional effort to tap the TAP rationale through the use of such designs, single-case researchers will be able to provide more powerful and persuasive evidence for the credibility of their intervention effects.

Credibility vs. Magnitude of Effects

One additional comment about Kratochwill's (this volume) Table 1.3 is needed. For his *Effect Size* and *Effect Impact* entries, "large" and "immediate," respectively, are seen as attributes that are important for validly attributing an observed effect to an intervention. I would agree with that assessment, as long as the particular intervention is *designed* or *assumed* to produce large and immediate effects. One can conceive of interventions that may not be potent or precipitate, but persuasive nonetheless (e.g., a well-controlled study of the effect of enforced homework on school achievement, in which small, delayed, but genuine improvements in school performance might be observed). That is, one must be careful not to confuse the credibility of a treatment's impact (an internal-validity aspect of the research methodology, over which the investigator has considerable control) with the magnitude of that effect (a treatment-related outcome, which is not under the control of the investigator).

Large and immediate effects may indeed be indicators of an intervention's *importance*, but they should not be used as indicators of an intervention's *credibility*. Similar distinctions are commonly made between the notions of "practical" or "clinical" significance, on the one hand, and "statistical" significance, on the other. That said, however, it should also be noted that enhancing the methodological, statistical, and psychometric properties associated with studying an intervention's impact (through improved treatment implementation, more efficient experimental designs, and more reliable and valid measurement of outcomes) can certainly have a direct impact on the magnitude of the effects observed.

Statistical Assumptions

As was mentioned earlier, the occasion of this volume has also afforded authors with yet another occasion to inform the single-case research community of the underlying assumptions required for proper use of the various statistical procedures they discuss (see also Kratochwill, 1978). Thus, it should come as no great surprise to hear once again arguments about the inappropriateness of applying traditional analysis-of-variance models to the analysis of single-case data (e.g., Busk & Marascuilo; Busk & Serlin; Edgington), particularly as far as matters of nonindependence and autocorrelation are concerned.

What must be added to that discussion, however, is what might be termed "analysis illusions" or "analysis delusions." These are simply alternative-to-ANOVA analyses that give researchers the illusion/delusion that they are performing or proposing a "proper" analysis—proper in the sense of not requiring (or circumventing) certain statistical assumptions of common ANOVA models by selecting their alternative analyses. In what follows: (a) A case in point will illustrate conceptual confusion about the assumption of independence of errors;

and (b) a heretofore unrecognized statistical assumption will be introduced.

Nonparametric approaches have been heralded as the great distribution- and assumption-free panacea for the analysis of single-case data. Unfortunately, however, serious misinterpretations have arisen about exactly what is distribution- and assumption-free in such approaches. It is certainly true that binomial tests and exact randomization tests (and their rank analogs) do not require an assumption of normality for them to be validly performed. However, simply collecting single-case data in the usual way and conducting nonparametric analyses at the level of individual observations does not alleviate the basic problem associated with analyzing single-case data. As Edgington (this volume), Levin, Marascuilo, and Hubert (1978), and other have pointed out, the problem is one of both the units of analysis and the randomization scheme underlying the data.

Units of Analysis.   In particular, Rose (1978) reported having performed a randomization test to assess the effect of food coloring on hyperactivity. The test, however, was based on the individual A (no food coloring) and B (food coloring) data points within essentially an ABABA design; that is, based on the individual within-phase observations, rather than on the randomized phase summary units that are needed to satisfy the assumptions for that type of analysis (Levin et al., 1978). Given the proper randomization units of three control and two experimental phases for the Rose (1978) study, the lowest significance probability possible is $\frac{1}{10}$ (i.e., $p = .10$), and not the probabilities ranging from .0001 to .009 that were claimed by Rose (1978). Thus, the concerned consumer must be aware that just because a "randomization test" is reported does not mean that it was appropriately conducted. The same can be said for improper use of the binomial sign test, as has been documented by Crosbie (1987).

Variance–Covariance Homogeneity.   As a second example of distributional confusion or neglect, consider the statistical assumption of homogeneity of variance that is required for parametric t and F tests of mean differences. There are two interesting little-known empirical facts about this assumption. The first concerns the purported "robustness" (Type I error control) of the t and F tests to violation of the assumption when sample sizes are equal (e.g., Glass, Peckham, & Sanders, 1972). Contemporary confidence in that assertion is waning, however, in view of recent empirical findings that even when sample sizes are equal, in the presence of unequal variances the obtained significance probabilities do not correspond well with their nominal values (e.g., Randolph, Barcikowsi, & Robey, 1990; Sawilowsky & Blair, 1991; Tomarken & Serlin, 1986).

What do these parametric based results have to say about the analysis of single-case data? This brings us to the second little-known fact. In order for one's conclusions to have some degree of sample-to-population generalizability, an assumption of homogeneous variances (and covariances, in the case of within-subject, repeated-measures designs) is required when testing the identical-population hypothesis via nonparametric tests of location.[1] Violating that assumption has been found to have serious Type I error-inflating consequences (e.g., Harwell, Hayes, Olds, & Rubinstein, 1990; Harwell & Serlin, 1989; Pratt, 1964). Nonparametric tests encompass the randomization-test approaches that have been proposed for analysis of single-case data (see, for example, Levin et al., 1978, Wampold & Worsham, 1986, and the chapters by Edgington and by Busk and Marascuilo in this volume). In a single-case context, then, unless the randomized phase summary measures are associated with equal variances, one's reported significance probabilities may well be distorted. For a randomization test applied to an ABABAB design, for example, in order to satisfy the homogeneity-of-variance assumption, the variance associated with the three A phase means must be comparable to that associated wth the three B phase means. Otherwise: (a) the randomization-test assumption that each possible relevant combination of the data is equally likely is not tenable; which in turn implies that: (b) one's ability to generalize beyond the particular sample's data configuration is severely impaired.

Summary.   Thus, to reiterate an earlier message of this section: Nonparametric procedures are nice, but they are not the single-case data analyst's cure-all. This statement is certainly true of misapplied or misinterpreted nonparametric approaches (e.g., Rose, 1978), and it is possibly true in the presence of heretofore unconsidered assumption violations—in particular, when the to-be-compared conditions (e.g., intervention and baseline) include summary measures with different degrees of variability and/or covariability.

Time-series Extensions

Few would argue that time-series analysis of single-case data (e.g., McCleary & Welsh, this volume) provides the most sophisticated, most precise, and most statistically appropriate method of analyzing single-case (time-series) data. Yet, few would also argue that the time-series approach represents the most computationally complex of the various statistical approaches to analyzing such data. Certainly in this day and age (i.e., in the 1990s), and as was mentioned earlier, objections based solely on computational complexity can be easily dismissed on the grounds of improved computer technology and associated software to combat the complexity (e.g., Crosbie & Sharpley, 1989). As a result, modern- and future-day researchers might become more inclined to consider applying time-

---

[1]Despite the distressing nature of this news, I am nonetheless grateful to Ron Serlin for bringing it to my attention. Strictly speaking, the requisite assumption for within-subject designs is known as "sphericity," which is generally connected with (but is less stringent than) the equal variance, equal covariance assumption known as "compound symmetry" (see for example, Kirk, 1982).

series analyses in as yet unconsidered situations. Research now in progress is examining the potential of adapting "replicated" time-series analyses to multiple-baseline and multiple-N designs. No news to report yet, but perhaps for the next volume.

CONCLUDING COMMENTS

I conclude with a vivid *déjà vu* (Levin et al., 1978), which was evoked by the present Parsonson–Baer case extolling the virtues of visual analyses for single-case data. As in 1978, I feel that the single-case researcher is obliged to answer two questions: (1) Is it necessary or important that an inferential-statistical test be performed on the data? and (2) If so, which statistical test is most appropriate (in terms of both meeting the test's assumptions and providing the most sensitive assessment of intervention effects)? Clearly, if one's primary concern is for attaining some predetermined criterion of success or clinical significance, then a measure of statistical significance seems superfluous (especially if it is based on spurious significance levels because of test-related assumption violations). In such situations, then, the answer to Question 1 ought to be "no" and graphical plots of the data should suffice. On the other hand, if one's primary concern is for assessing the likelihood of a particular intervention-based outcome (basically for Cook & Campbell's, 1979, "statistical conclusion" validity purposes), Question 1 should be answered affirmatively and Question 2 would need to be addressed in terms of the various statistical procedures and issues specified in this book.

I could easily endorse Parsonson and Baer's visual-analysis viewpoint were it not for two major impediments to that way of thinking. First, with the exception of a few notable journals, there are external pressures imposed by journal editors and reviewers to conduct statistical analyses of reported data—even when the analyses recommended or performed are not warranted, given the nature of the data. In that sense, pressures to analyze single-case data statistically are frequently yielded to because of pressures to publish. Second, it is this author's opinion that many researchers cannot (or do not) distinguish between exploratory (hypothesis-generating) research investigations, on the one hand, and confirmatory (hypothesis-testing) studies, on the other. Whereas visual analysis and other informal inspection methods represent legitimate exploratory-research vehicles for communicating what "is interesting to the eye" or what "merits further study," corroborating predicted outcomes on the basis of formal statistical analysis is often mandatory for confirmatory-research studies. My point here is simply that both single-case researchers and others alike should try harder to match the strength of their conclusions with the persuasiveness of their data and accompanying analyses: All else being equal, visual analysis of exploratory studies should be associated with more tentative, speculative statements; and replications or confirmed predictions with supporting probability-based statistical analyses (and, hopefully, substantial effect sizes) should be communicated with a greater sense of conviction.

Final Tribute

As a sad footnote, my comments in this volume have afforded me an opportunity to pay final tribute to my mentor, colleague, and jovial friend. "Dr. M.": Leonard A. Marascuilo. The illuminating Busk–Marascuilo chapter in this book was one of his last scholarly efforts. A little giant in the arena of educational statistics, Len Marascuilo is one individual whose insightful contributions to the analysis of individual $N = 1$ data will be sorely missed—not just by me personally, but by two other of his close collaborators and comrades (Ron Serlin and Pat Busk), as well as by the entire educational-research community. Lennie, this one's for you!

REFERENCES

Baer, D. M. (1988). An autocorrelated commentary on the need for a different debate. *Behavioral Assessment, 10,* 295–298.

Busk, P. L., & Marascuilo, L. A. (1988). Autocorrelation in single-subject research: A counterargument to the myth of no autocorrelation. *Behavioral Assessment, 10,* 229–242.

Campbell, D. T., & Fiske, D. W. (1959). Convergent and discriminant validation by the multitrait–multimethod matrix. *Psychological Bulletin, 56,*81–105.

Campbell, D. T., & Stanley, J. C. (1966). *Experimental and quasi-experimental designs for research.* Chicago: Rand McNally.

Cook, T. D., & Campbell, D. T. (1979). *Quasi-experimentation: Design & analysis issues for field settings.* Chicago: Rand McNally.

Crosbie, J. (1987). The inability of the binomial test to control Type I error with single-subject data. *Behavioral Assessment, 9,* 141–146.

Crosbie, J. (1989). The inappropriateness of the C statistic for assessing stability or treatment effects with single-subject data. *Behavioral Assessment, 11,* 315–325.

Crosbie, J., & Sharpley, C. F. (1989). *DMITSA: A statistical program for analyzing data from interrupted time-series.* Department of Psychology, Deakin University, Victoria, Australia.

DeProspero, A., & Cohen, S. (1979). Inconsistent visual analysis of intrasubject data. *Journal of Applied Behavior Analysis, 12,* 513–519.

Edgington, E. S. (1989). *RANDPACK: Randomization tests.* Department of Psychology, University of Calgary, Alberta, Canada.

Furlong, M. J., & Wampold, B. E. (1982). Intervention effects and relative variation as dimensions in experts' use of visual inspection. *Journal of Applied Behavior Analysis, 15,* 415–421.

Gardner, W., Hartmann, D. P., & Mitchell, C. (1982). The effects of serial dependency on the use of chi-square for analyzing sequential data in dyadic interactions. *Behavioral Assessment, 4,* 75–82,

Glass, G. V. (1976). Primary, secondary, and meta-analysis of research. *Educational Researcher, 5,* 3–8.

Glass, G. V., Peckham, P. D., & Sanders, J. R. (1972). Consequences of failure to meet assumptions underlying the fixed effects analyses of variance and covariance. *Review of Educational Research, 42*, 237–288.

Harwell, M. R., Hayes, W. S., Olds, C. C., & Rubinstein, E. N. (1990, April). *Summarizing Monte Carlo results using methods of research synthesis: The one-way fixed-effects ANOVA case*. Paper presented at the annual meeting of the American Educational Research Association, Boston.

Harwell, M. R., & Serlin, R. C. (1989, March). *An empirical study of the nonparametric Friedman test under variance and covariance heterogeneity conditions*. Paper presented at the annual meeting of the American Educational Research Association, San Francisco.

Hersen, M., & Barlow, D. H. (Eds.). (1976). *Single case experimental designs: Strategies for studying behavior change*. Oxford, England: Pergamon.

Huitema, B. E. (1985). Autocorrelation in applied behavior analysis: A myth. *Behavioral Assessment, 7*, 107–118.

Kirk, R. E. (1982). *Experimental design* (2nd ed.). Belmont, CA: Brooks/Cole.

Knapp, T. J. (1983). Behavior analysts' visual appraisal of behavior change in graphic display. *Behavioral Assessment, 5*, 155–164.

Kratochwill, T. R. (Ed.). 1978). *Single subject research: Strategies for evaluating change*. New York: Academic Press.

Kratochwill, T. R., & Levin, J. R. (1978). What time-series designs may have to offer educational researchers. *Contemporary Educational Psychology, 3*, 273–329.

Levin, J. R. (1989). A transfer-appropriate-processing perspective of pictures in prose. In H. Mandl & J. R. Levin (Eds.), *Knowledge acquisition from text and pictures* (pp. 83–100). Amsterdam: Elsevier.

Levin, J. R., Marascuilo, L. A., & Hubert, L. J. (1978). $N =$ nonparametric randomization tests. In T. R. Kratochwill (Ed.), *Single subject research: Strategies for evaluating change* (pp. 167–196). New York: Academic Press.

Maytas, T. A., & Greenwood, K. M. (1990). Visual analysis of single-case time series: Effects of variability, serial dependence, and magnitude of intervention effects. *Journal of Applied Behavior Analysis, 23*, 341–351.

Morris, C. D., Bransford, J. D., & Franks, J. J. (1977). Levels of processing versus transfer appropriate processing. *Journal of Verbal Learning and Verbal Behavior, 16*, 519–533.

Ottenbacher, K. J. (1990). When is a picture worth a thousand *p* values? A comparison of visual and quantitative methods to analyze single subject data. *Journal of Special Education, 23*, 436–449.

Phillips, J. P. N. (1983). Serially correlated errors in some single-subject designs. British *Journal of Mathematical and Statistical Psychology, 36*, 269–280.

Pratt, J. W. (1964). Robustness of some procedures for the two-sample location problem. *Journal of the American Statistical Association, 59*, 665–680.

Publication Manual of the American Psychological Association. (3rd ed.). (1983). Washington, DC: American Psychological Association. and Statistical Psychology, *36*, 269–280.

Randolph, E., Barcikowski, R., & Robey, R. R. (1990, April). *Type I error of the ANOVA revisited using power analysis criteria*. Paper presented at the annual meeting of the American Educational Research Association, Boston.

Revusky, S. H. (1967). Some statistical treatments compatible with individual organism methodology. *Journal of the Experimental Analysis of Behavior, 10*, 319–330.

Rose, T. L. (1978). The functional relationship between artificial food colors and hyperactivity. *Journal of Applied Behavior Analysis, 11*, 439–446.

Sawilowsky, S. S., & Blair, R. C. (1991, April). *A more realistic look at the robustness and Type II error properties of the t test to departures from population normality*. Paper presented at the annual meeting of the American Educational Research Association, Chicago.

Scruggs, T. E., Mastropieri, M. A., & Casto, G. (1987). The quantitative synthesis of single-subject research: Methodology and validation, *Remedial and Special Education, 8*, 24–33.

Sharpley, C. F. (1986). Fallibility in the visual assessment of behavioral interventions: Time-series statistics to analyse time-series data. *Behaviour Change, 3,* 26–33.

Sharpley, C. F., & Alavosius, M. P. (1988). Autocorrelation in behavioral data: An alternative perspective. *Behavioral Assessment, 10,* 243–251.

Suen, H. K., & Ary, D. (1987). Application of statistical power in assessing autocorrelation. *Behavioral Assessment, 9,* 125–130.

Tomarken, A. J., & Serlin, R. C. (1986). Comparison of ANOVA alternatives under variance heterogeneity and specific noncentrality structures. *Psychological Bulletin, 99,* 90–99.

Toothaker, L., E., Banz, M., Noble, C., Camp, J., & Davis, D. (1983). N = 1 designs: The failure of ANOVA-based tests. *Journal of Educational Statistics, 8,* 289–309.

Wampold, B. E., & Furlong, M. J. (1981). The heuristics of visual inspection. *Behavioral Assessment, 3,* 79–92.

Wampold, B. E., & Worsham, N. L. (1986). Randomization test for multiple-baseline designs. *Behavioral Assessment, 8,* 135–143.

White, O. R. (1987). Some comments concerning "The quantitative synthesis of single-subject research." *Remedial and Special Education, 8,* 34–39.

Wilkinson, L. (1987). *SYGRAPH: The system for graphics.* Evanston, IL: Systat, Inc.

Author Index

Subject Index